Cybercrime among companies

CYBERCRIME AMONG COMPANIES

Research into cybercrime victimisation among small- and medium-sized enterprises and one-man businesses in the Netherlands

SANDER VEENSTRA, RENSKE ZUURVEEN AND WOUTER STOL

eleven

international publishing

Published, sold and distributed by Eleven International Publishing
P.O. Box 85576
2508 CG The Hague
The Netherlands
Tel.: +31 70 33 070 33
Fax: +31 70 33 070 30
e-mail: sales@elevenpub.nl
www.elevenpub.com

Sold and distributed in USA and Canada
International Specialized Book Services
920 NE 58th Avenue, Suite 300
Portland, OR 97213-3786, USA
Tel.: 1-800-944-6190 (toll-free)
Fax: +1-503-280-8832
orders@isbs.com
www.isbs.com

Eleven International Publishing is an imprint of Boom uitgevers Den Haag.

ISBN 978-94-6236-652-7
ISBN 978-94-6274-486-8 (E-book)

Printed in The Netherlands

Foreword

Until this report was published, there was a lack of knowledge about the prevalence of cybercrime among small and medium-sized enterprises (SMEs) and one-man businesses. Since information about the nature and extent of crime is required to effectively tackle, this report contributes to the fight against cybercrime.

The cooperation of SMEs and one-man businesses has been crucial to the realisation of this report. It would have been detrimental to the value of our research findings if the companies would not have shared their cybercrime experiences with us. So it is for this reason that all the entrepreneurs who worked with us in this research project deserve our thanks.

Alongside business people, various professionals engaged in the security of companies, both online and in the real world, and interest groups representing SME and one-man businesses also contributed to this report. We would like to thank them too for their efforts.

Finally, six student assistants helped us to conduct the research underlying this report: Job Blaas, Wessel Doldersum, Martijn Poel, Ruben Schutte, Wouter Taal and Kim Weijer: thank you for your contribution.

We hope you enjoy reading this report and that you can benefit from the knowledge contained in it.

Sander Veenstra
Renske Zuurveen
Wouter Stol

Executive summary

Background and research design

The internet has become part and parcel of everyday life in the Netherlands. Virtually all businesses and members of the public use it. The digitisation of society goes hand in hand with the digitisation of crime. Earlier research conducted among young people and other members of the public has already demonstrated that cybercrime is having a serious impact on Dutch society. Yet there is a lack of understanding about the degree to which small and medium-sized enterprises (SMEs) and one-man businesses in the Netherlands are being confronted with cybercrime. That knowledge gap is the reason for this study.

The ultimate objective of this report is to contribute to the fight against cybercrime among the SMEs and one-man businesses in the Netherlands. Fighting crime requires an understanding of the nature and extent of the problem. With this in mind, this study gives answers to the following main questions:[1]

1. What activities do businesses undertake in cyberspace?
2. What protective measures do businesses take against cybercrime?
3. What is the nature and extent of cybercrime victimisation among businesses and what actions are taken by businesses in the Netherlands who have fallen victim to cybercrime?
4. What factors are associated with victimisation among businesses?
5. Which role do companies assign to public and private parties with regard to tackling cybercrime?

In this report, 'cybercrime' is defined as crime in which IT plays an essential role in the realisation of the offence. This study takes into account types of cybercrime in which IT is not only the means but also the goal of the crime, like DoS attacks (denial of service attacks) and malware, as well as traditional types of crime which are now committed online, such as e-fraud.

---

1. Wherever 'companies' or 'businesses' are referred to in the objectives and research questions, these terms are understood to mean the SME sector and one-man businesses in the Netherlands.

SAMPLE AND METHODOLOGY

Research into cybercrime was carried out among the SME sector in the Netherlands from the beginning of 2013 to March 2014. At the request of the Minister of Security and Justice, a similar research was conducted into cybercrime among one-man businesses directly after this (from March 2014 to April 2015). Similar research methods were deployed for both of these research projects: desk research, online surveys and interviews were used.

In both studies, the desk research was twofold. First, desk research was used to develop online questionnaires for SMEs and one-man businesses. Secondly, a literature study was conducted to clarify the survey findings. In this study, we searched for literature that was specifically related to the nature and extent of cybercrime among SMEs and one-man businesses. It became apparent that hardly any research into this subject had been conducted. Previous research into cybercrime among businesses generally concerned organisations which are larger than the ones that were the focus of this study (up to 50 employees). Furthermore, the publications which we found generally did not have a sound methodological justification, which means that their value is limited.

In addition to desk research, interviews contributed to the development of the online questionnaires. For this purpose, eight semi-structured face-to-face interviews were conducted in the spring of 2013 for the research among the SME sector. To further develop the questionnaire that was used for the research among one-man businesses, three semi-structured telephone interviews were conducted a year later. The interviews were conducted with representatives of interest groups from the SME sector and one-man businesses and with professionals engaged in the security of such businesses. The interviews threw light on specific knowledge gaps the questionnaires should contribute to. In addition to this, the interviews were meant to gain an understanding of cybercrime developments among SMEs and one-man businesses based on signals from professional practice as well as on information from experts. However, it emerged that those interviewed knew very little about these subjects.

Two comparable questionnaires were developed and tested on the basis of the input from the desk research and the exploratory interviews. A questionnaire for the SME sector was developed in the spring of 2013. An online survey was conducted in June and July of 2013. For this, 8,000 SMEs were invited to take part in the survey. These businesses were selected randomly from the Chamber of Commerce commercial register (active companies in the Netherlands with 2 to 50 members of staff). Ultimately, 1,203 SMEs completed the questionnaire. Based on the SME questionnaire, a questionnaire for one-man businesses was subsequently developed in the spring of 2014. In June 2014, 10,000 one-man businesses were invited to complete the questionnaire. The sample for this survey was also drawn from the commercial register of the Chamber of Commerce. Of the total sample, 1,622 one-man businesses completed the questionnaire.

Selectiveness in the response cannot be excluded. There is a good chance that victims of cybercrime were more likely than non-victims to be prepared to take part in the online survey. This means that victimisation rates may be lower in reality than indicated in this research. Based on available material, it cannot be determined how much lower victimisation rates may be.

Finally, in-depth interviews were conducted with representatives of SMEs as well as one-man business owners after the online survey had been conducted. Five telephone interviews were conducted with SMEs who had fallen victim to cybercrime in the autumn of 2013. Thirty-one in-depth interviews were conducted with one-man business owners in December 2014: 8 interviews with victims and 23 interviews with non-victims. The interviews contributed to the (correct) interpretation of the quantitative findings.

Results

The results regarding SMEs and one-man businesses can largely be compared to each other, because a similar research methodology was used in both studies. The results in the summary that follows are therefore described in combination as much as possible.

IT and internet use

Among one-man business owners, the use of computers and the internet are closely intertwined: more than 95 per cent use the same computer for both business and private purposes. Convenience was the reason mentioned most often. SMEs are more likely to use different computers for business purposes.

The SME and one-man business sectors are both active on the internet. Virtually all business people[2] use e-mail and internet banking facilities and carry out targeted searches for information on the internet. Ordering online is an activity that both the SME and the one-man business sectors also carry out frequently. Typical business activities, for instance, online placement and processing of orders and online bookkeeping, are activities which are carried out more frequently by SMEs than by one-man businesses. On the other hand, online chatting, using WhatsApp, for instance, is a typical one-man business activity, probably because private and business internet usage are intertwined.

The interwoven relationship between private and business internet use in the one-man business sector may also explain the difference between the extent to which SMEs and one-man businesses use social media. More than 60 per cent of those in the Dutch SME sector and virtually 90 per cent of the one-man business sector use one or more social networking sites. Although it is possible that one-man business

---

2. For the sake of the readability, 'entrepreneurs' and 'business people' are terms used to refer to SMEs and one-man businesses in this text.

owners also use their private profiles for business activities, almost 46 per cent of those in the one-man business sector also have a specific profile for business purposes. YouTube, Facebook, Twitter and LinkedIn are the most popular social networks among SMEs and one-man businesses alike.

Protection against and awareness of cybercrime

By their own admission, entrepreneurs are dependent on IT to a very large degree. More SMEs (73.9%) are dependent on IT than one-man businesses (63.2%). The functioning of IT is, therefore, vital to business operations.
Confidential information is also stored on company computers. Of those in the one-man business sector, 45.1 per cent admitted to having confidential information on their computers to a large or very large extent. The percentage of SMEs who said that they store confidential information to a large or very large degree is considerably higher (65.1%).
Considering that business people are dependent on IT and store confidential information on their computers, it is no surprise that most felt it is important or very important to protect company-related information. However, a higher percentage of those in the SME sector stated that they attach importance to this than those in the one-man business sector (83.7% versus 67.7%). In addition, SMEs are more inclined to engage external parties for information security than one-man businesses were. One-man businesses tend to take care of data protection themselves.
Entrepreneurs take a variety of measures to protect themselves against cybercrime. Virtually all business people (>99%) take one or more technical measures, for instance, installing a virus scanner, a firewall, keeping software up to date and backing up files. In addition to this, one-man businesses apply one or more rules themselves for safe internet practices (96.5%), such as rules for opening potentially unsafe files or when making online payments. More than three quarters of the SMEs surveyed apply at least one policy measure, such as raising awareness among staff about online risks or drawing up rules for responsible internet use.
Finally, almost 78 per cent of SMEs and almost 60 per cent of one-man businesses use physical measures, for instance, securing rooms where (vital) IT equipment is kept or securing computers using cable locks. More than half of those in the SME and one-man business sectors have confidence or a great deal of confidence in the measures they have taken.

Victimisation

More than a quarter of the Dutch businesses with a workforce of up to 50 members of staff had fallen victim to cybercrime: 28.5 per cent of Dutch SMEs and 27.9 per cent of the one-man businesses were confronted with at least one type of cybercrime in the year prior to the research. The most common types of cybercrime with which business people were confronted were malware, e-fraud, phishing and hacking. Previous research among members of the public and larger companies also showed that these kinds of cybercrimes occurred most frequently. The most common types of cybercrime therefore affect not only the SME and one-man business sectors, but can be characterised as a society-wide phenomenon.

Risk factors for victimisation

Risk factors for cybercrime victimisation have only been studied among the one-man business sector (so not among SMEs). It emerged from this research that victims of cybercrime mainly distinguish themselves from non-victims in that the former are more active on the internet. In addition, victims are younger (45 years and younger) and have less self-control. Protective measures (physical or technical) hardly contributed at all to preventing victimisation. What is important, however, is to exercise caution when on the internet. Self-imposed rules, like abiding by rules when disclosing information on the web or making online payments, can contribute to the prevention of victimisation.

The way in which cybercrime is committed

Entrepreneurs who fell victim to cybercrime knew little about the perpetrator(s) and their modi operandi. It was not generally known who the perpetrator was, from which country the most recent cybercrime they encountered was committed, and how the perpetrator set to work. There is a lack of knowledge in particular about the modi operandi for cybercrimes in the narrow sense (hacking, malware), more so than about the way criminals set to work for cybercrimes in a broader sense (such as e-fraud). This is not surprising because in e-fraud cases the perpetrator and the victim often communicate with each other, while the people responsible for a malware infection or those who hack computers tend to keep out of sight.

A finding that may influence police practice is that cybercrime crosses national borders: although most of the cases, insofar as victims are aware of the place cybercrime is committed from, were national by nature, 8.4 per cent of the SME victims and 14.8 per cent of one-man businesses indicated that the cyber criminal they had encountered operated from abroad. So when cases such as these are reported, the police have to deal with a suspect operating from a foreign country.

Despite the fact that not much was known about the way cybercriminals work, 83 SMEs and 185 one-man business owners described how the most recent cybercrime that they encountered was (presumably) committed. Based on this, it is not possible to make a generalisable statement about the modi operandi of cyber criminals. That said, the combined results do give an indication. Here is a summary of the (presumed) criminal methods used by offenders to commit the most common forms of cybercrime:

- Malware is principally the consequence of the web user's own (unwittingly high-risk) internet behaviour. Downloading, visiting infected (ostensibly trustworthy) websites and opening infected (links in) e-mails lead to malware infections.

- E-fraud generally involves purchasing and advertising fraud. This involves buying products that are not delivered and/or paying phantom invoices.
- Entrepreneurs regularly receive phishing e-mails; often these are e-mails which are apparently from (trustworthy) financial institutions. These e-mails contain requests for confidential information, like passwords.
- Hackers use various methods to gain unauthorised access to IT. They try to find out the entrepreneur's login information, for instance, using computer-generated scripts or fake websites. Hacking is a means of achieving another objective, like sending spam, disabling sites or stealing company data.

Impact and damage

Cybercrime does not by definition lead to damages: more than two fifths of the entrepreneurs who fell victim to cybercrime did not suffer any damage. The perceived severity of cybercrime is related to this: the greater the financial damages, the worse entrepreneurs feel about becoming a victim of cybercrime. Therefore, by no means all business people would label cybercrime victimisation as serious. However, more than a quarter (26.3%) of SMEs and a third (34.2%) of one-man businesses described the most recent cybercrime incident as serious. Loss of time, financial damages and limited access to data are the most common kinds of damage. Moreover, damage is offence specific: for instance, hacking leads to information being unavailable, lost or corrupted, while e-fraud leads to financial damages.
In terms of percentages, there is little difference in the percentages of one-man businesses (21.5%) and SMEs (20.6%) who were financially disadvantaged by cybercrime. There is no point in trying to extrapolate the reported financial loss to a nationally generalisable figure, because the number of respondents who reported financial loss is relatively small and the reported damages vary significantly. We did, however, calculate the total damages for both groups in the sample. The 59 SMEs that reported financial damages together suffered 442,953 euro in damages. One SME sector company, however, reported 240,000 euro in damage; this outlier increases the total amount considerably. The 89 one-man businesses that reported financial damages together suffered 235,568 euro in damages.

Reactions of victims

Almost a quarter of the SME sector businesses and virtually a fifth of the one-man businesses did not undertake any action after falling victim to cybercrime. When entrepreneurs become cybercrime victims, they are self-reliant. The biggest group solved the problems arising from cybercrime themselves and/or took measures to prevent cybercrime victimisation in the future. Moreover, reactions were specific to cybercrime: victims of 'cybercrime in the narrow sense' (malware, hacking), in particular, showed their self-reliance. E-fraud victims were more likely to engage third parties.

The extent to which SMEs and one-man businesses contacted the police differed: one-man businesses were more likely to do so (12.8%) than SMEs (7.2%). There is a correlation between contacting the police and the degree of damage suffered as a consequence of cybercrime: the greater the financial damage, the more likely the victim is to contact the police. The perceived severity of the incident and the entrepreneur's capability of solving the problems arising from the cybercrime also influence the deliberations regarding whether or not the police should be called in. Furthermore, confidence in the police plays a role: almost a quarter of the entrepreneurs expect that the police 'won't do anything anyway' when they report cybercrime. Confidence in the police is not as strong when it comes to fighting cybercrime as it is when it involves tackling traditional crime.

Entrepreneurs who do turn to the police do so mainly because they want to notify the police or file a report on the crime.[3] For this, they contact the police in person as well as electronically. Contacting the police electronically is mainly done for convenience and because it saves time. Choosing to visit the police station is principally inspired by the need for personal contact.

Entrepreneurs are more likely to be very satisfied or satisfied with their contact with the police than they are to be very dissatisfied or dissatisfied. The research among one-man businesses shows that their level of satisfaction about the police action is associated with the response of the police: entrepreneurs whose notifications were registered or whose reports were filed were more satisfied about the police than entrepreneurs who elicited another kind of response from the police. Because of the small number of SMEs who contacted the police, it is not possible to demonstrate that same connection for SMEs.

Although entrepreneurs are generally more likely to be satisfied with their contact with the police than dissatisfied, the SME and one-man business sectors identified various areas for improvement in the police response. According to the entrepreneurs, the areas requiring improvement mainly related to feedback about the way the police handles notifications/reports, increased certainty that a case would be handled and the speed at which the police works. Another opportunity for strengthening the police approach to cybercrime would be to use police volunteers to a greater extent: at least 15 per cent of one-man business owners – which also includes IT experts – offered their help in this regard.

The fact that 12.8 per cent of one-man businesses and 7.2 per cent of SMEs contacted the police means that cybercrime falls largely outside the police force's field of vision. However, the extent of the cybercrime dark number also depends on the police response to the cybercrime workload. When entrepreneurs contact the police, the police does not always register the cybercrime reports. As a consequence, cybercrime is still not being included in recorded crime statistics. For this reason, we did not only

---

3.   Where 'notify the police' or 'notification' is mentioned in this study is understood to mean that no report was actually filed. 'File a report' means that a report was filed, regardless of whether an investigation followed.

study to what extent entrepreneurs contact the police, but it was also investigated to what extent the police actually registers cybercrime notifications and reports. Of the one-man businesses who fell victim to cybercrime, 4.5 per cent said the police registered a notification and according to 4.3 per cent the police registered an official report. For SMEs, these percentages were 1.0 and 3.6 per cent, respectively. This means that the cybercrime dark number among entrepreneurs is higher than among members of the public because, according to Statistics Netherlands (CBS, 2015), 13 per cent of the general public notified the police about cybercrime and 7 per cent filed an official report with the police. So the police lack insight into the nature and extent of cybercrime, particularly where it affects businesses.

Despite the fact that the police are generally not called in when businesses fall victim to cybercrime, the majority of SMEs and one-man businesses stated that they would report future incidents of cybercrime victimisation to the police. They would preferably do so electronically. There is thus a difference between intentions to report incidents to the police and what happens in reality: the majority of the entrepreneurs said that they would report this kind of crime to the police, but when they are actually confronted with cybercrime, they tend not to contact the police.

The role of public and private parties when tackling cybercrime

Six per cent of entrepreneurs (6.0% of SMEs and 5.6% of one-man businesses) called in an interest group as a consequence of the most recent cybercrime incident. Interest groups are thus playing a minor role in the fight against cybercrime. Nevertheless, entrepreneurs consider various other parties, in addition to themselves, to have a shared responsibility for the safety on the internet. More than 80 per cent of entrepreneurs consider banks/financial institutions, internet service providers and software manufacturers to be responsible for internet security. It is notable that one-man businesses are more likely to feel that other parties are responsible (or share the responsibility) for security on the internet than their counterparts in the SME sector. One-man businesses feel that the police are the last on the list of responsible parties for security on the internet, which is a sentiment shared by those in the SME sector.

Respondents from the one-man business sector were asked about the extent to which they were aware of government initiatives against cybercrime, for instance, waarschuwingsdienst.nl or the National Internet Fraud Reporting Centre [*Landelijk Meldpunt Internet Oplichting* (LMIO)]. We also asked them whether they used these initiatives. Of the one-man businesses, 42.4 per cent knew one or more of these initiatives against cybercrime. Only 7.3 per cent used one or more of the initiatives. One-man businesses do not deploy these government initiatives because, according to them, they are capable of protecting themselves and/or of counteracting cybercrime. So again, entrepreneurs state that they are self-reliant. At the same time, one-man businesses mentioned during the in-depth interviews that they would appreciate more support when it comes to preventing and fighting cybercrime, particularly from interest groups in their sector.

Conclusions

Below we present the principle conclusions from this report point by point.

Online activities

- Those in the SME sector as well as those who have one-man businesses are all active internet users. The internet is principally used for traditional business processes, for instance, communicating (e-mails), searching specifically for information and managing banking affairs. Although entrepreneurs also use social media, targeted use of business-related profiles is less evident.

Protective measures

- The functioning of IT is vital for entrepreneurs. Consequently, data protection is something they value highly.
- Those in the SME sector as well as those with one-man businesses take a variety of measures to protect themselves against cybercrime. Obvious technical measures are the ones taken in the main, but policy rules about safe internet practices and physical measures are no exception.

Victimisation

- SMEs and one-man businesses are likely to fall victim to cybercrime to a similar degree: 28.5 per cent of Dutch SMEs and 27.9 per cent of one-man businesses were confronted with cybercrime.
- Businesses are mainly confronted with malware, e-fraud, phishing and hacking. These types of cybercrime can be typified as phenomena that affect society as a whole: not only SMEs and one-man businesses, but also members of the public and larger companies fall victim to these kinds of cybercrime most often.
- One-man business owners that fell victim to cybercrime distinguished themselves from non-victims by their younger age, their more active internet behaviour and their lower levels of self-control.
- Victims do not know much about the way in which cybercrime is committed.
- More than two fifths of entrepreneurs who fell victim to cybercrime did not report any damage. In line with this, entrepreneurs do not always refer to cybercrime victimisation as serious. So although it is not rare for companies to become cybercrime victims, the consequences must not be overestimated.
- Loss of time, financial damages and restricted access to information are the most common kinds of damage. Reported claim amounts varied from between 14 to 240,000 euro. The wide range of amounts spread over a relatively small number of victims who reported financial damages render it impossible to make

meaningful general statements about the (average) damage suffered by entrepreneurs through cybercrime victimisation.

Reactions of victims

- A quarter of the SME sector businesses and virtually a fifth of the one-man businesses did not undertake any action after falling victim to cybercrime. Victims who did take action proved to be self-reliant: they took action to solve the problems themselves and/or took measures to prevent cybercrime in the future.
- The majority of the entrepreneurs did not contact the police when falling victim to cybercrime. This can mainly be attributed to the fact that they did not experience any damage.
- The percentages of those who did contact the police as a consequence of cybercrime victimisation were 7.2 per cent for SMEs and 12.8 per cent for one-man businesses, the latter being significantly higher. Contacting the police does not always mean that notifications or official reports are registered. Of the victimised SMEs, 1.0 per cent said the police officially registered a notification and according to 3.6 per cent an official report was filed. Of the one-man businesses, 4.5 per cent said the police registered a notification and 4.3 per cent actually filed an official report with the police. Rates for notifying the police and filing reports were higher among members of the public (respectively 13% and 7%). So the police lack insight into the nature and extent of cybercrime, particularly where it affects businesses.
- Entrepreneurs who called in the police were more likely to be very satisfied or satisfied with the police action they experienced than they were to be very dissatisfied or dissatisfied. Nevertheless, various areas for improvement were identified, including feedback about the way the police handles notifications and reports, the certainty that a case was being handled and the speed at which the police worked.
- There is a difference between intended and actual reporting of incidents to the police. More than three fifths of entrepreneurs interviewed said that they intended to report cybercrime to the police were they to fall victim to cybercrime in the future. When entrepreneurs actually do become cybercrime victims, the vast majority do not report it to the police. This means that the police must not base their policy on what members of the public say they will do if they fall victim.

The role of public and private parties when tackling cybercrime

- Entrepreneurs agree that security on the internet is a responsibility to be shared by private and public parties alike. They assign themselves an important role in this.
- From the research among one-man businesses, it is evident that not much is known about government initiatives against cybercrime. Moreover, fewer than one in ten entrepreneurs used these initiatives. At the same time, those in the one-man business sector said during the interviews that they needed support to be able to arm

themselves against cybercrime, and that this support should come mainly from their own sector organisations. To gain insight in more effective strategies to help entrepreneurs in their battle against cybercrime it would thus be advisable to assess how the organisation of current government initiatives to support companies can be improved

Final considerations for police and other strategies for tackling cybercrime

- Since virtually all entrepreneurs take technical measures, our research could not demonstrate whether these measures, such as virus scanners, contribute to the prevention of victimisation. After all, if everyone took technical measures, then no comparison can be made between a group that did and a group that did not use such measures. That this research could not demonstrate that taking technical measures reduces the likelihood of victimisation thus does not mean that such measures are not important in the prevention of cybercrime.
- Exercising caution when on the internet reduces the risk of victimisation. Self-imposed regulations may help in this. Given that prevention is better than cure, it is important that entrepreneurs are informed about safe internet behaviour. The results show that it would not be logical for the police to take this prevention task upon themselves. It is more a job for national government and sector or interest groups.
- To effectively fight crime it is essential to understand its nature and extent. Given that insight into cybercrime is lacking in recorded crime statistics, encouraging people to contact the police is important. However, the police should not focus solely on increasing the amount of registered cybercrime reports. After all, the lack of knowledge and capacity within the police raises the question whether the police would be capable to effectively conduct the consequential cybercriminal investigations. By using the information the police gathers from notifications and reports of cybercrime, the police should also focus on achieving successes that transcend individual cases. In addition, the police can use the information that derives from the increased notifications and reports to, in collaboration with other parties, develop knowledge that can contribute to the self-reliance and problem-solving capacities of entrepreneurs who are confronted with cybercrime. Combining various police strategies would lead to a selection process: most of the cases can be dealt with by registering a notification and advising entrepreneurs on solving and preventing cybercrime problems. The police then contributes to the self-reliance of entrepreneurs. Other cases may require (case transcending) criminal prosecution. The police can then focus more specifically on this selection of cases.
- Most cybercrimes are committed within national boundaries rather than from outside the country. To start with, a national cybercrime policy needs to be put in place. That said, the police will inevitably have to deal with cross-border crime in their battle against cybercrime. As a consequence, an investigative policy for addressing 'everyday' international cybercrimes is unavoidable.

TABLE OF CONTENTS

1 | Introduction

1 | INTRODUCTION

Society is digitising and so is the business sector. According to recent figures published by Statistics Netherlands, all companies have an internet connection.[1] The same applies to their customers: 97 per cent of the Dutch households are connected to the internet.[2] The Netherlands is leading Europe in this respect.[3] The turnover from online shopping in the Netherlands amounted to almost 14 billion euro in 2014, an increase of 8.4 per cent in comparison with 2013.[4] In short, the digital world is crucial for entrepreneurs.

The internet has offered new opportunities not only to businesses, but to criminals too. Traditional forms of crime, like fraud, have been given a 'digital guise', while new kinds of crime, like DoS attacks, have emerged. This research focuses on both kinds: (1) new digital crime and (2) the old types of crime which are now also committed via the internet. In this report both types of crime have been grouped here under one term: cybercrime. Cybercrime will be explained in greater detail in Chapter 2.

It is suggested in the media that cybercrime impacts the business sector. On Thursday, 7 March 2013, for instance, an article appeared in the *Algemeen Dagblad*, a major Dutch newspaper, under the headline 'Online theft kills one-man business'. In this article it is claimed that internet criminals have got it in for one-man businesses and SMEs in particular. Banks are becoming less inclined to compensate for damages. Ton Geuzendam, a consultant in safe business practices at the Chamber of Commerce, says the following on the subject in that article: 'Although there are a few exceptions, in most cases companies are not compensated at all. Victims have to demonstrate that they are not liable at all, but try proving that … Cybercrime can hit hard, particularly for one-man businesses. Internet theft can easily result in bankruptcy. It has already happened.'[5]

---

1. <http://statline.cbs.nl/StatWeb/publication/?DM=SLNL&PA=81934NED&D1=a&D2=a&VW=T>. Retrieved most recently on 7 April 2015.
2. <http://statline.cbs.nl/Statweb/publication/?DM=SLNL&PA=71098NED&D1=33,69-72&D2=0& D3=0,l&HDR=G1,G2&STB=T&VW=T>. Retrieved most recently on 7 April 2015.
3. <www.cbs.nl/nl-NL/menu/themas/bedrijven/publicaties/digitale-economie/artikelen/2012-3636-wm.htm>. Retrieved most recently on 7 April 2015.
4. <www.thuiswinkel.org/bedrijven/nieuws/2721/nederlanders-besteden-in-2014-bijna-14-miljard-online>. Retrieved most recently on 7 April 2015.
5. <www.ad.nl/ad/nl/5601/TV-Radio/article/detail/3405380/2013/03/07/Diefstal-via-internet-nekt-zzp-er.dhtml>. Retrieved most recently on 7 April 2015.

On Wednesday, 13 March 2013 (as a consequence of this newspaper article), Members of Parliament (MPs), Mulder and Oskam, by letter, asked the ministers of Economic Affairs and of Security and Justice about the extent of cybercrime among businesses. Recent research has thrown light on the nature and extent of cybercrime victimisation among members of the public and among specific groups, such as young people.[6] However, less is known about cybercrime victimisation among companies.[7] At the time that the parliamentary questions were asked, a research project into cybercrime victimisation among small and medium-sized enterprises in the Netherlands was already conducted. The police commissioned this research as part of their former National Programme Against Cybercrime.[8] The minister of Economic Affairs wrote the following in his answer to the parliamentary questions: 'The minister of Security and Justice has asked the police to include the one-man business sector in the research'.

Policies on crime require an understanding of the nature and extent of the problem. The lack of insight into cybercrime victimisation among SMEs and one-man businesses in the Netherlands was the reason behind this research. The findings of the research among SMEs have already been reported separately (Veenstra, Zuurveen, Jansen, Kloppenburg & Stol, 2014). Research into the extent of cybercrime victimisation among one-man businesses was added during the research project. This report includes the results of the research among SMEs as well as among one-man businesses, and the two target groups are compared in the process.

1.1   READER'S GUIDE

Research into cybercrime was carried out among SMEs in the Netherlands from the beginning of 2013 to March 2014. On the orders of the minister of Security and Justice, that research project was expanded to include the one-man businesses. So comparable research into cybercrime was carried out in the one-man business sector in the Netherlands from the beginning of 2014 to March 2015. The (comparable) design of these two research projects is described in Chapter 2. In the chapter, the demarcation, research objectives and research questions are explained. In Chapter 3, the research methodology is justified. Chapter 4 discusses the results relating to the SME sector and Chapter 5 describes the results about cybercrime among one-man businesses. In Chapter 5 the results regarding one-man businesses are also compared with the results from the SME sector where possible. Finally, Chapter 6 presents the conclusions and final considerations.

---

6. See, for instance, special issues on this subject published by *Justitiële Verkenningen* (2012/1), *Tijdschrift voor Veiligheid* (2012/2) and *Tijdschrift voor de Criminologie* (2013/4).
7. See Sections 3.1.2 and 3.2.1 for an inventory and evaluation of previous research.
8. Veenstra, Zuurveen, Jansen, Kloppenburg and Stol (2013).

<table><tr><td>**2**</td><td># RESEARCH DESIGN</td></tr></table>

2.1 SUBJECT AND DEMARCATION

This report describes two separate but comparable studies which were carried out as an extension of each other. Both studies were about cybercrime. The first study was conducted among SMEs in the Netherlands. The target population of the second research was one-man businesses. In this section, we discuss the demarcation of the subject and the target populations that are central to this report.

2.1.1 Cybercrime

Cybercrime is crime in which IT plays an essential role in the committing of the offence (Stol, 2012). A distinction is made within this definition. Firstly, there are traditional types of crime that are now (also) being committed in cyberspace, such as online fraud and cyber extortion. These kinds of crime are sometimes called cybercrime in the broad sense (or computer-assisted crime). Secondly, new kinds of crime have emerged in which IT is not only the means but also the objective of the crime ('cybercrime in the narrow sense' or computer-focussed crime). Examples of these are hacking and DoS attacks.

There is a debate about whether cybercrime in the broad sense should fall under the term cybercrime (see also Domenie, Leukfeldt, Van Wilsem, Jansen & Stol, 2013). The argument against this is that a classification of crimes must be derived from the nature of the act (or the rights that are violated by it) and not by the means used in the act. We endorse that argument (compare Stol, 1999). However, for practical reasons, we will use the term 'cybercrime' as defined in the previous paragraph. The term is useful, and, as it stands now, it is in line with how society talks about this contemporary form of crime.

The definition of cybercrime states that IT must play an essential role in the committing of the offence. Although this demarcates the term 'cybercrime', it does not provide a sharp boundary. For instance, it is not clear when IT is essential to the crime and when IT is merely a tool. This lack of clarity does not, however, form a compelling objection for this study because our departure point is a set of predetermined types of cybercrime.[1] The reason behind the research was the lack of insight into the extent to which companies fall victim to cybercrime, regardless of whether this refers to

---

1. Listing crimes referred to by the term 'cybercrime' is a proven way of delineating the term (COE, 1990).

cybercrime in the broad or narrow sense. In consultation with the commissioning party, we therefore decided to investigate various kinds of cybercrime (see Table 2.1).

Table 2.1   Cybercrimes covered by this research[2]

(D) DoS attack	Defacing	Malware
Cyber extortion	Theft of data carriers[b]	Unauthorised use of the
Cyber blackmail	Theft of data	internet or company network
Cyberstalking[a]	Fraud/scams online	Phishing
Cyber defamation	Hacking	Skimming
Cyber espionage	Identity abuse online	Destruction of data

[a] On the basis of evolving insights, the nature and extent of this type of cybercrime was not investigated in the research conducted among SMEs but was included in the research among one-man businesses.

[b] Theft of data carriers does not take place online and therefore does not fall under 'cybercrime'. Norwegian research has shown that theft of data carriers is one of the most common kinds of crime among businesses (NSR, 2012). Given that it does involve theft of digital company information, it was decided in consultation with the commissioning party to include this type of crime. However, theft of data carriers is not taken into consideration in the results sections on cybercrime victimisation given that it does not involve cybercrime.

2.1.2   *Small and medium-sized enterprises*

First, the research was conducted into the nature and extent of cybercrime among Dutch SMEs. For the term 'SME', we first attempted to correspond with the EU definition (2003/361/EC).[3] According to the EU definition, the number of staff in the workforce and the company's financial position (turnover and balance sheet total) determine whether a company should be labelled as an SME. SMEs are distinguished into three types: medium-sized, small and micro (Table 2.2).

Table 2.2   EU criteria for SME

Company category	Workforce	Turnover	Balance sheet total
Medium-sized companies	<250	≤€50 m	≤€43 m
Small companies	<50	≤€10 m	≤€10 m
Micro companies	<10	≤€2 m	≤€2 m

In the Netherlands, however, a different definition is used. According to the EU, businesses comprising one person fall under the category 'SME', but according to the Dutch Chamber of Commerce, they do not. Statistics Netherlands also applies different boundaries to the ones used by the EU. Statline has the latest figures about

---

2.   The glossary contains definitions of the types of cybercrime referred to in the survey and the accompanying offences.

3.   <http://ec.europa.eu/enterprise/policies/sme/facts-figures-analysis/sme-definition/index_en. htm>. Retrieved most recently on 7 April 2015.

the business sector in the Netherlands.[4] There are more than 1.4 million businesses. Table 2.3 shows how the number of employed people is distributed across companies in the Netherlands. The EU limit of 250 employees does not exist in these statistics. The Dutch approach also does not include the EU criteria of turnover and balance sheet total. We therefore decided to abandon the EU criteria and use the Dutch approach as a starting point.

Table 2.3   Number of employees in companies in the Netherlands in 2012

Number of employees	Business sector share NL	Cumulative
1	74.5%	74.5%
2 - 9	21.2%	95.7%
10 - 49	3.4%	99.1%
50 - 99	0.4%	99.5%
100+	0.5%	100%

Most (74.5%) Dutch companies have a staff complement of one person. In Dutch terms, these are not SMEs but one-man businesses, or *Zelfstandigen Zonder Personeel* (ZZP'ers). Then, there is a group of companies (24.6%) who have 2 to 50 members of staff and finally a small group (0.9%) with 50 or more members of staff.

In consultation with the commissioning party, we limited the SME study to companies with 2 to 50 members of staff. The most important considerations for this were as follows:

1. Private and business use and security of computers are intertwined in one-man businesses. The fact that they operate solo means that they do not have any special company-related options to enhance their resilience. This means that they may have their own problems, which deserve special attention.
2. Businesses larger than 50 members of staff comprise a small group (0.9%) and are in a better position than most to get their digital resilience in order because of their size.

2.1.3   One-man businesses

The research among Dutch SMEs was extended by a study into the nature and extent of cybercrime among one-man businesses. The Social and Economic Council of the Netherlands (SER, 2010, p. 51) defines one-man businesses as follows:

A one-man business owner is an entrepreneur who does not employ any people, whereby the following criteria, as applied by the Tax and Customs Administration in the context of income tax, are used to determine whether this person is an entrepreneur:
- autonomy in the organisation and implementation of their own work;

---

4.   <http://statline.cbs.nl/StatWeb/publication/?VW=T&DM=SLNL&PA=81589NED&LA=NL>.
     Retrieved most recently on 13 November 2014.

- carrying out work for their own account and risk;
- aimed at and having the prospect of making profit;
- announcing the entrepreneurship;
- aiming to have several clients.

On the basis of that definition, all entrepreneurs who do not employ any staff were included in the target population of the research.

SMEs and one-man businesses together make up 99.1 per cent of all Dutch businesses.

2.2 OBJECTIVE AND RESEARCH QUESTIONS

The ultimate objective of this report is to contribute to the fight against cybercrime among SMEs and one-man businesses in the Netherlands. The specific research goals are to offer insight into:
- the online activities of businesses;
- the extent to which businesses protect themselves against cybercrime;
- the nature and extent of cybercrime victimisation among businesses and gaining an understanding of the actions that victims of cybercrime take against it;
- risk factors for cybercrime victimisation among companies; and
- the role that companies assign to public and private parties with regard to tackling cybercrime.

2.2.1 *Research questions*

The main questions emanating from the aforementioned objectives for this research are as follows:
1. What activities do businesses undertake in cyberspace?
2. What protective measures do businesses take against cybercrime?
3. What is the nature and extent of cybercrime victimisation among businesses and what actions are taken by businesses in the Netherlands who have fallen victim to cybercrime?
4. What factors are associated with victimisation among businesses?
5. Which role do companies assign to public and private parties with regard to tackling cybercrime?

These main questions have been elaborated into sub-questions. The research among one-man businesses was conducted after the research among the SME sector was completed. Based on an evolving understanding, minor changes were made to the sub-questions for the one-man business research compared to the research questions for the SME research. In addition to this, some sub-questions were added for the research among one-man businesses. Table 2.4 lists all the sub-questions discussed in this report. The table indicates to which target population each sub-question applies.

Table 2.4   An overview of the research questions for the research under SMEs and one-man businesses

Sub-question	SMEs	One-man businesses
Internet activities		
To what extent do one-man businesses separate IT use for work and private purposes?	X	X
What activities do businesses undertake on the internet?	X	X
Protective measures		
To what extent are companies aware of online risks?	X	X
To what extent have companies taken protective measures against cybercrime?	X	X
Cybercrime victimisation		
Which kinds of cybercrime do companies fall victim to?	X	X
How often does cybercrime victimisation among businesses occur?	X	X
What is the impact of victimisation on companies?	X	X
What is the direct damage from cybercrime victimisation among businesses, expressed in monetary terms?	X	X
How do companies fall victim to cybercrime (modi operandi)?	X	X
To what extent are the perpetrators of cybercrime known to their victims? What is the relationship between businesses that are victims of cybercrime and the perpetrators?	X	X
How serious do companies think becoming a victim of cybercrime is?	X	X
What actions do companies who are victims of cybercrime undertake?	X	X
To what extent do companies who are victims of cybercrime contact the police? Why? Why not?	X	X
How (and through which channel) do companies contact the police?	X	X
How willing will companies be to report cybercrime in the future and how can willingness to report be enhanced?	X	X
To what extent do companies use forms of settlement other than prosecution under criminal law? Which do they prefer? Why?	X	X
Risk factors for victimisation		
Are there relationships between victimisation and company attributes, personal attributes, computer knowledge and skills, cyberspace activities, protective measures and/or government measures?	-	X
Tackling cybercrime		
Who is responsible for security on the internet according to companies?	X	X
To what extent do companies have confidence in the police when it comes to fighting cybercrime?	X	X
To what extent are one-man businesses prepared to help the police with their knowledge and expertise, for instance, as police volunteers?	-	X
To what extent are one-man businesses familiar with and use government measures which are intended to help one-man businesses against cybercrime?	-	X
What are the motives for one-man businesses to either use or not use these supportive government measures (for instance, the websites *Digibewust* and *Bescherm Je Bedrijf* (respectively, 'Digital awareness' and 'Protect your company' in Dutch)?	-	X

Despite a few differences, the sub-questions in both research projects were largely the same. To make it possible to compare the results from both studies, identical questions were used as much as possible in the questionnaires. Chapter 4 presents the findings for the SME sector research. In Chapter 5, the results of the research among one-man businesses are described and where possible compared to the results from the study among the SMEs. In addition to direct comparisons based on statistical data files, literature was also used for comparison and interpretation of the results.

3 | RESEARCH METHODOLOGY

In this chapter, we first account for the methodology used to conduct the research into the nature and extent of cybercrime among SMEs (Section 3.1). Section 3.2 describes the research methodology which was used for the research among one-man businesses.

3.1 METHODOLOGY FOR SME SECTOR RESEARCH

In this section, we account for the methodology used for the study among SMEs. First, we explain that the research methods and instruments used have been used in earlier research projects. We go on to explain that we used three research methods for this research project, namely desk research, interviews and a questionnaire-based online survey. In the process, we also explain how each method has contributed to the research findings.

3.1.1 Digital Cybercrime Desk for Businesses Evaluation

Prior to the research among the SME sector, we investigated the functioning of the police force's Digital Cybercrime Desk for Businesses [*Digitaal Bedrijvenloket Cybercrime* (DBC)] (Jansen, Veenstra & Stol, 2013a). There is an overlap in terms of content between that evaluation research and the study into cybercrime among SMEs. Efforts undertaken in the context of evaluating the DBC contributed as much as possible to the research into cybercrime among SMEs and its preparation. For instance, it was used to develop the questionnaire. So we repeatedly refer to Jansen et al.'s report in the account that follows.

3.1.2 Desk research

The objective of the desk research was twofold. First, the desk research contributed to the development of the questionnaires. For this purpose, we used the survey questions posed by Koldijk (2011), the Chamber of Commerce (2009), Syntens (2006) and the research into cybercrime victimisation among members of the public in the Netherlands (Domenie et al., 2013). We also carried out a search on the web to identify and list the protective measures that companies can take against cybercrime. We examined the following websites: www.waarschuwingsdienst.nl, www.digibewust.nl and the website of the police force's DBC (www.politie.nl/ondernemer).

In addition to this, the objective of the desk research was to find national and international articles and research reports about cybercrime victimisation among small- and medium-sized enterprises. The focus of the literature research was to find prevalence rates derived from research with a comparable research methodology conducted either in the Netherlands or abroad. We also searched for literature about other sub-topics examined in the report, for instance, the online operations of businesses, the extent to which they are aware of and protect themselves against cybercrime, and the reactions of businesses that fall victim to such crime. Publications about traditional crime against medium-sized and small businesses were consulted so that we could put the problem into perspective.

Various scientific databanks and search engines were consulted. These included ScienceDirect, EBSCO Host, IEEE Xplore, Google Scholar and the Research and Documentation Centre databank. In addition to this, we searched potentially relevant scientific journals that deal specifically with small- and medium-sized enterprises. Examples of these are *OECD Small and Medium Enterprise Outlook, SME Update* and *OECD Studies on SMEs and Entrepreneurship.* We also consulted several scientific journals in which cybercrime was the focal point. Examples of these are *CyberPsychology & Behavior* and the *International Journal of Cyber Criminology.*

We used search terms such as 'SME cybercrime' and 'SME security online'. Because national and international literature was consulted, we also searched for 'SME(s) cybercrime', 'SME(s) online security' and 'SME(s) information security'. In addition, we used related search words such as 'MKB/SME malware' and 'MKB/SME e-fraud'.[1] This produced 34 publications in total.

Publications that not are based on empirical research were not taken into consideration and so two articles were dropped for this reason. These were articles in 'popular' magazines in which cyber security experts give their opinion on online security of businesses and how to promote it. We then evaluated the extent to which the remaining publications had sufficient common ground with this study in terms of their content. It became apparent that some of the remaining 32 studies were not relevant for this reason (n = 6). For instance, although a theoretical explanation about strategies for fighting cybercrime was given in these publications, the extent to which businesses are confronted with cybercrime and what they do to prevent or fight cybercrime was not explained on the basis of empirical data.

We then investigated the extent to which there were scientifically sound findings in the remaining 26 publications. For this, we used the following criteria:

---

1. The actual search terms used here were the Dutch equivalents, respectively: 'MKB cybercrime'; 'MKB veiligheid online'; 'MKB/SME malware' and 'MKB/SME e-fraud(e)'.

- The extent to which the literature research incorporated in the publication was accounted for (search strategy, quality of the studies found and criteria for selecting relevant studies).
- The extent to which the development of the research instruments (for instance, a questionnaire) was accounted for.
- The extent to which the recruitment of respondents was accounted for:
  - gross and net sample;
  - gross and net response rate and
  - reasons for non-response.
- The extent to which the final population composition (and its representativeness) were ultimately accounted for.

Finally, in order to assess the comparability of the studies we consulted with this research, we investigated the extent to which the research was done among the same target group, namely companies with a workforce of 2 to 50 employees.

It became apparent from literature study that the (scientific) value of the studies we consulted is too limited and the results are therefore of little use as reference material for this research. This can be attributed to the following factors: a lack of common ground from a content point of view; generally unsound accounts of the methodology used and the fact that the target populations researched in those studies generally differed from the target group in this study. Despite these deficiencies we, in order to get an impression of the available studies that offer insight into cybercrime within the business sector, included the results of these 26 reports where relevant.

3.1.3 Two kinds of interviews

Interviews were conducted at two points in time during the research. Interviews with experts were conducted during the preparatory phase of the study. The results of these interviews were used to develop the questionnaire for the survey. In addition to this, and based on the results of the quantitative analysis, in-depth interviews were conducted among companies to help in the interpretation of the quantitative results. Below we give an account of the methodology used for each type of interview.

Interviews for developing the questionnaire
Eight face-to-face interviews were conducted with a total of nine professionals; these interviews contributed to the development of the survey questionnaire. The interviews were semi-structured in nature and were conducted on the basis of respondent-specific interview protocols. The respondents worked for the police force, private detective agencies and interest groups. All were professionals involved in the online security of companies. Given that the interviews were also partly concerned with the functioning of the DBC, they were conducted during that research project (July, October and November 2012). The interviews each lasted around one hour. Table 3.1 gives an overview of the respondents' jobs and the organisations for which they worked.

Table 3.1   Questionnaire development for respondents

Organisation	Position in organisation
Police – Northern Regional Crime Squad	Deputy Police Chief
Police	DBC Project Manager
Police – Central Unit	Investigative Advisor
Police – Department of International Police Information	Strategic Development Team Leader
YourRequest (developer: DBC)	Director
Chamber of Commerce – Regional Platform on Crime Control	Advisor on the Regional Economy
Almere Business Association [*Vereniging Bedrijvenkring Almere*]	Director
Fox IT	Lead Expert at the 'Audits & Readiness' Business Line
Hoffman Corporate Investigations	Cybercrime & audits coordinator

In addition to the persons mentioned above, we approached five other professionals and requested interviews with them. Two of them worked for the police but did not consider themselves appropriate for participation in the research. Three others worked for interest groups [Confederation of Netherlands Industry and Employers (VNO-NCW) and the Chamber of Commerce]. Of these, two gave as a reason for not participating that they had nothing to do with cybercrime in their professional capacity. The third representative of the interest group did not respond to our request for an interview.

Interviews used to analyse the quantitative results in greater depth
In the final phase of the research, five semi-structured in-depth interviews were held with victims of cybercrime. The objective of these interviews was to gain a better understanding of how entrepreneurs feel about falling victim to cybercrime; what the consequences of victimisation are and how victims perceive the tasks and responsibilities of various parties involved in preventing and fighting cybercrime. The interviews took place using an interview protocol. Because the perceptions of the entrepreneurs were the focus of these interviews, respondents were given the opportunity to tell their story.
The respondents were recruited from the database of participants to the online survey. Entrepreneurs were given the opportunity in this survey to indicate whether they would be prepared to be respondents in in-depth interviews. On the basis of the quantitative analyses, it was decided to only approach those entrepreneurs who had indicated on the questionnaire that they had been confronted with cybercrime during the previous year and who had suffered damage as a consequence (n = 17). The expectation was that this group of respondents would be in the best position to contribute to the objective of the in-depth interviews, namely to offer better insight into experiences with cybercrime, the consequences that businesses suffered as a result and the way they would like to see it tackled. Ten of the seventeen entrepreneurs were contacted within the available time. On further consideration, three of the entrepreneurs said that they were too busy to be interviewed. Two of the entrepreneurs were not

available for an interview within the timeframe set aside for this research. Ultimately, telephone interviews were conducted with five entrepreneurs. The interviews lasted between 20 minutes and 1 hour. Table 3.2 gives an overview of the type of company in which the various respondents worked and the type of cybercrime to which they had fallen victim.

Table 3.2   Cybercrime victims interviewed

Company	Cybercrime
Print shop	Hacking
Hairdressers	Hacking
Wholesaler	Hacking, defamation and threats
Furniture shop	Malware
Consultancy firm	Malware

We tried to interview victims of the most common types of cybercrime (see Section 4.2). As Table 3.2 shows, we did not manage to interview victims of e-fraud and phishing. The reason for this was that none of the companies who suffered damage and were available for an interview were victims of phishing. In addition, only one respondent who fell victim to e-fraud and suffered damage as a consequence indicated to be willing to be interviewed in the questionnaire. This respondent was repeatedly approached for an interview, but the researchers were unable to get through to the company.

The results relating to the nature and extent of cybercrime among SMEs are discussed in Chapter 4. Several quotes from the interviews are given in Chapter 4. Names are mentioned in the text boxes containing these quotes. In order to protect the respondents' anonymity, these names are fictitious.

3.1.4   *The online questionnaire*

Below we explain how the online questionnaire was developed and how the interviews were conducted.

Questionnaire development

The questionnaire for the quantitative measurement is based on the questionnaire used for assessing the DBC (see Jansen et al., 2013a). Those questions specifically related to evaluating the DBC were not taken into consideration in this research; instead questions about company internet activities were included.

The questionnaire was quantitatively pre-tested during the period between the end of 2012 and the beginning of 2013. For this purpose, all companies in Flevoland Province with 2 to 49 people employees were selected from the Chamber of Commerce commercial register. All in all, 9,675 businesses met these criteria. The address information for these companies was entered into SPSS so that a random sample of

1,000 companies could be drawn. These companies were then invited by letter to complete the online questionnaire. Eighteen of the invitation letters turned out to be undeliverable. Overall, 982 businesses received an invitation letter and a reminder. Of these, 139 businesses eventually completed the questionnaire, which boils down to a response rate of 14.2 per cent. However, 25 of these were one-man businesses and 11 were companies with more than 50 members of staff, which meant that the results from these companies could not be included. Therefore, a total of 103 SMEs took part in the quantitative pre-testing of the questionnaire (response rate = 10.5%).

The pre-test threw light on areas for improvement in the questionnaire. For instance, it became apparent that it was important to also include questions about *attempts* at cybercrime, because companies reported attempts as victimisation and were subsequently not in a position to answer follow-on questions about victimisation properly. We then discussed an adjusted draft questionnaire with the consultative group. On the basis of this discussion, the questionnaire was improved and coded so that it could be used in an online environment. The consultative group and fellow researchers at the Cybersafety Research Group were asked once more for their comments and criticisms of the online version. After having taken the suggested areas for improvement into account, the final version was drafted in June 2013.

One of the difficulties when developing the questionnaire was formulating the questions precisely. To illustrate: to what extent can a *company* have confidence in the police? Or considered from the opposite perspective: to what extent does the confidence that one respondent may have in the police say anything about the way other employees in the company may think? The question is therefore: how do we measure what we intend to measure? To continually make it clear to respondents that it was not about their own experience or opinion, but rather about those of company, the questions were formulated as much as possible from the company's point of view. So not, for instance, 'How much faith do you have in the police?' but rather 'How much faith does your organisation have in the police?' We are aware that this does not remove the fundamental problem: we are looking for company attributes but are gathering information at an individual level. An organisation is, however, more than an individual or the sum of individuals. So, when interpreting the results, it should be taken into account that the respondents' answers may not necessarily reflect the experiences of the organisations about which they are reporting.

Recruitment
At the time of the research among SMEs, approximately 333,900 addresses of businesses with 2 to 50 employees were registered in the Chamber of Commerce commercial register. Each 41st company was selected from the alphabetical list of addresses. After drawing this sample, the Chamber of Commerce provided 8,264 addresses of companies which belonged to this target population according to the information in the commercial register. Given that our intended sample size was 8,000 companies, we then drew a random sample of 8,000 addresses (gross sample) in SPSS.

Making a public link known online would have made it difficult to control which companies completed the questionnaire. For this reason, we approached the companies selected for the sample by invitation letter only. We opted to send a traditional invitation letter because an interview respondent indicated that it annoys businesses when they receive such invitations by e-mail. The invitation letter was addressed to the director/owner of the businesses in the sample. The director/owner could then decide whether they themselves would complete the questionnaire online or whether a member of staff would do it. To gain access to the questionnaire, each company who received an invitation was given a unique login code. The questionnaire could only be completed once using the login code. We opted for an online survey because conducting interviews on site or by telephone was not feasible for financial and practical reasons.

The invitation letters were sent and signed on behalf of Patricia M. Zorko, Central Unit police chief/subject specialist for digitisation and cybercrime. The contents of the letter were discussed with the communication department of the police force's Programme Against Cybercrime. The invitation letters were subsequently sent from the police organisation, i.e. on police letterheads and in police envelopes. We opted for this approach because it became apparent during the pre-test that entrepreneurs find it strange if they are approached to take part in research by a knowledge institute (NHL University of Applied Sciences/Cybersafety Research Group).

Response rate

The gross sample comprised 8,000 SME sector businesses registered with the Chamber of Commerce. Not all 8,000 businesses were reached due to incorrect addresses. In total, the maximum number of businesses that actually received the letter was 7,925[2] (the net sample) after the original invitation letter (17 June 2013) and a reminder letter (2 July 2013) were sent.

Various steps were taken to increase the response rate to ensure that it would be as high as possible. These measures were based on the pre-test and on experiences with previous victim research conducted among members of the public and included the following:

- The invitation letters were sent in police envelopes and on police letterheads. Because the National Police Force was undergoing changes at the time, an invalid police web address was given in the metadata in the first letter. This incorrect information was corrected in the reminder letter. The reminder letter was sent in colour, on high-quality paper and with reference to the appropriate police web address.
- The letter also mentioned that it was important for the research that companies that had not fallen victim to cybercrime and/or that hardly used computers also completed the questionnaire.

---

2. It is always possible that letters were sent to the wrong address and that the person who received the letter did not return it to sender.

- Because it became apparent from the pre-test that suspicious entrepreneurs some-times call the (local) police to verify the legitimacy of the research, the National Police in the Netherlands were informed about the research (for example by a notification on the intranet).
- A message was also placed on politie.nl and the police twittered about it. The police bulletins were also copied by other websites, for instance security.nl.[3]
- The questionnaire was hosted via a secure connection.

Businesses had the options of contacting the research team by telephone as well as by e-mail if they had any questions about the research. The research team received 27 e-mails and registered more than 70 telephone calls. Entrepreneurs mainly got in touch to excuse themselves from the research (n = 38). The most important reasons for this were that the company did not use a computer or the internet;[4] because business operations had already stopped or were due to be halted in the near future or because they had doubts about the legitimacy of the research. In this case, vigilant business people wanted to verify whether the research project was indeed legitimate. Some entrepreneurs did so because according to them they are by definition cautious when dealing with requests to disclose company information. In part suspicions arose because the initial invitation letter was printed in black and white on cheap paper – according to the entrepreneurs – and, as noted above, it contained an invalid police web address. Other reasons why entrepreneurs contacted the research team varied. Several entrepreneurs called to say that they could not find the site despite the fact that the letter gave an explanation supported by an illustration on how the questionnaire could be found (i.e. by entering www.vragenlijstonderzoek.nl/mkb in the address bar of the web browser). Many of these entrepreneurs entered the web address in the Google search bar instead of in the address bar. In addition to this, entrepreneurs contacted the team because they doubted whether they belonged to the relevant target population; they were not sure whether it was obligatory to cooperate; they had already completed the questionnaire but had received a reminder letter; they wanted to know how their privacy would be guaranteed or because they were keen to have access to the research findings.
Data collection ended on Friday 19 July. Of the 1,606 businesses that started completing the questionnaire, 1,481 went on to complete it in full. That equates to a gross response rate of 18.7 per cent.[5] The responses from some of the 1,481 businesses that

---

3. <www.security.nl/posting/41541/Politie+start+onderzoek+naar+cybercrime+onder+MKB>. Retrieved most recently on 22 August 2013.
4. In the introduction, we mentioned that all companies in the Netherlands have access to the internet according to the Statistics Netherlands. This research showed, however, that there are indeed SMEs that do not use the internet. This was not only a reason why companies turned down participation in the research project; 16 companies who started completing the questionnaire indicated that they do not use the internet and for this reason, they were not part of the target audience for this research.
5. Of the 7,925 companies who eventually received an invitation letter, 1,481 completed the questionnaire in full.

completed the questionnaire had to be disregarded, however. Of these businesses, 262 did not fall within the definition of an SME applied in this research: 149 respondents reported that their company was in fact a one-man business and 113 indicated that their company had a workforce of 50 or more employees. This finding means that the sample supplied by the Chamber of Commerce was not up to date, i.e. the sample did not consist exclusively of companies for whom 2 to 50 people were employed. In addition to this, 16 of the entrepreneurs who completed the questionnaire did not use the internet for business purposes. So a total of 1,203 respondents completed a questionnaire that was fully usable for the analyses. The results are based on the responses of these 1,203 respondents. The net response rate was 15.2 per cent (at least).[6,7] On average, the questionnaires took 10 minutes and 45 seconds to complete.

3.1.5   *The generalisability of the findings and data analysis*

According to the definition of SME used in this research, the Netherlands had a total of 357,295 SMEs at the time of the study.[8] A total of 1,203 businesses which belonged to the study's target group completed the survey in full. That means that statements can be made about the population as a whole with a 99 per cent confidence level and a confidence interval of plus or minus 4 per cent (rounded up). So suppose that it becomes apparent from this research that 8 per cent of the businesses fell victim to hacking, then it can be concluded with a confidence level of 99 per cent that the number of victims of hacking out of all SMEs (the total population) is between 4 and 12 per cent.[9]

In addition to the confidence level of the net response rate, we also calculated the extent to which the size of SMEs, expressed as the number of employees, that participated in this research differs from the size of all SMEs in the Netherlands. Table 3.3 shows how company sizes, expressed as the number of employees, are distributed in the Netherlands (in absolute numbers as well as in percentages).

---

6. The comparability of our response rate with the response rates of prior studies is – due to a lack of methodological justification in earlier studies – limited.
7. 'At least' because, even though the companies that did not fall under the definition for SMEs used for this research were indeed removed from the response, we could not remove them from the sample provided by the Chamber of Commerce. (The sample they provided turned out to be 'contaminated'.) For this reason, the response rate was calculated on the basis of a sample that was too large and the response rate is therefore lower than it would have been if the ineligible companies had been removed from the original sample.
8. <http://statline.cbs.nl/StatWeb/publication/?VW=T&DM=SLNL&PA=81589NED&LA=NL>. Retrieved most recently on 24 December 2013.
9. This 4 per cent has been rounded up and applies to a population proportion of 50 per cent (maximum distribution). The margin would in fact be smaller for smaller or larger population proportions.

Table 3.3   Distribution of size of the company, expressed as the number of employees, within the SME sector in the Netherlands (on the basis of Statistics Netherlands figures, see Footnote 8)

Size of the company	Number in NL	Portion in %
2 - 4 employees	242,480	67.9
5 - 9 employees	63,975	17.9
10 - 19 employees	31,685	8.9
20 - 49 employees	19,155	5.4
Total SMEs	357,295	100

On the basis of Table 3.3, it is possible to calculate what distribution according to company size should be in the net sample. If 67.9 per cent of SMEs in the Netherlands have 2 to 4 employees, then in theory 816 of the companies that took part in the study should have 2 to 4 employees. Using a chi-square test, we analysed the extent to which the expected number of businesses per category differs from the number which participated in the research per category (see Table 3.4).

Table 3.4   A comparison between the expected size of the company on the basis of Statistics Netherlands data and the actual size of the companies that participated in this research

Size of the company	Expected number in net sample	Actual number in net sample
2 - 4 employees	816	561
5 - 9 employees	215	315
10 - 19 employees	107	192
20 - 49 employees	64	135
Total SMEs	1,203	1,203

The distribution of businesses that participated in the survey differs significantly from the distribution in the total population of SMEs in the Netherlands ($p < 0.01$). There is under-representation of SMEs with 2 to 4 employees and over-representation of the rest. There is no obvious explanation for the difference in response rate according to the size of the company.

The difference means that our research is not representative of the SME sector in the Netherlands as far as size of the company is concerned. It should therefore be taken into account when interpreting the results that the larger SMEs are over-represented and the findings therefore do not automatically apply to the group of small SMEs. We did not investigate the extent to which the research is representative in terms of the other company attributes (such as sector, turnover and geographical location).

Previous research has shown that sending invitations for research in the name of the police (on police letterheads and in police envelopes) elicits a higher response rate compared to sending invitations from a research institute (Domenie, Leukfeldt & Stol,

2011). The aforementioned research also shows that not only the response rate but also the percentage of victims is higher when police invitations are used.[10] This means that the measures taken to increase the response rate may have led to a selective response: victims of cybercrime may well be more inclined to respond to an invitation from the police.

Respondent characteristics may also influence the victimisation rate. In this context, we investigated which position in the organisation the respondent had and the extent to which respondents were involved in the company's IT security. This investigation showed that 79 per cent of the respondents were owners of the companies participating in the research. The remaining 21 per cent were employees of the SME. In addition, 72.9 per cent of the respondents were involved in IT security for their organisation. The respondent's position in organisation or the extent to which the respondent is involved in IT security for the company does not affect the victimisation rates presented in the chapter on findings.

Data analysis
The analyses were carried out using SPSS, a statistical software package. In addition to standard statistical analyses like frequency analyses, we also carried out in-depth analyses to interpret differences or indicate correlations, for example. Unless otherwise indicated, a chi-square test was used in these analyses. Asterisks in the tables indicate significant differences One asterisk indicates a significant difference based on a confidence level of 95 per cent (* $p < 0.05$). Two asterisks indicate a difference based on a confidence level of 99 per cent (* $p < 0.01$). If the difference or correlation is not significant or the test does not lead to reliable results, for instance, because the number of respondents is too small, then the results were not taken into consideration.

3.2   METHODOLOGY FOR ONE-MAN BUSINESS SECTOR RESEARCH

This section accounts for the research methodology used in the research among one-man businesses. We describe how the desk research, interviews and online survey contributed to the research findings. In addition to this, we consider the extent to which the findings and the data analysis can be extrapolated to the general population which underlies the research (generalisability).

---

10. For financial and interpersonal cybercrimes together, Domenie et al. (2013) found: 6.7 per cent victimisation in response to an invitation from the police (n = 358) and 2.3 per cent victimisation in response to an invitation from NHL University of Applied Sciences (n = 175). The difference between the two percentages is significant (Z-score for proportions: $p < 0.05$). The difference is not only significant, it is also relevant: using invitations from the police, Domenie et al. found the percentage of victims to be almost three times higher than when invitations from the NHL were used. We do not know which of the two percentages best reflects reality.

3.2.1   Desk research

In 2013, research was conducted into cybercrime victimisation among Dutch SMEs. A questionnaire was developed for the research (see Section 3.1.4) and this questionnaire was used as the departure point for the one-man business sector survey. Despite already having a questionnaire to work with, we once again carried out a media analysis and a literature study for the purposes of developing the questionnaire for this study.

In addition to this, we searched and used (scientific) literature to gain an understanding of the nature and extent of cybercrime victimisation and risk factors for this type of crime among one-man businesses. The objective of the literature study was to contribute to the interpretation of the quantitative survey findings (see Section 3.2.3). Below we account for the way in which the desk research was carried out.

Media analysis
We searched Lexis Nexis for news articles about one-man businesses and cybercrime. The objective of this was to gather leads to potentially relevant research publications and/or institutions that could possibly contribute to the development of the questionnaire. The number of search results for unqualified search terms used in isolation, like cybercrime or one-man business (ZZP in Dutch), was too large and contained too many irrelevant publications. For this reason, we opted to use a combination of search terms. The (combined) search terms used included: cybercrime, cyber criminality, one-man businesses, cybercrime, businesses and (independent) entrepreneur(s). Depending on the (combination) of search terms used, between 0 and 483 articles were found. The combined search term 'cybercrime' AND 'businesses' produced the most search results (n = 483). We then made a selection of articles published in *national* newspapers. As a result, the number of search results dropped to 188 search results (26 March 2014). These 188 search results were screened by title. All articles whose title made a statement about the nature and extent of cybercrime among companies were then read.

In total, 19 articles provided leads to potentially relevant research or institutions that could be consulted for the purposes of developing the questionnaire. Various potentially useful publications were downloaded based on the references in the news articles. These included, for instance, publications from the National Cyber Security Centre (NCSC), such as the National Cyber Security Strategy 2.0 and trend reports; research reports from large consultancy and advisory organisations like KPMG and Ernst and Young, for instance the IT Barometer and trend reports from companies that develop security software, such as Symantec and Kaspersky Lab. An overview of the studies that ultimately contributed to the development of the questionnaire is given in the explanation of how the questionnaire was developed (Section 3.2.3).

In addition to references to potentially useful reports, the news articles also regularly referred to professionals who represent small entrepreneurs and/or have information about cyber problems among this population. With questionnaire development in mind, the intention was to interview (a selection of) such professionals. So the media analysis contributed in this way to the identification and listing of the interest group representatives/experts to be interviewed. Section 3.2.2 accounts for the way these exploratory interviews were organised and conducted.

Literature study

In 2013, literature research was conducted for interpreting the quantitative results from the research into cybercrime victimisation among the Dutch SME sector. The most important conclusion was that the scientific value of the literature found was limited and that the studies were of little use (see Section 3.1.2). Even though the studies were about cybercrime, the research was seldom methodologically sound and about the nature and extent of cybercrime among comparably sized companies. Nevertheless, we collected 26 publications which we, for the purposes of developing the questionnaire, also consulted for the research among one-man businesses. In addition, we once again searched for scientific literature about cybercrime in relation to companies and/or one-man businesses (in March 2014).

The BoomLemma journal databank can be searched for scientific articles about cybercrime (whether or not in relation to the business sector) in the most relevant Dutch journals.[11] The following combined search terms were used (among others) to search in this databank for relevant publications: one-man business (and its Dutch acronym, ZZP), small business(es), cybercrime, cyber and company. Although we did find articles about cybercrime, no publications were found about cybercrime which were relevant to companies and/or one-man businesses in these Dutch journals.

In addition to this, we searched for literature in various international databanks in which searches can be done in several scientific journals at the same time. The databanks which were searched were EBSCO Host, IEEE Xplore, IBSS, ScienceDirect, SAGE Journals, Springer Link, Taylor & Francis and Wiley e-Journals. The initial search was based on the term 'cybercrime'. Depending on the databank, 'cybercrime' produced thousands of search results. For this reason, we used combined search terms, for instance 'cybercrime AND business' or 'cybercrime AND self-employed', in some databanks, like ScienceDirect. The titles of the publications we found were then scanned and potentially relevant articles, in which statements were made about cybercrime, its nature and extent among companies, were filtered out.

We also used Google and Google Scholar to find relevant publications. We used various search terms for this (those previously mentioned), sometimes in combination with each other. Because this search method is less restricted to scientific publications, searching using Google and Google Scholar produces publications which are varied in nature. For instance, it also finds (online) news articles which contain references to publications about cybercrime in the corporate sector. The publications mentioned in these publications were, if potentially relevant, also collected.

---

11. Magazines regarding safety and security: *Justitiële verkenningen, Sociologie, Tijdschrift voor Criminologie* and *Tijdschrift voor Veiligheid*.

The literature study produced about 30 publications. None of them, however, was specifically related to one-man businesses. Despite this, the results presented in the publications as well as the research instruments upon which the studies were based, such as questionnaires that were completed by (larger) companies, could contribute to the development of the questionnaire for the one-man businesses. The publications we gathered were consulted with this objective in mind.

In addition to literature research into studies about the nature and extent of cybercrime among businesses, we also searched the aforementioned (international) scientific databanks for (validated) instruments to measure computer skills, awareness of online risk and self-control (see the sub-questions in Table 2.4). To find a validated instrument for measuring computer skills, we used search terms such as: measuring (of) computer skills, (measuring) computer skills, computer self-efficacy and self-assessment, either on their own or in combination. We searched for instruments to measure risk awareness, online or otherwise, using (combined) keywords such as (online) risk awareness and (risk) awareness. To search for a validated instrument to measure self-control, we searched on the basis of search terms like self-control, measuring self-control and self-control scale. Since constructs are often based on previous research, we also used the snowball method to find other relevant publications. We account for the extent to which the publications actually contributed to developing the questionnaire in Section 3.2.3.

We also used (scientific) literature for the interpretation of the quantitative results. For the research among the SME sector we, despite their limited comparability and methodological soundness, already gathered and used several studies about cybercrime in the corporate sector. An impression of cybercrime in the corporate sector in general has thus already been sketched. Therefore, the literature study that was conducted for the research on the one-man business sector specifically focussed on cybercrime among one-man businesses. Literature about cybercrime in the corporate sector in general was disregarded.

The results from searches carried out previously showed that there was hardly any literature (in which the methodology had been properly accounted for) on the subject of cybercrime among small companies and/or one-man businesses. However, these literature studies (for the SME research and the development of the questionnaire for one-man businesses) were conducted in 2013 and at the beginning of 2014. Given that the analysis of the quantitative data from the online survey for one-man businesses was completed in the autumn of 2014, there was a possibility that new and relevant publications may have been published. For this reason, we once again searched for literature specific to the one-man business sector at the beginning of 2015. Using, among others, the (combined) search terms: 'self-employed, entrepreneur, cybercrime' and their Dutch equivalents, we once more searched Google and Google Scholar, the online database of BoomLemma Journals and the international databanks mentioned previously.

The (Dutch) Google search generally led to websites which made mention of this research project. In addition to this, there were websites containing 'advice about security' and/or a few insurance websites explaining that entrepreneurs could insure themselves against cybercrime. A few websites contained articles with facts and figures about cybercrime, albeit not scientific and without an account of the methodology used. As we had discovered earlier, there is a significant number of (scientific and other) publications about cybercrime. However, none of the publications found via Google and Google Scholar related specifically to cybercrime among one-man businesses. The same applies to the publications found in the BoomLemma database. Even though various articles on cybercrime were found, we still did not manage to find publications about cybercrime in the one-man business sector in relevant Dutch language scientific journals.

The search in international scientific journals produced more than 500 search results. We looked at all titles and, if the title prompted it, we also read through some of the abstracts of the publications we found. Once again, none of the publications we found were about cybercrime among one-man businesses.

In short, there are no publications on cybercrime among one-man businesses as far as the research team is aware. This is not a new finding: other researchers have also established that, as it stands now, there is a lack of knowledge about cybercrime among entrepreneurs. For this reason, they have suggested that future cybercrime research should focus on this (Hernandez-Castro & Boiten, 2014; McGuire & Boiten, 2013; Schaper & Weber, 2012). On the one hand, this finding confirms the need for this research. On the other hand, it makes it difficult for us to put our observations into perspective. Nevertheless, in order to make an attempt to do so, we mainly used the international literature about the nature and extent of victimisation among members of the public. After all, one-man businesses are in fact individuals who use IT for private and business use interchangeably (see also Sections 3.2.3 and 5.1.1). We used Dutch as well as international (English) victim research, where possible. Insofar as these publications were not found on the basis of the search described above, these publications were not gathered by searching an academic databank because the researchers (generally) already knew of their existence and therefore searched specifically for them. The snowball method was then used to gather publications mentioned in the publications already collected. Finally, we also used, where relevant, research and other publications we had already gathered which were relevant to the corporate sector (even though they did not specifically discuss the issue of cybercrime among one-man businesses).

3.2.2 *Interviews*

Interviews were conducted at two points in time during the research. During the preparatory phase of the study, exploratory interviews were conducted with professionals from interest groups for the one-man business sector. After the quantitative data collection, interviews were conducted with one-man business owners. These interviews were used to interpret the quantitative results. Below we account for the method used for each type of interview.

Exploratory interviews (n = 3)
The primary objective of the exploratory interviews was to contribute to the development of the online questionnaire. With this in mind, we tried to gain insight into the knowledge and research requirements of organisations that advocate for the interests of the one-man business sector. In addition to this, our intention was to, based on the concerns from professional practice as well as on the knowledge of experts, identify and list trends in cybercrime among one-man businesses. Finally, we used the interviews to raise awareness for this study and to create a support base for it.
Based on the media analysis (see Section 3.2.1), we established which organisations and/or experts could contribute to the aforementioned interview objectives. The following is an overview of the relevant organisations and/or experts:

- The Foundation for One-Man Businesses in the Netherlands [*Stichting ZZP Nederland*] is the largest interest group advocating for the one-man business sector in the Netherlands. This foundation maintains close contacts with one-man businesses and so is aware of developments within this professional group.
- The media analysis showed that the Chamber of Commerce organised information meetings for entrepreneurs about cybercrime in 2012 and 2013. The concerns that business people voiced during these Chamber of Commerce meetings may offer insight into the developments of cybercrime among entrepreneurs. In addition to this, the Chamber of Commerce also advocates for the interests of one-man businesses.
- News reports repeatedly made mention of 'the help button for cybercrime' and the 'stopcybercrime.nu' (Dutch for 'stop cybercrime now') campaign. These initiatives are intended to raise awareness of cybercrime among business people. The 'SME service desk' developed the campaigns in consultation with the Ministry of Security and Justice. The SME service desk is an online platform (www.mkbservicedesk.nl) which tries to answers questions from entrepreneurs. The SME service desk indicated that there is a need for a similar kind of service desk for the one-man business sector and went on to set up such a desk for one-man businesses. In short, the SME service desk is engaged in various initiatives concerning cybercrime and raising awareness about it; it registers reports of cybercrime among entrepreneurs and represents their interests.
- The media analysis showed that the Centre for Crime Prevention and Security [*Centrum voor Criminaliteitspreventie en Veiligheid* (CCV)] carried out a study into cybercrime among 8,500 small businesses. We approached the CCV for an interview because of the knowledge that they had acquired through their study and because of the role that the CCV plays in informing entrepreneurs.
- The news reports made mention of the 'action plan for crime against the corporate sector' set up by the Ministry of Security and Justice. That plan of action shows that

the National Platform for Crime Control [*Nationaal Platform Criminaliteitsbeheersing (NPC)*] concerns itself (among other things) with fighting cybercrime among small companies. For this reason, we also contacted the NPC.

In total, interviews were conducted by telephone with 3 of the 5 prospective respondents. We spoke to representatives of the Foundation for One-Man Businesses in the Netherlands and the SME/one-man business service desk, and an interview was conducted with the Chamber of Commerce's consultant for safe business practices. We approached the CCV four times for an interview. After the first request by e-mail failed to get a response (1), we called the organisation's secretarial department (2). We then sent a targeted request once more by e-mail within the organisation (3), but once again failed to get a response. After that, we sent one last reminder by e-mail, but we did not get a response to that either. It was therefore not possible to interview the CCV within the timeframe set aside for the exploratory interviews.[12] We did not find a direct e-mail address for the NPC on the internet, so we contacted them by telephone. During this telephone call, we were given a direct e-mail address for a member of staff at the Ministry of Security and Justice who deals with cybercrime issues. We requested an interview with this staff member twice by e-mail. A response followed six weeks after the first request for interview was made, once the survey was in full swing. In the response we were told that the person concerned was still prepared to be interviewed. Given that the objective of the exploratory interviews was to develop the questionnaire, we indicated that conducting an exploratory interview at that stage was pointless, but that we would request another interview if the findings of the survey gave us reason to do so.

The interviews were semi-structured in nature. We used a generic interview protocol in which the following subjects were discussed:

- the way one-man businesses should be addressed in a questionnaire (as private individuals and/or as entrepreneurs);
- internet activities that one-man businesses undertake;
- online risk awareness among one-man businesses and the extent to which they take protective measures;
- cybercrime victimisation and the actions that one-man businesses subsequently take;
- the knowledge requirements of interest groups and
- tips for increasing the response rate and raising awareness for the research via interest groups.

The interviews were conducted in the spring of 2014 and each lasted around one hour.

---

12. We were also not able to find the research that the CCV, according to the media analysis, conducted. Hence, the CCV members of staff were not able to provide it (even at a later stage). The researchers were referred to the Dutch Federation of Small- and Medium-Sized Enterprises for the research.

In-depth interviews (n = 31)
Ultimately, 1,622 one-man business owners completed the online questionnaire (see Sections 3.2.3 and 3.2.4). At the end of the questionnaire, respondents were asked whether they would be willing to take part in an in-depth interview based on the survey findings. Eleven per cent of the respondents said that they would be prepared to take part in an in-depth interview (n = 179). In accordance with agreements reached with the commissioning party, we aimed to conduct 30 in-depth interviews: 20 with victims and 10 one-man business owners that had not fallen victim to cybercrime. We analysed the extent to which potential interview respondents had fallen victim to cybercrime based on the respondents' answers in the questionnaires. Of the one-man businesses that were willing to participate in the interviews, 65.9 per cent (n = 118) had not fallen victim to cybercrime; the remaining 34.1 per cent (n = 61) had been victims. Because we expected that there would be non-response for the in-depth interviews, we selected a total of 75 potential interview respondents to approach for in-depth interviews: 50 victims and 25 non-victims. The assumption was that if 40 per cent of the group of non-victims and 40 per cent of the victims were still prepared to take part in an interview, then we would be able to reach our objective of 20 interviews with victims and 10 interviews with non-victims.[13]
Twenty-five potential non-victim respondents were selected randomly from the group of 118 potential interview respondents who had not fallen victim to cybercrime according to the survey results. Respondents for the interviews with victims were mainly selected from those who fell victim to the most common kinds of cybercrime according to the survey results. The most common types of cybercrime are malware, e-fraud, phishing, hacking, bankcard skimming and DoS attacks (see Section 5.3). Table 3.5 shows the percentage of respondents prepared to be interviewed for each common type of cybercrime.

Table 3.5   The percentage of victims of the most common types of cybercrime prepared to take part in an in-depth interview

Cybercrime	Number of potential interview respondents	Proportion in %
Malware	28	34
E-fraud	15	18
Phishing	13	16
Hacking	8	10
Bankcard skimming	11	13
DoS attack	7	9
Total	82	100

13. That is: if 40 per cent of a total of 50 who were eligible for the victim interviews agreed to be interviewed, then that would mean a total of 20 interviews with victims. And if 40 per cent of a total of 25 who were eligible for the non-victim interviews agreed to be interviewed, then that would mean a total of 10 interviews.

We attempted to select the 50 respondents for the in-depth interviews according to the same proportion, rounded off into 5.[14] This meant that ideally 15 victims of malware, 10 victims of e-fraud, 10 victims of phishing and 5 victims each of hacking, skimming and DoS attacks should have been selected.

Table 3.6   The intended distribution of the number of selected respondents for each cybercrime

Cybercrime	Victimisation in percentages	Number of interview respondents to be selected per type of cybercrime[a]	Number of respondents to select, rounded off to 5
Malware	34	17	15
E-fraud	18	9	10
Phishing	16	8	10
Hacking	10	5	5
Bankcard skimming	13	6.5	5
DoS attack	9	4.5	5
Total	100	50	50

[a] The numbers in this column were calculated using the following formula: victimisation in percentages/100 * 50 (the total number of victims to approach for the in-depth interviews).

However, as is clear in Table 3.5, the total number of potential interview respondents amounts to 82 while only 61 victims said that they would be prepared to participate in an in-depth interview. The explanation for this is that some respondents fell victim to several (frequently occurring) types of cybercrime. For this reason, it was not possible to select enough individual victims for interviews for each type of cybercrime. Six instead of the intended ten individual phishing victims and four instead of the intended five DoS victims were available for interviews. The shortage of potential interview respondents was supplemented with one-man business owners that were also prepared to take part in an interview and were victims to a cybercrime other than one of the six most common types of cybercrime.

We opted to select victims of the most common types of cybercrime for the interviews with victims because the focus was also mainly on these victims in the quantitative results. It was important to get in-depth information about precisely these types of cybercrime to be able to interpret the quantitative results. Furthermore, this method was in line with the method used in the research among Dutch SMEs.

---

14. Deciding to round off the numbers at 5 each was a pragmatic decision. Five student assistants conducted the interviews. Each student assistant was given a batch of respondents which had been divided in the same way. Numbers rounded off to the nearest 5 can be divided by 5: so each student assistant was given the contact details of 3 malware victims (3 malware victims * 5 student assistants equals 15 malware victims in total) and 2 victims of e-fraud and phishing (2 e-fraud/phishing victims * 5 student assistants equals 10 e-fraud/phishing victims in total).

Five 4th-year students undergoing a higher professional education conducted the interviews in November and December of 2014. These students had all acquired interviewing experience during their studies. An interview protocol, which the researchers had drafted beforehand based on the quantitative analysis results, was used. A briefing – during which the design and results of the research up until that time were discussed – was also held prior to the interviews. During the briefing, the researchers furthermore explained the interview protocol and the interview method to be used. The objective of the briefing was to enhance the quality of the interview results.

From a total of 75 one-man businesses selected for the interviews, 67 were asked whether they were still prepared to take part in a telephone in-depth interview.[15] The non-response was as follows: 22 respondents were not reached despite repeated attempts to reach them by telephone (maximum of five attempts). In addition, 14 respondents said that they were not prepared to be interviewed by telephone, despite having said on the questionnaire that they would be prepared. The most important reasons for not wanting to participate were as follows:

- No time (n = 6)
- Could not remember the research (n = 3)
- Other/no particular reason (n = 3)[16]
- Did not feel like being interviewed (n = 2).

Ultimately, 31 in-depth interviews were conducted by telephone with one-man business owners. Based on the answers that the interviewed respondents gave to the survey questionnaire, it was expected that 27 victim interviews and 4 non-victim interviews would be conducted. For ethical reasons and because it was up to the respondents to decide which incident they wanted to talk about, the respondents were not told during the interviews which type of cybercrime they said they had fallen victim to in their answers to the survey questionnaire. Remarkably, according to the interview results, a total of 8 interviews were conducted with victims and 23 interviews with non-victims. So there was a discrepancy between the number of interviews we expected to conduct and those that we actually conducted, with victims and non-victims, respectively. An explanation for this discrepancy is that some respondents reported cybercrime attempts as victimisation in the survey questionnaire. In addition to this, some respondents could probably no longer remember that they had been victims.

Table 3.7 shows the types of companies owned by the one-man business owners who were interviewed. The table also shows whether one-man business owners indicated during the interviews whether or not they had fallen victim to cybercrime and, if so, to what type of cybercrime.

---

15. We would have preferred to have conducted these interviews face-to-face but, in the interests of saving the researcher's and the respondents' time, we opted instead for telephone interviews.
16. One respondent asked us to call back. We did not manage to call the respondent back at a convenient moment during the timeframe set aside for the in-depth interviews. We were asked once to send the questions by e-mail and once no specific reason was given.

Table 3.7   One-man business people interviewed

Company	Victimisation
Administrative office	Advertising fraud
IT firm	Identity abuse
Driving school	Malware
Garden landscaping and maintenance	Malware
Architectural consultancy firm	Malware
Housing rentals	Malware
Bookbinder for miniature books	Malware
Webshop and animal caretaker	Skimming
Freelance journalist	Non-victim
Consultancy firm	Non-victim
Driving school	Non-victim
IT firm	Non-victim
Software development	Non-victim
Odd-jobs firm	Non-victim
Care sector	Non-victim
Photographic studio	Non-victim
Consultancy/design studio	Non-victim
Coaching	Non-victim
Sales of gems and minerals	Non-victim
Lego salesperson	Non-victim
Administrative office	Non-victim
Administration and consultancy	Non-victim
Journalist, copywriter and publisher	Non-victim
Photographer	Non-victim
Firm specialising in sound	Non-victim
Masseur	Non-victim
Design studio and system management	Non-victim
Cleaning and administration	Non-victim
Consultancy firm	Non-victim
Translation bureaus	Non-victim
Webshop for skin care products, coach and communication staff member	Non-victim

The results relating to the nature and extent of cybercrime among one-man businesses are discussed in Chapter 5. Chapter 5 also gives examples from the interviews so that greater depth is given to the survey results. In these examples, names are mentioned. To protect the respondents' anonymity, these names are fictitious.

3.2.3   *Online questionnaire development*

In this section, we account for the way the online survey among one-man businesses was conducted and describe how the questionnaire was developed. In the process, we explain the contents of the questionnaire.

Existing questionnaires as a basis

In 2011, research was conducted into cybercrime victimisation among members of the public in the Netherlands (Domenie et al., 2013) and in 2013, research was conducted into cybercrime victimisation in the Dutch SME sector. People who own one-man businesses can be considered to be members of the public in the sense that they can fall victim to cybercrime as individuals. One-man businesses can, however, also be approached as companies in the sense that their owners are not only active in cyberspace as private individuals but also as business people. It goes without saying that the research questions (Section 2.2) were the departure point when developing the questionnaire. However, considering that the research questions strongly resembled the research questions that were central to the SME research, and had attributes from the research conducted among members of the public, many of the questions in survey were based on the research among members of the public and the questionnaires from the SME sector research.

Those parts of the questionnaire that were derived from previous victim research conducted by the Cybersafety Research Group were – in summary – developed on the basis of literature research and interviews with members of the public, interested parties and cybercrime experts. In addition, professionals in the field and fellow researchers provided feedback on the existing questionnaires several times. The existing questions were also tested extensively in the studies which have already been carried out. For a detailed explanation of existing sections of the questionnaire, see Domenie et al. (2013) and Section 3.1.4.

Some questions and/or response categories from the existing sections of the questionnaire were improved as a result of new insights from the literature. For instance, previous research carried out by the Cybersafety Research Group did not pay any attention to working on the cloud and the attendant risks, yet it was mentioned in the literature (Hoevenagel, 2013; Motivaction, 2012). Also the question of the extent to which entrepreneurs take technical measures was supplemented based on the literature: one of the technical measures that the literature discussed was the use of biometric security methods, like fingerprint readers (Hagen, Sivertsen & Rong, 2008; RAND, 2008). Furthermore, the questionnaire now reported that cybercrime had led to the bankruptcy of a firm and that access to information had been temporarily restricted or leaked due to cybercrime (Kjaerland, 2006).

Also, insights gained during the analyses of the SME research, which was very similar to this research, contributed to improving sections of the questionnaire. The objective of one of the research questions posed in both the research among Dutch SMEs and this study among one-man businesses was to offer insight into the impact and financial damages that cybercrime has. In the SME research, respondents were only asked about the impact and the damage suffered as a consequence of the last encountered cyber incident. However, entrepreneurs may well have fallen victim to cybercrime more than once. Given that the SME research only asked about damage suffered as a consequence of the most recent incident, some of the damage that occurred may not have been taken into consideration. For this reason, respondents in the research among one-man businesses were asked about damage from the most recent incident but also about damage from other incidents, if applicable. Despite this, only the results pertaining to the most recent incident are discussed in Chapter 5, the chapter which specifically discusses the results for the one-man business research. The research findings on the impact and damage that related to the most recent incident are in fact broadly comparable to the results on the impact and damage suffered as a consequence of all cybercrime incidents. Moreover, the results presented about the impact and damage among SMEs can be compared to the results relating to the impact and damage suffered by one-man businesses.

The development of new questionnaire sections

In addition to improving existing sections of the questionnaire, additional survey questions were formulated as a consequence of several new research questions. The new research questions related in particular to risk factors for victimisation. The additional survey questions which were formulated about 'new' risk factors were intended to measure computer and internet skills, awareness of online risk and self-control. Below we account for the way in which the new constructs were developed.

Computer and internet skills

To measure the computer and internet skills of one-man business people, a construct comprising 14 items was included in the questionnaire. The construct was based on the Computer Self-Efficacy Scale (Murphy, Coover & Owen, 1989; Sam, Othman & Nording, 2005; Torkzadeh & Koufteros, 1994) and the General Computer Skills Questionnaire (Klinkenberg, 2004). Both instruments include more items than the set of questions that were used in this research. It was necessary to shorten the original lists because of their length and the time required to complete the questionnaire. Thus, we removed items that strongly resembled other items in the construct. In addition to this, items which had become outdated were not taken into consideration. Also, questions about the use of applications were posed at a higher level of abstraction than in the existing instruments. In the original question sets, for instance, respondents were asked about particular skills in Excel, Word and PowerPoint, while in the new questionnaire, they were asked about the extent to which they were capable of using software on their own computers – for instance Word, Excel or PowerPoint. Respondents could answer the 14 statements using a four-point Likert scale ranging from 'to a very large extent' to 'to a very limited extent'. The reliability of the scale is $\alpha = 0.96$.

Risk awareness

We were unable to find a validated scale for measuring awareness of online risk. Various studies have, however, researched risk awareness in general. The questions in these studies depend on the risk being measured (for instance, the risk of a disaster). What is noticeable in the various studies in which risk awareness was measured is that they all use the same method of working: using various items, respondents are asked how great they consider the chance that a certain risk may occur. Response options for these are commonly based on the Likert method (see for instance: Featherman & Pavlou, 2003; Foubert, 2012; Hong & Cha, 2013; Ma, Ono-Kihara, Cong, Pan, Xu, Zamani, Ravari & Kihara, 2009; Mullan, Wong & Kothe, 2013; Ochsner, Scholz & Hornung, 2013; Rundmo & Nordfjærn, 2013; Scholz, Nagy, Göhner, Luszczynska & Kliegel, 2009).

In addition, another method is used to measure risk awareness. In this method, respondents are not asked about the perceived chance of a risk occurring. Instead, they are asked about the extent to which concerns about a risk lead to certain safe behaviour (see Domenie et al., 2013; Ng, Kankanhalli & Xu, 2009; Ngo & Paternoster, 2011).

Based on the literature, a set of nine questions was developed. Statements made by Ng et al. (2009) and statements from the victim research among Dutch members of the public (Domenie et al., 2013) were used as the departure point. Respondents could rate the statements using a four-point Likert scale. The reliability of the scale is α = 0.78.[17]

In addition, two questions were inserted, partly based on the literature, in which one-man business people could indicate how great they estimated the risk to be that they themselves, as well as other one-man businesses, would fall victim to cybercrime.

Self-control
Grasmick, Tittle, Bursik and Aneklev (1993) developed a set of 24 questions to measure self-control based on Gottfredson and Hirschi's General Theory of Crime (1990). The 'Grasmick Scale' is a popular instrument used in criminology to measure self-control. The self-control concept comprises six basic features: impulsivity, a preference for simple tasks, risk-seeking behaviour, physicality, self-centeredness and temperament. Higgins (2007) reduced this set of questions to 16 items in which the six basic features were kept. The 16 items in English and the response categories used in Higgins' study (four-point Likert scale) were used as the departure point and translated into Dutch. Because there were existing Dutch instruments, or Dutch translations of instruments, to measure impulsivity (one of the six basic elements within the concept of self-control), the items for measuring impulsivity were based on the Dutch translation of the 'Dickman Impulsivity Inventory' [as applied, for instance, by Van Wilsem (2010)]. The scale has a reliability of α = 0.78.

Finally, this research also investigated the extent to which one-man business people were aware of and use government measures to counter cybercrime. For this, we first

---

17. At the time of this research project, the NHL University of Applied Sciences investigated awareness of online risk among students. The graduate intern who was involved in that research project developed an instrument specifically for the project but also tested the question design used in this study. The pretest conducted among 100 NHL students showed that the scale had a reliability of α = 0.71.

identified and listed government initiatives to counter cybercrime based on the media analysis and a search on Google. A grid question was then compiled in which entrepreneurs could indicate whether they were aware of the government measure and whether or not they had used it.

Questionnaire optimisation and final content
After improving the existing sections of the questionnaire and including new survey questions based on the research questions, a draft version of the questionnaire was presented to fellow researchers and the consultative group for feedback.
In the draft version of the questionnaire, a distinction was made between private and business use of computers by one-man business owners. The members of the consultative group and the fellow researchers felt that it would not be feasible to make a distinction in the questionnaire between private and business use of the internet by people operating one-man businesses, because these two types of usage are probably too closely intertwined. As this suspicion was confirmed in the exploratory interviews, private and business use of computers and the internet were combined in the final version of the questionnaire. At the same time, questions were asked at the beginning of the questionnaire which could be used to determine whether the same computers were used for both private and business purposes.
Based on the feedback of the consultative group and fellow researchers, the sequence of the questions was also changed. In the draft version, the question designs to determine computer and internet skills, awareness of online risks and self-control were posed one after the other. In addition, all the questions formulated for this were asked before the substantive questions about cybercrime were raised. The members of the consultative group and the fellow researchers remarked that many respondents would presumably stop completing the questionnaire prematurely because of this. For this reason, we opted to disperse these concepts more widely in the questionnaire. Finally, the comments and criticisms concerned improving the consistency in word use; formulating the questions more clearly, i.e. so that they were less open to interpretation and a few grammatical and spelling errors were discovered.
After improving the questionnaire, five one-man business owners pre-tested the questionnaire from a qualitative point of view. The pre-test respondents came from various backgrounds. They were as follows: an artist, a construction worker, a recruiter/HRM consultant, a one-man business owner in the care sector and a web-shop owner. To recruit respondents for the pre-test, we initially used addresses from the Chamber of Commerce commercial register. For the online survey, the Chamber of Commerce was asked to provide 10,000 addresses of one-man businesses. The file they provided, however, contained more than the requested 10,000 addresses. Thirteen people operating one-man businesses in the vicinity of the researchers' place of work were selected from the surplus addresses. From these, only two were able to carry out the pre-test during the timeframe set aside for it. For this reason, the remaining three respondents for the pre-test were recruited based on a convenience sample.

The one-man business respondents were asked to fill in the questionnaire in the presence of a researcher, question by question, by thinking aloud. This method clarifies comments and criticisms and brings ambiguities to light. For those questions for which there were doubts about their validity on forehand, the researchers also asked a number of targeted questions to test whether the respondents interpreted these questions as intended. These questions mainly focussed on the question of whether private and business use of computers and the internet are indeed combined when one-man business respondents complete the questionnaire.

Overall, one-man business owners understood the questionnaire. Despite this, the pre-test led to some modifications to the questionnaire. Several questions were asked about the internet use of one-man business owners. The pre-test respondents indicated that it is important to keep repeating that 'internet use' in the questionnaire is understood to mean using the internet, also via mobile devices like laptops, tablets and smartphones. Initially, this was only mentioned once in an introductory paragraph of the questionnaire. However, the respondents tended to forget this introduction after a few questions, and some of them had not even read it at all. The one-man business respondents also discovered that in some parts of the questionnaire, a distinction was still mistakenly made between private and business internet use, as indeed was the intention originally. We also made changes to the way the questions and/or response options were formulated in a few places to clarify what was meant by the question and/or response option. The word 'activities' was changed to 'internet activities', for instance, because otherwise a painter, for example, might think 'activities' refer to his sanding and paint work instead of internet use. In addition, some examples were given to clarify question formulations. For example, respondents were no longer asked whether they used computer hardware, but instead they were asked whether they used hardware like CD/DVD players, USB ports and printers. Finally, it became apparent from the pre-test that the relevance of the questions that were intended to measure self-control was not understood. As a result, the 16-point question was found to be frustrating. Therefore, we explained in the questionnaire that these questions were intended to investigate the extent to which personal attributes influence cybercrime victimisation.

Based on the qualitative pre-test, the questionnaire was adjusted again and subsequently ISIZ, a firm that specialises in the programming of online surveys, programmed it and put it online. The questionnaire was then tested online by various fellow researchers and a member of the consultative group. Some final minor modifications were made based on the feedback from this round of testing. In the online test version of the questionnaire only the NHL University of Applied Sciences logo was included. Based on the feedback, and in order to enhance the perceived reliability of the research, a police logo was also placed on the link. We also displayed question numbers in the test version. This was found to be confusing because in some cases questions are, due to previous answers, skipped. Therefore, question numbers were removed. Finally, we processed a few minor suggestions for improvement in the formulation of the introductory texts, questions and response categories.

The final version of the questionnaire was put online on 2 June. From then onwards, one-man businesses owners that had received an invitation (see 'response rate') were able to access the questionnaire. Respondents were given the opportunity to contact the researchers for questions and remarks about the study. During the first few days, the researchers received various reports which showed that the term 'ZZP' (the Dutch acronym for 'one-man business owner'), which was used in the introductory text to the questionnaire and in a few questions, caused confusion. Some one-man business owners do not consider themselves to belong to the one-man business sector. They considered themselves 'entrepreneurs' and felt as if the term ZZP downgraded their status. The second question was however: 'Did you work as a one-man business owner (ZZP'er) during the previous year?' If the answer to this question was negative, then that is where the questionnaire ended. Entrepreneurs without staff who did not view themselves as one-man business owners, even though they are according to the Social and Economic Council's definition (2010), therefore stopped completing the survey prematurely, which was not the intention. For this reason, a few minor changes were made on 5 June so that such misunderstandings could be avoided during the remaining survey period. We spoke of 'entrepreneurs' in the questionnaire's introductory text instead of one-man business owners, and the acronym 'ZZP' was avoided in the actual questions. On 5 June (at 10:54 a.m.), the modified version of the questionnaire went live. Up to that point in time, 364 respondents had completed the questionnaire.

The final questionnaire contains a few questions to demarcate the survey's target population (one-man businesses that use the internet), followed by questions about:
* company attributes;
* computer and internet activities;
* awareness of online risk and the extent to which one-man business owners take protective measures against cybercrime;
* cybercrime victimisation;
* actions that victims of cybercrime undertake and the perceived role of public and private parties in fighting cybercrime;
* the way one-man businesses will act in the event of future victimisation;
* awareness and use of government measures;
* confidence in the police and
* personal attributes of one-man business owners.

3.2.4 *Recruitment and response rate*

In April 2014, the Chamber of Commerce had the address information of 441,911 active Dutch enterprises for which not more than one person worked. This selection does not include entrepreneurs who indicated to the Chamber of Commerce that they did not want their information to be given to third parties. The researchers asked the Chamber of Commerce to draw a random sample of 10,000 from the commercial register of active businesses for which one person worked. Each 43rd company was selected each from the alphabetical list of addresses (n = 441,911). So the address information from a total of 10,277 businesses was supplied. Given that our intended sample size was 10,000 companies (gross sample), we then drew a random sample in SPSS of 10,000 addresses from the 10,277 which were provided.

We approached the companies selected for the sample by invitation letter. We opted to send a traditional invitation letter addressed to the owner of the company. We purposely did not opt to recruit the respondents by e-mail because previous experience had taught us that companies find it annoying to receive invitations in this way. The invitation letter included a unique login code which gave access to the online questionnaire. Using a targeted approach to recruit respondents and a unique login code prevents the final database from being contaminated with questionnaires that have not been completed by one-man businesses (from the sample). We opted for an online survey because conducting interviews on site or by telephone was not feasible for financial and practical reasons.

The invitation letters were sent on behalf of and signed by Patricia M. Zorko, who holds the portfolio for Digitisation and Cybercrime at the National Police in the Netherlands. The researchers drafted the letter and it was then sent to Mrs Zorko's secretarial department for approval. The letters were then printed and sent by the police organisation. Police letterheads and envelopes were used to convince entrepreneurs of the legitimacy of the research and because previous research has shown that this kind of approach increases the response rate (Domenie et al., 2011).

Response rate
The gross sample comprised 10,000 active enterprises for which one person worked, according to the Chamber of Commerce. As was the case during the SME research, it turned out that the Chamber of Commerce commercial register was not up to date. This became apparent because 107 letters were returned to the research team after the original invitation letter had been sent on 2 June and a reminder letter on 16 June. These letters were undeliverable because the addresses were incorrect or incomplete or were returned to sender because the addressees were not reachable at those addresses. So all in all a maximum of 9,893 respondents were reached (net sample).[18]
Various steps were taken to ensure the response rate would be as high as possible:
- The invitation letters were sent on police letterheads and in police envelopes.
- After the first letters and the reminder letters had been sent, the Netherlands police force put a news bulletin about the research project on its website (www.politie.nl/ nieuws). In addition, police officers were informed of the research via the intranet.
- Thanks to the exploratory interviews, news bulletins were placed on the websites of various interest groups or parties affiliated to these groups as well. The Foundation for One-Man Businesses in the Netherlands [*Stichting ZZP Nederland*]

---

18. It is always possible that letters were sent to the wrong address and that the people who received the letters did not return them to sender.

informed its members via the news page on its website.[19] The research project was also mentioned on the one-man business service desk website.[20] Thanks to the involvement of the SME/one-man business service desks in nation-wide information campaigns, the research was also mentioned on the stopcybercrime.nu website.[21]

- The media attention created with the help of the interest groups led to coverage on the research appearing elsewhere on the internet. For instance, the news report was adopted by 'NUzakelijk' (a Dutch online news channel)[22] and was reported on the news page of the Centre for Crime Prevention and Public Safety.[23]
- The questionnaire was hosted via a secure connection. The police force logo was included in the online environment where the questionnaire was completed.
- Finally, entrepreneurs were offered the opportunity to contact the researchers, as previously mentioned.

The research team was contacted 265 times in total. Most of these entrepreneurs got in touch to excuse themselves from the research (n = 143). Reasons for this varied: many respondents said that they do not use a computer and/or the internet; some companies who received the letter had more than one member of staff; many companies were inactive or had since ceased to operate; a few of the entrepreneurs did not speak Dutch well enough to be able to complete the questionnaire and some entrepreneurs were simply too busy.

In addition to this, the researchers were contacted 46 times to verify the legitimacy of the research project. These entrepreneurs indicated that they wanted to avoid giving information to a party whose intentions were not above board. In 4 of the 46 cases, the entrepreneur did not call the researchers themselves; on behalf of the entrepreneurs, the police called the research team to check whether it was a bona fide research project. The police officers with whom the researchers spoke were themselves not aware of the research, despite it being mentioned on politie.nl and on the intranet.

Thirty-seven entrepreneurs reported that they had had trouble logging in. Most of this group of entrepreneurs did not enter the web address for the questionnaire in the address bar of their web browser, but instead used the search bar on their home page (like Google). Because this also caused problems in the earlier research, we included an image of a web browser in the invitation letter which showed where the web

---

19. <www.zzp-nederland.nl/nieuws/10103-onderzoek-naar-cybercrime-onder-zzpers>. Retrieved most recently on 11 July 2014.

20. <www.zzpservicedesk.nl/348/groot-onderzoek-naar-zzp-ers-cybercrime.htm>. Retrieved most recently on 27 April 2015.

21. <www.stopcybercrime.nu/1585/nhl-start-cyberonderzoek.htm>. Retrieved most recently on 11 July 2014.

22. <www.nuzakelijk.nl/zzp/3792232/politie-onderzoekt-cybercrime-zzpers.html>. Retrieved most recently on 11 July 2014.

23. <www.veiligondernemenbeginthier.nl/nieuws/details/article/onderzoek-naar-zzpers-en-cybercrime/>. Retrieved most recently on 27 April 2015.

address needed to be entered. Despite this, some of the entrepreneurs did not manage to do it on their own.

A further ten entrepreneurs contacted us because they received reminder letters despite having completed the questionnaire. In order to have the reminder letter ready in time for dispatch, the text of the letter and the address file had to be delivered to the printing department of the Central Police Unit by 6 June (less than a week after the research project had commenced). Even though the addresses of the businesses that had already completed the questionnaire had been removed from the address file that was sent to the printing department, the reminder letter was only sent ten days later (16 June). So some entrepreneurs received a reminder letter even though they had already completed the questionnaire. To prevent questions being raised about this, the reminder letter did point out that if the recipient had already completed the questionnaire, the letter should be ignored.

Other reasons for contacting the researchers varied: some respondents had comments about the content of the questions; some entrepreneurs wondered whether it was obligatory to complete the questionnaire and a few questions were asked about the way privacy was being safeguarded.

The data collection phase ended on Tuesday 1 July 2014. A total of 2,088 entrepreneurs started completing the questionnaire. Of these, 112 stopped answering the questions prematurely. The remaining 1,976 respondents completed the questionnaire in full. So the gross response rate was 20.0 per cent.[24] The responses of some ($n = 354$) of the respondents were not taken into consideration because these respondents did not belong to the target population for the research. Of these companies, 182 which had more than one member of staff; 135 of the businesses had not operated during the previous year and in 37 cases, the entrepreneurs did not use the internet. The results are thus based on the responses of the remaining 1,622 entrepreneurs. This brought the net response rate to 16.4 per cent.[25] On average, the questionnaires took 17 minutes and 23 seconds to complete.

3.2.5   *Generalisability of the findings*

According to the definition of one-man businesses used in this research, the Netherlands had a total of 441,911 one-man businesses at the time of writing. A total of 1,622 one-man businesses completed the survey in full. That means that statements can be made about the population as a whole with a 99 per cent confidence level and a confidence interval of plus or minus 3 per cent (rounded up). So suppose that it becomes apparent from this research that 8 per cent of the businesses fell victim to hacking, then it can be concluded with a confidence level of 99 per cent that the number of

---

24. Of the maximum of 9,893 companies who eventually received an invitation letter, 1,976 completed the questionnaire in full.
25. That is, 1,622 usable and fully completed questionnaires divided by a maximum of 9,893 entrepreneurs who received the invitation letter.

victims of hacking out of all one-man businesses (the total population) is between 5 and 11 per cent.[26]

Non-response to the research

In addition to the size of the net sample, other factors may influence the generalisability of the findings. A non-response study conducted to determine the selectiveness of the response rate (Doldersum, 2015). For this, a random sample was drawn of 80 one-man business owners that had been approached for the research and who, as far as the research team were aware, had been reached but had not participated in the research. These 80 one-man business owners also did not contact the research team to opt out of the research. We found the telephone numbers of the selected one-man businesses via 'Company.info' and the Dutch version of 'Google my business' [*Google mijn bedrijf*]. All 80 people operating one-man businesses were then approached for a telephone interview in which they were asked for their reasons for not wanting to take part in the survey. In a similar way to the survey, the non-response group was also asked about whether they had fallen victim to cybercrime. As a result, the percentage of victims obtained by the survey could be compared to the percentage of victims in the non-response group. Any difference between the two would indicate that the generalisability of the findings is limited.

Of the 80 one-man business owners in the non-response group, 14 could not be reached because the telephone number was no longer in use and no other number could be found. In addition to this, eight people operating one-man businesses did not pick up the telephone despite various attempts to reach them. A total of 58 respondents were therefore reached. Of these, 55 per cent (n = 32) said that they were not willing to take part in the telephone non-response study. The most important reason given was a lack of time. This may also explain why one-man businesses did not take part in online survey. Of the people with one-man businesses that were part of the non-response group, 45 per cent (n = 26) did take part in the telephone interview.

Respondents gave various reasons for not participating in the online survey. Table 3.8 provides an overview of the reasons for non-response.

Table 3.8   Reasons for non-response

Reason	Number	Proportion in %
No time	12	46.1
Have not been confronted by cybercrime	4	15.4
Threw it straight into the waste paper bin	3	11.5
Did not read it	3	11.5
Could not log in	2	7.7
No particular reason	2	7.7
Total	26	100

---

26. This 3 per cent has been rounded up and applies to a population proportion of 50 per cent (maximum distribution). The margin would in fact be smaller for smaller or larger population proportions.

Not having enough time to take part in surveys was the most important reason given for non-response. 'Time is money', according to many people operating one-man businesses, which is why they generally do not respond to requests to take part in research. A shortage of time for completing an online questionnaire is not immediately a reason to assume that the online survey results are not representative for one-man businesses. After all, this reason for non-response is not substantive in nature but is instead a practical one. If the reason given for not taking part in the survey is that the one-man business does not have first-hand experience of cybercrime, however, this may point to selectivity in the response. It raises the suspicion, namely, that one-man business people who have encountered cybercrime may be more inclined to participate in the research.

To establish whether being confronted by cybercrime does in fact play a role in the decision to take part in online survey, we asked one-man businesses within the non-response group whether they had ever fallen victim to cybercrime. The questions posed about this were similar to the questions in online survey: we asked one-man business people whether they had been victims of the same kinds of cybercrime. As was the case in the survey, we also separated one-man businesses that were victims, those who were not victims and one-man businesses which encountered one or more attempts at cybercrime.

Two one-man business owners (7.7%) that took part in the non-response research reported that they had fallen victim to at least one type of cybercrime. One of the respondents had been a victim of 'online fraud/scams (financial damages incurred through fraud)'. The respondent received phantom invoices and thought that he had an outstanding bill and so paid it. The other respondent was a victim of 'bankcard skimming'. The remaining 24 respondents (92.3%) said that they had not been victims. Of these, 19 (79.2%) said that they had, however, experienced one or more failed attempts. These mainly involved phishing e-mails, online phantom invoices and malware.

Considering that the survey showed that 27.9 per cent of one-man businesses fell victim to one or more types of cybercrime (see Section 5.3), the findings from the non-response research suggest that the response may be selective. It seems that victims may have been more inclined to take part in the survey than one-man businesses that had not fallen victim to cybercrime. However, caution should be exercised when interpreting these findings because the number of respondents who participated in the non-response study is too small for reliable conclusions. Furthermore, while similar questions were asked during the survey and the telephone non-response interviews to determine the percentage of victims, the methodology had in fact been altered. It may well be that the difference in research methodology (online questionnaire as opposed to telephone interview) partly explains the difference in victimisation rates.

Measures taken to increase the response rate

Previous research has shown that sending invitations for research in the name of the police (on police letterheads and in police envelopes) elicits a higher response rate compared to sending invitations from a research institute (Domenie et al., 2011). That research also shows that not only the response rate but also the percentage of victims is higher when police invitations are used.[27] This means that the measures taken to increase the response rate may have led to a selective response: victims of cybercrime may well be more inclined to respond to an invitation from the police.

Selectiveness in the response cannot be excluded

In short, while the net response rate is large enough to be able to make reliable statements, it cannot be ruled out that the response to this study was selective. There is a good chance that victims of cybercrime were more likely than non-victims to take part in the online survey. This means that victimisation rates may be lower in reality than indicated in this research. Based on available material, it cannot be determined how much lower victimisation rates may be.

3.2.6   Data analysis

The analyses were carried out using SPSS, a statistical software package. In addition to standard statistical analyses like frequency analyses, we also carried out in-depth analyses to interpret differences or indicate correlations, for example. Unless otherwise indicated, the chi-square test or, for analyses of small numbers, the Fisher's exact test was used.

We also used logistic regression to compile victim profiles. This analysis method makes it possible to calculate the influence of various risk factors (verified against for each other) on the chances of becoming a victim of cybercrime. In addition, statements can be made based on this analysis about the extent to which several risk factors together explain why a one-man business person may be confronted by cybercrime (the so-called explained variance).

In the elaboration of the regression analyses (see Section 5.3.2) beta coefficients are included. The values of these coefficients indicate the direction of a correlation (without going into causality).[28] A positive value means that the probability of that

---

27. For financial and interpersonal cybercrimes together, Domenie et al. (2013) found: 6.7 per cent victimisation in response to an invitation from the police (n = 358) and 2.3 per cent victimisation in response to an invitation from NHL University of Applied Sciences (n = 175). The difference between the two percentages is significant (Z-score for proportions: p < 0.05). Moreover, the difference is not only significant, it is also relevant: using invitations from the police, Domenie et al. found the percentage of victims to be almost three times higher than when invitations from the NHL were used. We do not know which of the two percentages best reflects reality.

28. Only correlations between risk factors and victimisation were made in this research. The cause–effect relationship is not known. It is also possible that a third variable (so-called mediating variables) may explain the correlation.

risk factor is greater, while a negative value indicates that the risk factor is less likely to occur. For instance: if victims and non-victims are compared in a regression analysis and the beta value for the factor 'self-control' is negative, then this means that victims have less self-control than non-victims.

In addition to beta coefficients, the Odds Ratios (ORs) for each risk factor were also included in the regression analyses. Odds ratios represent the extent to which a risk factor increases or reduces the likelihood of victimisation, depending on the direction of the relationship (B-coefficient). Suppose the B-efficiency of the 'self-control' factor is negative and the odds ratio (rounded off) is 1.5, then this means that victims have less self-control than non-victims and that a lack of self-control increases the chance of victimisation by one and a half times.

The Nagelkerke R^2 is also reported in the regression models. This parameter measures the explained variance. The results of this were between 0 (no explanation) and 1 (perfect explanation). To illustrate a Nagelkerke R^2 of 0.147 in cybercrime victimisation means that the factors in the regression model explain 14.7 per cent of the variance in cybercrime victimisation.

Asterisks in the tables indicate significant differences ($p < 0.05$ = *, $p < 0.01$ = **). One asterisk indicates a significant difference based on a confidence level of 95 per cent. Two asterisks indicate a difference based on a confidence level of 99 per cent. If the difference or correlation is not significant or the test does not lead to reliable results, for instance, because the number of respondents is too small, then the results were not taken into consideration.

4 | CYBERCRIME AMONG SMEs

In this chapter, we discuss the results of the research among SMEs in the Netherlands.[1] The chapter is structured according to the main and sub-questions that are the focus of this research (see Table 2.4 on page 29). Section 4.1 offers insight into the online activities of the SME sector, their awareness of online risk and the extent to which they protect themselves against cybercrime. Section 4.2 covers victimisation among SMEs. This section not only describes the extent to which SMEs become victims, but also how cybercrimes are committed and their consequences. The concluding paragraph discusses the reactions of SMEs that were victims of cybercrime and the role they assign to the police in tackling such crime (Section 4.3).

4.1   ONLINE ACTIVITIES, RISK AWARENESS AND PROTECTIVE MEASURES

4.1.1   *Online activities*

The companies were asked about their online activities. Multiple answers were possible. Figure 4.1 summarises what percentage of companies carry out each activity. To get a general impression, the three response categories shown in the figure are stacked. The total percentage shown in a bar indicates what percentage of businesses engage in that internet activity, regardless of how often they do so. For example, 98.1 per cent of businesses do e-mail and 1.9 per cent of companies do not e-mail at all. The intensity with which companies use e-mail facilities is represented by the colour of the bar: the darker, the more frequent.

The companies in this study actively use the internet. Almost all companies look for specific information on the internet (98.8%), e-mail (98.1%) and/or do internet banking (96.4%). These three activities are done on a daily basis or continuously by 73.8, 91.1 and 54.5 per cent of the companies, respectively. Several studies have indicated that companies frequently undertake these activities (Hoevenagel, 2013; Motivaction, 2012).

Three quarters of companies maintain their own website (75.0%),[2] but also surfing (83.1%) and placing orders online (85.7%) are activities that are undertaken frequently. Video calls (24.6%) and chatting (26.2%) are relatively less common.

---

1. This chapter was completed in February 2014.
2. 83.5 per cent of companies have their own website.

Figure 4.1   General online activities (n = 1,203)[3]

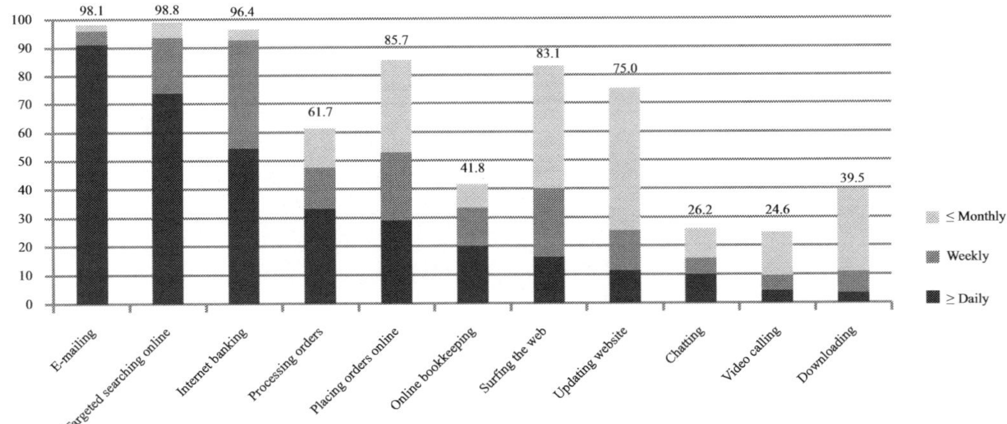

Social media

In total, 60.4 per cent of companies use social media (n = 727).[4] Once again, the intensity of social media use is illustrated by the colour: the darker, the more frequent (see Figure 4.2). Almost half of the companies use Facebook (46.9%), followed by LinkedIn (35.9%) and video sites like YouTube (32.6%). More than one in five even use Facebook on a daily basis or continuously (20.6%).

Figure 4.2   Social media activities (n = 1,203)

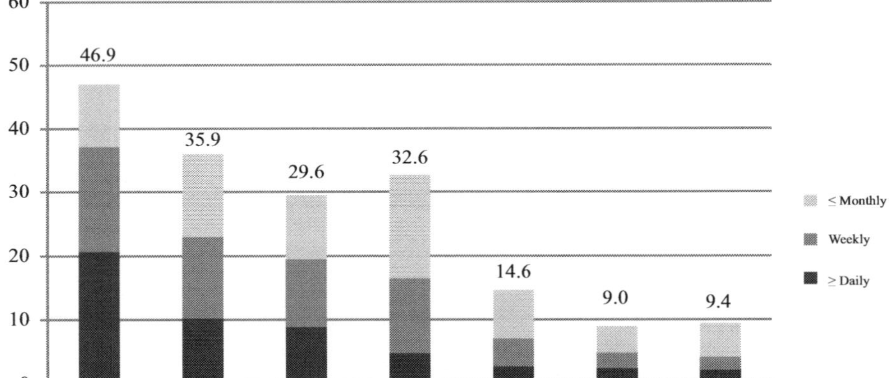

---

3. The response categories were: continuously (24/7) – daily – weekly – monthly – less frequently than monthly – not at all. In Figure 4.1 'continuously' and 'daily' are combined as '≥daily', and 'monthly' and 'less frequently than monthly' as '≤monthly'.

4. Social networking sites are used exclusively for business purposes by 46.5 per cent, and 40.0 per cent use these sites for business and private purposes alike.

Twitter is also used by a relatively large group of companies (29.6%). Fewer respondents indicated that their companies take part in community/discussion forums (14.6%) and blogs (9.4%). In the 'others' category, 9.0 per cent said that their companies use other social networking sites. They did not provide information about which sites they mean exactly.

4.1.2   Risk awareness

To give an indication of the extent to which companies are aware of cybercrime and the dangers associated with this, we first asked about the extent to which the organisation is dependent on IT. As shown in Figure 4.3, the largest group considers itself to be dependent on IT to a large or very large extent (73.9%). This means that they cannot operate their business if there is an IT outage. This is consistent with the conclusion that companies use their internet connection intensively for their more or less traditional business processes such as correspondence, placing orders and online banking. A much smaller group (11.8%) indicated that they were dependent on IT to a minor or very minor extent or not at all.

In the IT Barometer, 39.0 per cent of the surveyed companies indicated that operations would come to a complete stop without IT (Ernst & Young, 2011). Almost half of these companies are significantly dependent on IT. This study, too, indicates that companies are heavily dependent on IT.

Figure 4.3   Dependency on IT (n = 1,203)

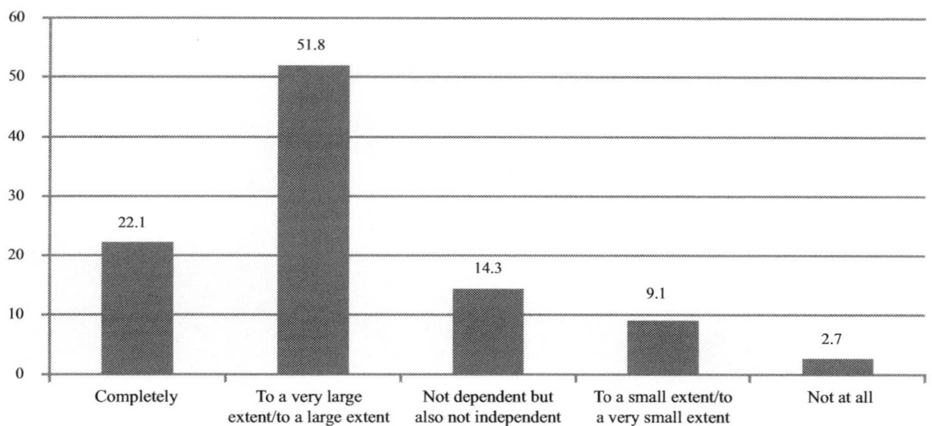

In addition, almost two thirds of companies (65.1%) said that they store confidential information on the company network and/or on company computers to a large or very large extent (see Figure 4.4). Here we have in mind customer and administrative information and information about product development.

We then asked about the extent to which they were aware of the online risks confronting their organisation (see Figure 4.5). Almost two thirds of the respondents said that they were aware or very aware of cybercrime (65.0%). This awareness is small or very small among 8.4 per cent of the respondents.

Figure 4.4   Extent to which confidential information is stored on the company network/ computers (n = 1,203)

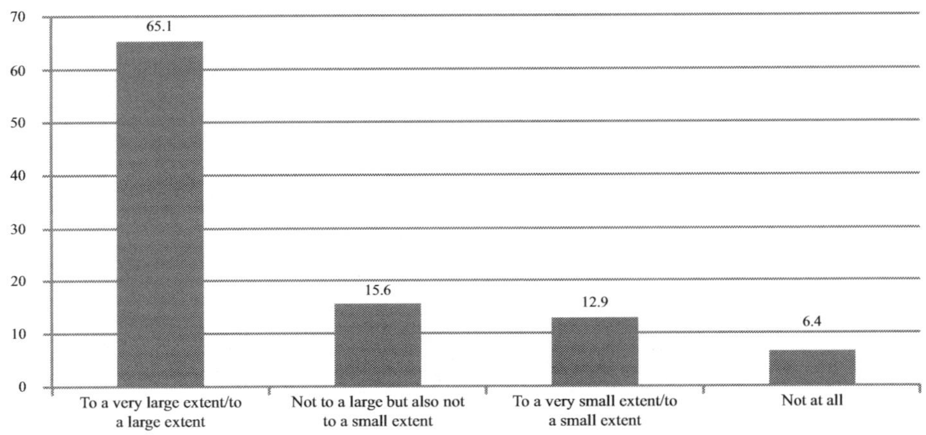

Figure 4.5   Awareness of cybercrime (n = 1,203)

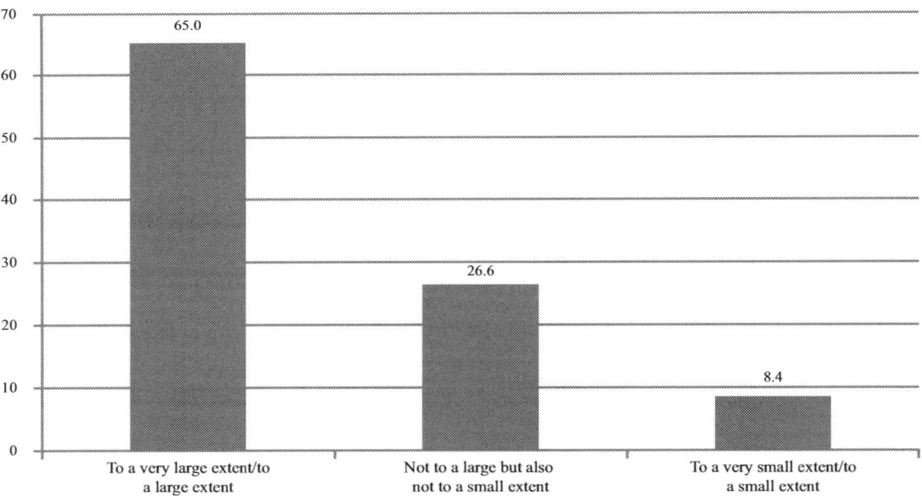

Figure 4.6 shows that a significant group feel that it is important or very important to protect company-related digital information. Only 4.1 per cent hold the opinion that it is unimportant or very unimportant and 12.2 per cent of the people surveyed had no clear opinion on this. Companies were also asked who is responsible for protecting company-related digital information. Almost half of the companies outsource information security (47.4%) to a third party. Slightly more than a quarter, however, arrange protection within the company and have one or more employees in service with affinity and knowledge of IT and/or information security (26.6%). In addition to this, 8.6 per cent of the businesses had their own separate department within the organisation (in some cases an IT department) that deals with securing digital information.

Figure 4.6   Importance of data protection (n = 1,203)

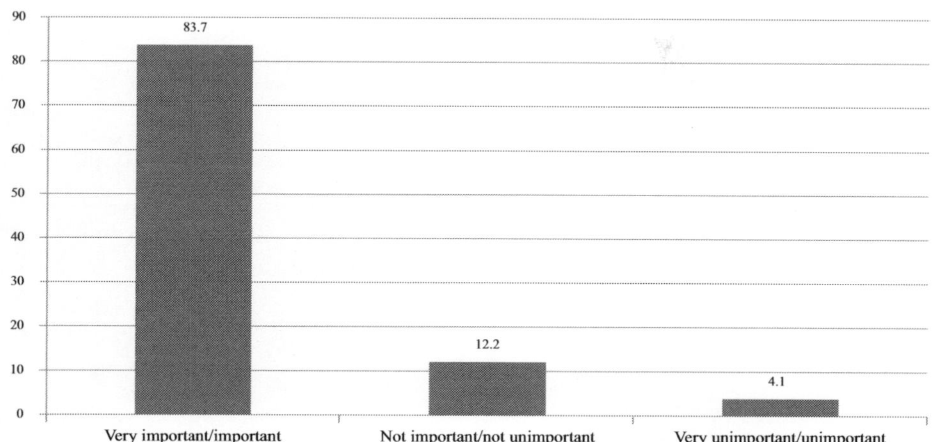

4.1.3   *Protective measures*

We asked the companies what measures, preventative or otherwise, they had taken to protect themselves from cybercrime. The measures are classified as physical, technical and policy measures. These three kinds of measures will be discussed in succession.

Physical measures
Of all the surveyed companies, 77.6 per cent had taken one or more physical measures to protect the company's IT. From Figure 4.7, it can be deduced that the most commonly applied physical measure is to protect the digital environment against disasters such as fire and flooding (57.9%). In addition, 44.9 per cent of the companies

Figure 4.7   Physical measures (n = 1,203)

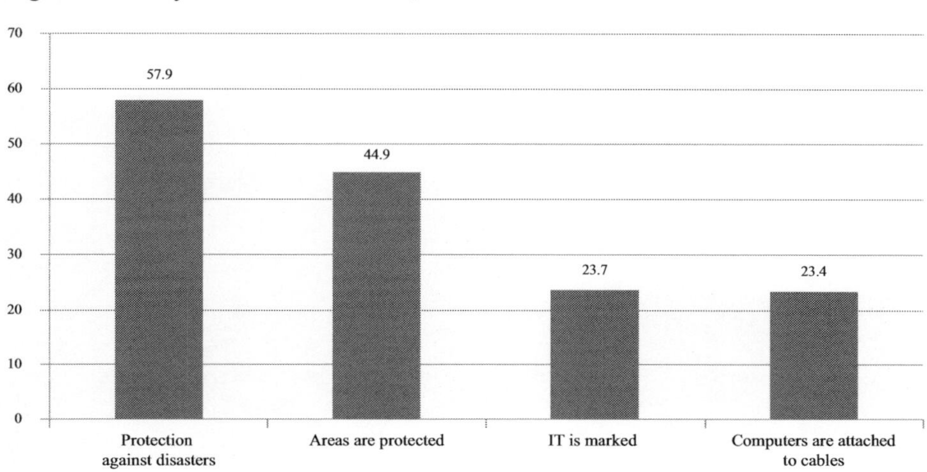

secure and/or lock the rooms where essential IT is kept. Almost a quarter mark IT equipment with a distinguishing feature which can be used to ascertain whether it belongs to the company. Attaching a cable lock to computers/laptops was a measure applied by 23.4 per cent of the companies.

Technical measures
One or more technical measures were taken by 99.4 per cent to limit the risk of cyber-crime as much as possible (see Figure 4.8). Practically, all businesses install virus scanners (96.8%) and/or firewalls (92.2%) on their computers. Previous studies have also shown that these two measures are the ones applied most (i.e. Ernst & Young, 2011; Federation of Small Businesses (FSB), 2013; Hagen et al., 2008; Motivaction, 2012). Securing internet connections, including wireless connections (89.6%) and keeping software up to date (88.6%) were also measures taken by a very large group.

Figure 4.8   Technical measures (n = 1,203)

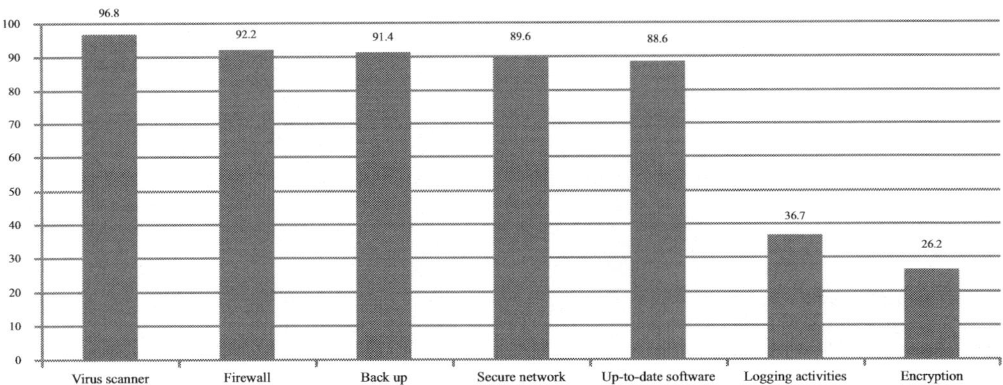

Backing up files on company computers and/or the company network regularly was a step undertaken by 91.4 per cent. In addition, 68.8 per cent stored backups outside the company premises. More than one third of the companies log internet and other activities on the company network (36.7%). These logs are checked and assessed (regularly) by 19.9 per cent of the respondent companies. Fewer respondent companies (26.2%) encode files containing confidential information, for instance using encryption, as a measure to protect information.

Policy measures
Of the respondents surveyed, 76.3 per cent had taken at least one policy measure (Figure 4.9). The most common policy measure applied was to raise awareness of online risks among employees (60.3%). Percentages from previous studies in relation to raising awareness range from 20 (FSB, 2013) to 55 per cent (Ponemon Institute, 2012). Even though these results can only be compared to a limited extent, it seems as though

Figure 4.9   Policy measures (n = 1,203)

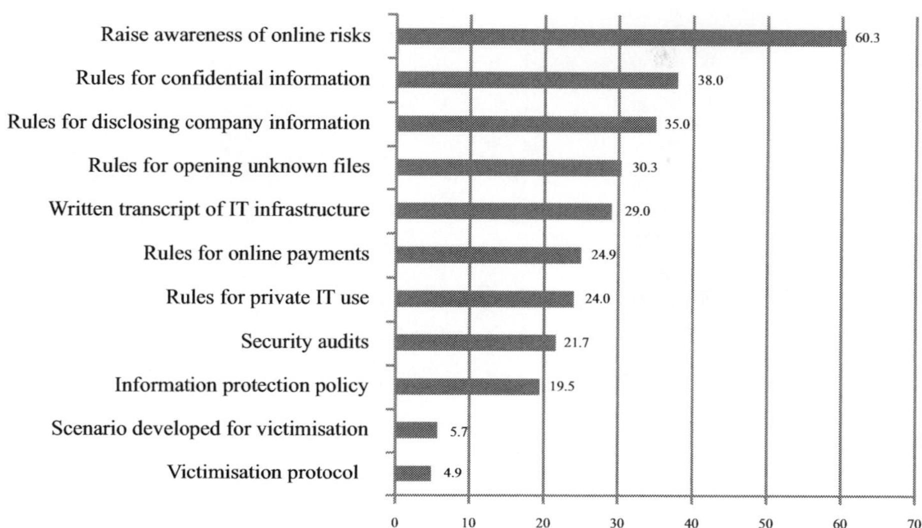

companies surveyed for this research are more inclined to choose to raise awareness among their employees of online threats compared to companies from other studies.[5] More than one third of the companies (38.0%) laid down written rules about handling confidential information like the personal details of customers. A slightly smaller number of companies (35.0%) did the same for providing company information when requested. Of the companies surveyed, 30.3 per cent laid down rules for opening unknown files, like e-mail attachments. Also, 24.9 and 24.0 per cent of the companies had rules about online payments and the use of IT for private purposes, respectively. Fewer than one third (29.0%) of the businesses had a written transcript available of their current IT infrastructure. Almost one in five of the surveyed companies had an information protection policy (19.5%). Regular security and other audits were carried out by 21.7 per cent of the companies.

The remaining two policy measures we asked about were applied to a lesser extent. Only 5.7 per cent of the companies had developed scenarios to describe how the organisation could fall victim to cybercrime. This could be a scenario in which a former employee steals confidential information. Fewer than 1 in 20 businesses had drawn up a protocol which outlines how to act in the event of cybercrime (4.9%).

Confidence in measures taken
Finally, we asked the companies how much confidence they have in the set of measures taken by the organisation to prevent online risks. An overview of the answers is

---

5.   Apart from the (scientific) value of the studies we consulted being limited (see Section 3.1.2), it is also not clear whether raising awareness among employees was measured in the same way in these various studies. After all, raising awareness can range from face-to-face training to sending e-mails to members of staff.

given in Figure 4.10. More than half of those surveyed said that they have much confidence or a great deal of confidence in the measures they have taken (54.7%).

Figure 4.10   Confidence in measures taken (n = 1,203)

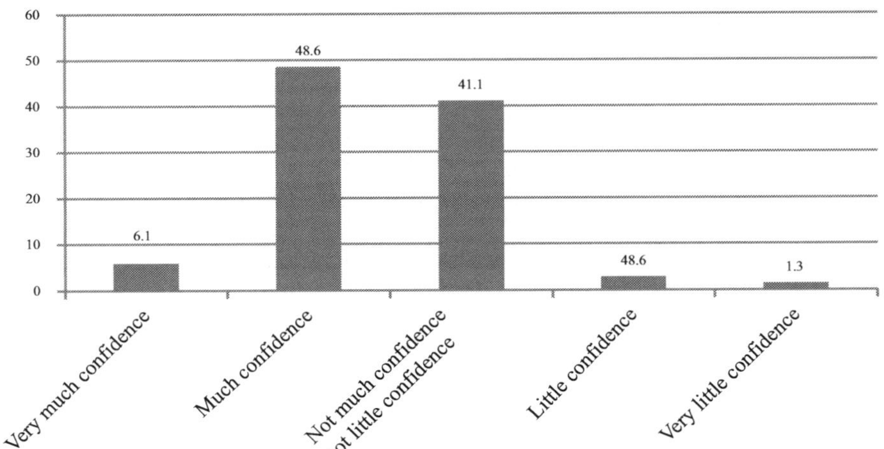

Summary
Companies frequently undertake online activities and for a variety of applications. Searching for specific information on the internet, e-mailing and internet banking are the ones mainly undertaken. These have become more or less traditional internet activities. Companies are also active on social networking sites, especially on Facebook. That said, almost 40 per cent of businesses do *not* use social networking websites. It may be concluded that, although companies with an internet connection use them intensively for more or less traditional business processes (getting information, corresponding, making payments), using the internet for profiling the company is less commonplace. Business processes are dependent on IT to a large or very large extent at most of the companies (73.9%). A significant proportion of the companies (65.1%) have a large or very large amount of confidential information on the company network. Companies indicated that they are aware of the risks associated with their online activities: the lion's share (83.7%) of businesses finds it important to protect the company's digital information. Almost half of the companies had chosen to engage an external party for this. Thus, it can be concluded that SMEs are not only dependent on IT, but they have also become dependent on the quality of the work of external IT specialists, and it is therefore important for them to assess their quality. Whether they are able to do so, and how they do it, is beyond the scope of this research.
Companies also protect themselves against the risks of cybercrime by taking measures to this effect. Three quarters undertook one or more physical measures and three quarters had taken policy measures. Policy measures relate mainly to drawing up company rules and raising awareness among company personnel about the risks of cybercrime. The most commonly applied physical measure is to protect the digital

environment against disasters. Virtually, all companies had taken one or more technical measures. These are generally 'standard' measures, like installing virus scanners and firewalls. Advanced security measures, logging of activities and using encryption were less common.

Despite the measures taken, companies are vulnerable because of their dependency on IT and the extent to which they store confidential information on their company networks. For instance, many companies do not have the obvious measures in place to protect themselves. For example, more than half do not protect the rooms in which (essential) IT equipment is kept; three quarters do not encrypt files containing confidential information and a substantial proportion of companies have not laid down rules, for instance, for online payments. Despite this, more than half of the companies had confidence in the measures they had taken to prevent cybercrime. The question is whether this confidence is justified. The confidence in the measures taken may explain why very few companies had drawn up a protocol stating how to act in the event of cybercrime.

All things considered, the following picture emerges. The SME sector has gone along with digitisation: business processes take place online and SMEs take security measures. But SMEs are not digital front runners: social media is not fully explored and taking advanced security measures is not standard practice. We could say that SMEs digitise within their comfort zone.

4.2 Cybercrime victimisation and the way in which cybercrime is committed

Cybercrime victimisation is the focus of this section. First, we describe the extent to which SMEs have fallen victim to the various kinds of cybercrime (Section 4.2.1). In the questionnaire, the most recent cybercrime incident to which SMEs had fallen victim was elaborated on. We therefore go on to outline by whom and how the most recent cybercrime was committed in Section 4.2.2. SMEs were also asked about the severity of the last cybercrime incident and the damage incurred. An explanation of the results on severity and damage is given in Section 4.2.3.

4.2.1 Victimisation

Previous publications offer no clear picture about the extent to which companies were victims of cybercrime. Prevalence rates range, for instance, between 23 [PricewaterhouseCoopers (PwC), 2011] and 87 per cent (PwC, 2013).[6] The scientific value of the studies we consulted is moreover limited (see Section 3.1.2). Also, the results

---

6. For instance, intermediate victimisation rates: 30 per cent (FSB, 2013), 45 per cent (McAfee, 2013) and 57 per cent (Hoevenagel, 2013).

are hardly comparable, if at all, because the companies studied ranged in size and because the ways used to measure cybercrime varied widely.

To gain an understanding of the extent to which SMEs fall victim to cybercrime, we asked in this study about the extent to which companies had experienced various forms of this kind of crime in the 12 months prior to the research. In the questionnaire, we gave a short clarification for each type of cybercrime. For each type of cybercrime, respondents could then indicate whether they had been confronted by it, whether they had to deal with a failed attempt, or whether they had been victimised (once or more than once) (Table 4.1).

Table 4.1   Types of cybercrime and the extent to which SMEs were confronted by these in the previous 12 months (in %) (n = 1,203)

	Do not know	Not at all	≥1 failed attempt (s)	Once	>Once	Total number of victims
Malware	6.5	49.5	26.0	11.7	6.2	17.9
Phishing	3.4	51.2	38.2	1.9	5.3	7.2
E-fraud	1.7	86.2	8.0	3.5	0.6	4.1
Hacking	5.2	87.2	4.2	2.6	0.8	3.4
DoS attack	3.3	91.7	2.0	2.3	0.7	3.0
Theft of data carriers	1.5	95.4	0.1	2.2	0.8	3.0
Cyber defamation/slander	3.5	93.0	0.7	1.7	1.1	2.8
Identity abuse	5.3	90.9	1.7	1.2	0.8	2.0
Defacing	1.4	96.3	0.3	1.2	0.7	1.9
Skimming – bankcard	2.7	93.8	1.8	1.5	0.2	1.7
Unauthorised use company network	6.6	90.4	2.0	0.6	0.5	1.1
Destruction of data	3.1	95.7	0.2	0.8	0.2	1.0
Theft of data	5.1	93.8	0.3	0.7	0.1	0.8
Espionage	9.6	89.3	0.8	0.2	0.1	0.3
Cyber blackmail	1.2	97.8	0.9	0.2	0	0.2
Cyber extortion	1.2	97.4	1.1	0.2	0	0.2
Skimming – payment system	2.2	97.3	0.5	0.1	0	0.1

Victims were defined as companies that had been victim of forms of cybercrime once or more in the year prior to the research (not counting failed attempts at cybercrime). If theft of data carriers is not taken into consideration (because it is not a cybercrime, see note b in Table 2.1 on page 26), 28.5 per cent of the companies in our study fell victim to one or more kinds of cybercrime (n = 343). The most recent Corporate Sector Crime Monitor (2011) of the Dutch the Research and Documentation Centre [*Wetenschappelijk Onderzoek- en Documentatiecentrum* (WODC)] shows that 31 per cent of businesses fell victim to one or more particularly traditional types of crime. This means that cybercrime among businesses occurs to more or less the same degree as traditional crime.

Comment on phishing victimisation

In the questionnaire, phishing was defined as 'using a fabricated story to extract information about your company via digital means, like e-mails'. So phishing victimisation occurs if company information is extracted (completed offence 'fraud', Section 326 of the Dutch Criminal Code). Merely sending a phishing e-mail is therefore an attempt at fraud. To avoid having companies report such attempts (receiving a phishing email) as victimisation, we offered respondents the opportunity to report attempts separately (see Table 4.1). Answers to open questions suggest that, despite this, some companies reported merely receiving a scam request to surrender company information as victimisation (see Text Box 4.5). So phishing victimisation in this research may not have been measured accurately. The percentage of companies from whom company information was extracted may be lower in reality. Caution should therefore be exercised when interpreting the results about phishing victimisation.

This possible inaccuracy may skew the total percentage of cybercrime victims (28.5%). For this reason, we also excluded phishing when calculating the victimisation rate. This did not change the results much. If phishing is not taken into consideration at all, the percentage of companies that fell victim to one or more kinds of cybercrime (n = 317) is 26.4 per cent. Based on this study, the victimisation rate, rounded off to some degree, is still between 25 and 30 per cent.

Phishing has not been excluded from the analyses on victimisation that follow, first because the doubts about the accuracy of the victimisation rate are based on only a few answers given to open questions. Second, many of the analyses do not relate to the total number of all cybercrimes, but instead they relate to individual kinds of offences (malware, phishing, e-fraud and hacking), which means that phishing can be assessed separately.

The most common types of cybercrime are malware, phishing, e-fraud and hacking. Nearly 18 per cent of the companies fell victim to malware; more than 7 per cent fell victim to phishing, 4 per cent had to contend with fraud and, according to the victims, more than 3 per cent fell victim to hacking.[7] Other research also shows that companies – albeit not necessarily comparable to the companies examined in this study – are mainly faced with these kinds of cybercrime (Ernst & Young, 2011; FSB, 2013; Hagen et al., 2008; Hoevenagel, 2013; McAfee, 2013; Motivaction, 2012). In a study into victimisation among members of the public in the Netherlands (so not companies, but individuals), malware is also the offence with the highest percentage of victims (16.7%), followed by hacking and e-fraud (respectively, 4.3% and 2.7%). Phishing was not included in the research among individuals (Domenie et al., 2013). Malware, phishing, e-fraud and hacking are therefore not typical SME sector problems but instead are general crime

---

7. This was a self-report study, so if hacking went unnoticed at a company, the respondent may have reported that they had not been hacked while they may well have been. This problem is inherent to self-report research on hacking. The actual percentage of hacked companies may therefore be higher in reality than reported here. So while we may suspect that phishing is over-reported (see text box), under-reporting may be the case for hacking.

problems associated with digitisation that affect the whole of society – and so SMEs as well. These problems are also persistent to a certain extent, given that hacking and e-fraud emerged as major problems in the first broad-based research into cybercrime in the Netherlands as well (Stol, Van Treeck & Van der Ven, 1999).

> **Cybercrime as a commonplace phenomenon**
> *Mr Delhaize has a print shop and sees successful and failed attempts at cybercrime on a daily basis: 'We have an FTP server at the shop and if I check to see how often people try to login, every day there's always someone. I kept track of it for a while and the attempts come from an address in Russia somewhere, or God knows where. I think it's more of a social problem than one which entails catching the crook. Catching that crook would be really difficult I think.'*

Table 4.1 shows that e-fraud is a relatively common kind of cybercrime. It is, however, an umbrella term under which various kinds of criminal behaviour are grouped. For this reason, we asked victims of online fraud or scams to specify which type of fraud they had been confronted with. In this way, we were able to chart cybercrime victimisation as specifically as possible. Figure 4.11 gives the findings.

Figure 4.11 Types of e-fraud that companies fall victim to (n = 49)

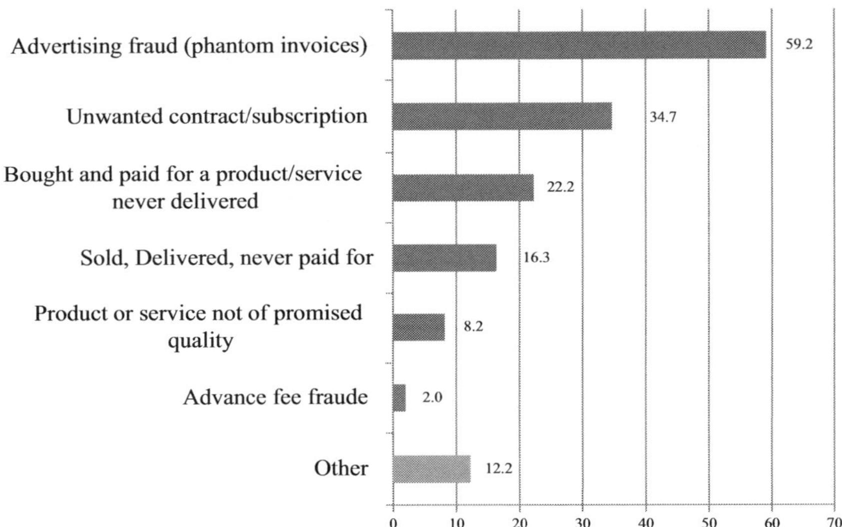

More than half of online scam victims were confronted with phantom invoices (n = 29).[8] Other kinds of online fraud occur less frequently but are not rare. Entrepreneurs

---

8. While it is also possible for companies to receive offline phantom invoices, we specifically asked about types of online fraud.

were also offered the opportunity to explain what had happened to them in an open answer field. Three of these notes were usable. Quotes from these entrepreneurs have been included in the text box below.

Text Box 4.1: Quotes from entrepreneurs about the kinds of fraud that they had fallen victim to
- *'Credit card fraud committed by a customer'.*
- *'Money cashed from the bank using invalid authorisation'.*
- *'Manipulated e-mails from supplier. Goods paid to a fraudulent bank account (man-in-the-middle attack)'.*

Summary

In summary, we can see that cybercrime seriously affects small and medium-sized enterprises in the Netherlands in terms of prevalence and indeed to a similar degree as traditional crime. Companies mainly fall victim to malware, phishing, hacking and various kinds of e-fraud. Taking other research into account, we can conclude that these are not typically SME sector problems but instead are general crime problems associated with digitisation that affect the whole of society and so SMEs too. However, when it comes to e-fraud, the indications are that the SME sector is confronted with specific modi operandi: advertising fraud (receiving phantom invoices) is the most common type of fraud within the SME sector.

4.2.2 The way in which cybercrime is committed

Once it had been established which types of cybercrime businesses were confronted with, we probed about the cybercrimes that SMEs encountered. We restricted the probing to the cybercrime that the company had experienced most recently because it would otherwise have cost respondents too much time to fill in the questionnaire. Theft of data carriers was not taken into consideration, because it is no cybercrime. So we selected 335 cybercrime incidents. The distribution of these incidents is shown in Table 4.2. In this selection, malware, phishing, e-fraud and hacking are the most common types of cybercrime, which logically corresponds to victimisation prevalence (Table 4.1 above).

Hereafter, these 335 most recently experienced cybercrime incidents are taken as the departure point for the discussion of the in-depth questions. The findings about the four most common cybercrimes have also been presented separately as far as possible. The answers from companies who most recently fell victim to malware, phishing, e-fraud or hacking are therefore compared to the answers of other victims.

Table 4.2 Cybercrimes which were probed (each time the most recent cybercrime with which a company was confronted)

	N	Per cent of the most recently experienced cyber incidents (n = 335)
Malware	155	46.3
Phishing	49	14.6
E-fraud	34	10.1
Hacking	27	8.1
DoS attack	17	5.1
Cyber defamation/slander	17	5.1
Identity abuse	11	3.3
Bankcard skimming	11	3.3
Defacing	6	1.8
Unauthorised use of company network	3	0.9
Cyber extortion	2	0.6
Destruction of data	2	0.6
Theft of data	1	0.3
Total	335	100

Note

It was not uncommon for companies to have fallen victim to cybercrime more than once during the 12 months prior to the research (see Table 4.1). But in this study they were only given the opportunity to report in detail about the most recent incident that they had encountered. The observations from that selection, i.e. 'each most recent cybercrime with which a company was confronted' (Table 4.2), are limited in terms of generalisability for all cybercrimes that the SMEs reported. An additional analysis reveals that the distribution from the 'each most recent cybercrime' selection differs significantly compared to the distribution of the 'all cybercrimes reported in this study'. As far as statements about individual types of cybercrime are concerned (malware, phishing, e-fraud or hacking), this difference is no cause for concern. The share of each type of cybercrime within the sample is, in that case, no longer relevant. After all, the only thing that matters than is the way in which *that type of cybercrime* was committed. The question remains, however, whether findings concerning a particular type of cybercrime in the 'each most recent cybercrime' selection is representative of the same type of cybercrime as in the selection 'all cybercrimes reported in this research project'. There is no obvious answer to this question because respondents were only asked about the way the most recent cybercrime was committed.

Knowing the perpetrator

Businesses were asked whether they knew who had committed the most recent cybercrime. Table 4.3 gives a schematic outline of the extent to which companies were aware of the perpetrator's identity.

Table 4.3   Does your organisation know who committed this cybercrime?

	Yes	Suspicion	No	Do not know
Total number of victims (n = 335)	10.1	5.4	79.4	5.1
Malware (n = 155)**	**0.6	3.2	**91.0	5.2
Phishing (n = 49)	2.0	2.0	*91.8	4.1
E-fraud (n = 34)	**38.2	8.8	**44.1	8.8
Hacking (n = 27)	11.1	7.4	77.8	3.7

*Difference with 'all other victims than those in this category' ** ($p < 0.01$), * ($p < 0.05$) (Z-score for proportions).*

Most of the companies did not know the identity of the perpetrator. For malware incidents, it is apparent that offenders were significantly more likely to be unknown than those committing other kinds of cybercrime. On the other hand, victims of e-fraud were significantly more likely to be aware of the perpetrator's identity.

In total, 15.5 per cent of the companies knew, or had a suspicion, who the offenders were in the most recently experienced incidents (n = 52). These companies mainly indicated that they were wronged by someone they did not know personally. At the same time, respondents were given the opportunity to indicate who had presumably committed the cybercrime, so several of them indicated who they suspected the offender to be (Text Box 4.2).

> **Text Box 4.2: Quotes about the identity of the perpetrator**
> - *'Company in Singapore'. (e-fraud victim)*
> - *'Company in China'. (e-fraud victim)*
> - *'Supplier'. (e-fraud victim)*
> - *'A person who deceived us using a false name and bank statement'. (e-fraud victim)*
> - *'A member of the family, but experts say that that is not possible…?' (hacking victim)*
> - *'PKK fighters organisation'. (hacking victim)*
> - *'A former employee from another company'. (victim of cyber defamation/slander)*
> - *'A former business partner. He admitted it. The police wouldn't even to listen to the story'. (victim of cyber defamation/slander)*

These quotes confirm that cybercrime offenders are often not known. If a company happens to know or suspect who the offender is, then it is usually someone that they do not know personally. That is a finding that also emerged from other studies on cybercrime among businesses: although insider threats do occur to a certain extent (McAfee, 2013), companies are mainly victims of cybercrimes which are committed from outside the organisation (Ernst & Young, 2011; PwC, 2011; Verizon, 2012). The consequence of this for police operations is that, as a rule the perpetrator, is not known: any criminal investigation has to therefore first focus on identifying the alleged suspect.

The internationalisation of cybercrime
In addition to questions about the extent to which the perpetrator was known, we also asked questions about the modus operandi. Previous research has shown that cybercrime regularly crosses national borders (Domenie et al., 2013; Leukfeldt, Domenie & Stol, 2010). We asked respondents in this study about whether the most recent cybercrime incident was committed from within the Netherlands. Table 4.4 demonstrates that more than 8 per cent of the most recent cybercrimes encountered by businesses were committed from abroad. The majority of the respondents, however, did not know from which country the offence had been committed. This means that the number of cybercrimes committed from abroad may be higher in reality. If the 'Do not know' category is not taken into consideration, then 19.2 per cent of e-frauds were committed outside the Netherlands (n = 5/26) and 30.4 per cent of the total of cybercrimes were committed from outside the Netherlands (n = 28/92). For police work, this means that the investigative work will not only have to focus on identifying the alleged perpetrator but also on an unknown perpetrator operating from abroad in a significant number of the cases. Conversely, it must therefore also be concluded that offenders operate from the Netherlands in the majority of cases (69.6%), which means that Dutch policy with regard to fighting 'SME cybercrime' must still be based on what is happening at a national level.

Table 4.4   Was the offence committed from within the Netherlands?

	Yes	No	Do not know
Total number of victims (n = 335)	19.1	8.4	72.5
Malware (n = 155)**	7.7	4.5	87.7
Phishing (n = 49)*	4.1	10.2	85.7
E-fraud (n = 34)**	61.8	14.7	23.5
Hacking (n = 27)	7.4	14.8	77.8

*Difference with 'all other victims than those in this category' ** (p < 0.01), * (p < 0.05).*

In addition, there were differences between the cybercrimes: for malware and phishing, the respondents were less likely to know whether the offenders operated from the Netherlands. So, it is possible that perpetrators of these kinds of crime are more likely to be operating from abroad. The opposite applies to e-fraud: companies that most recently fell victim to online scams were more likely to know from where the perpetrators were operating, and, in more than three fifths of the cases, they claimed that the criminal was operating from the Netherlands. Nevertheless, nearly 15 per cent of this group of victims were still deceived by someone who operated from abroad. These findings are not strange: it is plausible that e-fraud victims, as opposed to malware victims, interacted in some way with the perpetrators, for instance, via their website or when buying or selling.

The modi operandi of perpetrators
To gain an understanding of the modi operandi used by perpetrators, we then asked whether companies were aware of the way in which cyber criminals set to work. Table 4.5 answers the question of whether companies know how the most recent cybercrime they experienced was committed.

Table 4.5 Do you know how the cybercrime was committed?

	Yes	Suspicion	No
Total number of victims (n = 335)	20.3	14.6	65.1
Malware (n = 155)**	12.3	14.8	72.9
Phishing (n = 49)	22.4	12.2	65.3
E-fraud (n = 34)**	44.1	8.8	47.1
Hacking (n = 27)	18.5	7.4	74.1

*Difference with 'all other victims than those in this category' ** ($p < 0.01$), * ($p < 0.05$).*

Almost two thirds of the victims indicated that they did not know how the most recent cybercrime incident was committed. That percentage is significantly higher among the companies that fell victim to malware in the most recent incident than among victims from other kinds of cybercrime: almost 73 per cent of the malware victims did not know how the perpetrator had committed the cybercrime. For e-fraud, on the other hand, a significantly larger proportion of the companies were aware of, or at any rate suspected, how the cyber criminal had set to work.

> **Malware – difficult to spot**
> *Mr Veldhuizen has a furniture shop. One day his virus scanner reports that his computer is infected. He suspects that the virus arrived via an e-mail address on his website, but he does not know for sure. Mr Veldhuizen gets a lot of spam and sometimes finds it difficult to distinguish between e-mails he wants and unsolicited e-mails. As a result, he sometimes accidently opens e-mails that turn out to be spam. Because Mr Veldhuizen does not know what he should do about the message from his virus scanner, he gets in touch with a company that regularly helps him with his IT issues. However, no virus is found so Mr Veldhuizen gets in touch with the virus scanner company. It eventually takes this company five full working days to remove what turns out to be a new kind of malware from this computer.*

To understand how cybercrimes are committed, victims were asked to describe the perpetrators' modi operandi for the most recent offence that they had encountered. In total, 83 victims gave a usable description of the perpetrators' modi operandi.[9] Below we

---

9. A total of 94 respondents gave a description of the modus operandi based on the most recent incident they had experienced. However, 11 of the descriptions were unusable. Because the descriptions were too brief, it remains unclear in these cases how the cybercrimes were committed. Verbatim examples from, in this case, incidents reported by malware victims that lack an interpretation include: 'virus

describe in succession how malware, phishing, e-fraud and hacking are committed according to the victims. This is followed by an overview of the descriptions of the modi operandi used in other cybercrimes. The descriptions of the modi operandi are based on respondents' perceptions: so it may well be that respondents characterise something as a certain type of cybercrime while it is in fact another kind of cybercrime, or that it does not involve a crime at all. While the modi operandi described offer an illustrative insight into how businesses become victims of cybercrime, no generalisable statements can be made about the way each cybercrime is committed. The number of descriptions is too small and the content too diverse for this.

Modi operandi for malware
In total, 27 malware victims gave a usable description of the way in which the cybercrimes were committed. From these descriptions, it is evident that malware is mainly the consequence of the (unwittingly high-risk) internet behaviour of SME owners themselves and/or their own members of staff. Opening unsolicited e-mails and/or unknown files, downloading software and visiting high-risk websites lead to company networks being infected, for instance. Text Box 4.3 contains quotes from entrepreneurs who were duped because of their own (unwittingly high-risk) internet behaviour.

Text Box 4.3: Quotes from malware victims as a consequence of their own (high-risk) internet behaviour
- *'Virus concealed in spam e-mail that an employee opened'.*
- *'An .exe file was opened which then infected the PC with malware'.*
- *'A virus while consulting a website'.*
- *'Link in an e-mail'.*
- *'From visiting pirate bay (presumably)'.*
- *'Downloading files'.*
- *'An e-mail from a bankruptcy receiver who said that there was an outstanding amount at a company which had gone bankrupt. There was a link which you could use to see the invoice in question. After that, we had a Trojan horse'.*
- *'Via a website'.*
- *'After looking something up on the internet, we were infected by the ukash police virus. We eventually managed to remove it without any consequences, but it took us a long time (3 hours)'.*
- *'Phishing e-mails, or visiting the wrong sites or opening contaminated attachments. The malware (Trojan horse) reached our internal network, but was blocked and removed before it could mine data or cause damage'.*
- *'Obsolete version of virus scanner on computer'.*
- *'Via visits to contaminated websites'.*

---

planned Trojan horse after during a hack' or 'approached by an IP from neighbourhood as shown by the provider'.

- *'Via e-mail attachments'.*
- *'Importing files via a website we visited'.*
- *'Via an unprotected computer'.*
- *'By e-mail'. (twice)*
- *'From approaching a contaminated site and by e-mail'.*
- *'Phone call from someone who spoke English badly who masqueraded as someone working for Microsoft and claimed that all kinds of computer settings needed to be changed which would then give them access to the computer and networks'.*
- *'Received via e-mail when the virus scanner didn't yet have an "answer" for it'.*

It is not clear in some of the above descriptions whether the website, e-mail or files were ostensibly trustworthy. Having said that, it is clear from several other responses that cyber criminals try to use trustworthy parties to spread malware. It is no easy task for business owners in such cases to avoid becoming victims of cybercrime because cyber criminals make it difficult for entrepreneurs to recognise this type of crime.

Text Box 4.4: Quotes from entrepreneurs whose systems became infected with malware from ostensibly trustworthy parties
- *'Malware is often installed without you being aware of it when you install online software (unsolicited software). The most recent example that I have of this within our organisation is Hola Search. All my search engine settings were suddenly set to Hola Search when I installed Mozilla Firefox (browser)'.*
- *'MMS sent by e-mail so-called from Vodafone. Once we'd received ten of these messages in one week did we become suspicious, not the first time, partly because a genuine MMS had just been sent to a mobile phone'.*
- *'It was a Trojan horse (Conficker) which was on a laptop made available by a client (for test purposes). It was a Windows XP laptop which was missing a security patch'.*
- *'Through the NU.nl ad servers'.*
- *'Web server of a fireworks hosting provider had been hacked'.*
- *'Attachment from apparently trustworthy sender'.*
- *'From zip files which were included in e-mails that seemed trustworthy'.*
- *'Unsafe windows software'.*

Phishing modi operandi
Twelve of the entrepreneurs who most recently became victims of phishing gave usable descriptions of the perpetrators' modi operandi. Text Box 4.5 illustrates how phishing is committed according to the entrepreneurs. Of the 12 descriptions, 6 were related to the manipulation of electronic payment traffic. Cyber criminals try to extort money from companies, for instance, by asking for confidential bank details or by suggesting that an online payment has or should have been made or should be reversed. In the other

descriptions, but also once as an explanation about the modi operandi for malware, it emerged that criminals try to gain access to company computers 'remotely' through social engineering. In such cases, companies are called in an attempt to convince them that the person on the other side of the line has to get access to the company network remotely to ostensibly change computer settings.

Text Box 4.5: Quotes from entrepreneurs about phishing modi operandi

Electronic payment traffic

- *'The "standard" e-mails with a link re updating bank details. Incidentally, we have never fallen for this'.*
- *'They were always about imitations of ING or ABN AMRO websites with a request to login. We reported all of mails to these organisations and normally it wasn't possible to login to these websites anymore because ING or ABN AMRO had already intercepted the mails'.*
- *'They made a copy of our ING current account. It looked as though we had made a payment to an insurer. The next day it turned out to be a bogus company'.*
- *'Phishing via an e-mail from Rabobank'.*
- *'We regularly receive requests by e-mail to cancel iDEAL payments that we did not make or we receive fake invoices or fake letters from bailiffs'.*
- *'We receive fishing mails on a daily basis from various so-called banking institutions, e-mails from other institutions like iDEAL or e-mails from online suppliers and/or mail order companies, for example, H&M clothing. There are links in the e-mails to cancel orders. But these e-mails do not come from the original companies so I think the intention is that you click on the link in these ghost e-mails and then your computer gets hacked. Because we are a small organisation and everyone is well informed and instructed, and knows what is going on in our organisation and what is ordered, we remove these e-mails immediately I always send any fishing e-mails from the bank through to the bank in question'.*

Other

- *'...called by a so-called Microsoft help desk and they attempted to get remote access to our network'.*
- *'Phone call and then logged in to our computer'.*
- *'Sent an e-mail to administration with a request to send back information. It then became apparent that it was a enrolment form for a non-existent or hardly existing online address book. For six months the company tried to get a considerable amount of money for the registration. I suspect that while their conduct may have been legal, it was certainly bordering on a scam. Didn't pay'.*
- *'You've won the main prize, please send your bank details so that amount can be deposited'.*
- *'Having mail forwarded to another address'.*
- *'Confidential information requested via several e-mails'.*

Some companies who were confronted with phishing viewed themselves as victims, even though no company information was actually extracted from them. Evidently, these companies perceive being approached by cyber criminals to disclose company information for dishonest purposes as sufficient to speak of phishing victimisation, as opposed to the definition that the researchers had in mind (see Section 4.2.1) Other companies view themselves as victims if they have actually been caught by a phishing trap.

E-fraud modi operandi

Fourteen of the companies which fell victim to e-fraud described how the most recent cybercrime had been committed (Text Box 4.6). The working methods described illustrate that cyber criminals have and use a wide pallet of fraud types, as Figure 4.11 has already shown. Not paying for a product or service, not supplying products or services which have been paid for, delivering poor quality goods and advertising fraud are types of e-fraud that companies are confronted with.

Text Box 4.6: Quotes from e-fraud victims who described how the fraud was committed

Not paying for service or goods

- *'Agreements not met, payment for delivered services not made'.*
- *'Through mules who then don't pay'.*
- *'Sold old IT hardware to an online buyer. The buyer collected it and never paid the money. Later we read on the internet that he was a crook and no one ever got their money'.*

Paid but not supplied or poor quality

- *'Ordered several central heating boilers. Collected one of them after which it became very clear that fraud was involved. Filed an official report at the police station – sat there for almost 1½ hours – but the Roosendaal police did not deal with it seriously'.*
- *'Prepaid order not delivered'.*
- *'Ordered something, paid for it and never received it'.*
- *'A product was offered via Marktplaats (a Dutch online marketplace) for a reasonable price (did not suspect fraud). Product was not delivered after payment'.*

Advertising fraud

- *'Sent an invoice for a newspaper advert that was never placed and which the newspaper itself knew nothing about'.*
- *'Asked by phone to cancel a subscription by fax and then send it back by fax once signed. A couple of months later they sent a final demand and notice that you have to pay. So instead of cancelling the subscription, you're still tied to it according to the small print. This involved a website which you're on but with useless information'.*
- *'Phantom invoice sent via a company set up'.*

Other

- *'Stolen credit card details from a customer'.*
- *'Texts subsequently added in an e-mail exchange'.*

- *'Via an invalid authorisation at the bank. The description on the bank statement came from "multipay"'.*
- *'Asking for bank details'.*

Hacking modi operandi

Hacking is one of the most common types of cybercrime among businesses. Six entrepreneurs who reported hacking as the most recently encountered cyber incident described how the perpetrators operated. Text Box 4.7 shows how businesses fall victim to hacking.

Text Box 4.7: Quotes from victims about the perpetrators' hacking modi operandi
- *'Received it via an infected file. After that, the settings in our system were regularly changed and our computer was used to send spam. We had to buy a new server'.*
- *'Brute force hacking of our customers' passwords'.*
- *'Hacking of remote desk top which was open'.*
- *'It involved a hospital department – the hospital's website was copied and staff passwords were stolen.'*
- *'Software was installed after opening an e-mail'.*
- *'I reckon it was via a copied page'.*

Some of these quotes confirm the findings of previous research (Leukfeldt et al., 2010). That research showed that in fact hacking often serves as a means to achieve an underlying goal. For example, the quotes here suggest that hacking was done to extract passwords or to send companies spam via the network. Various methods are used to carry out the hacking, such as copying login websites or infecting computers with malicious software that gives the hacker access to the company network.

Modi operandi for other cybercrimes

Other usable descriptions of modi operandi related to defamation/slander, skimming, defacing, identity abuse and a DoS attack. Given that the number of victims for each offence for which the modi operandi was described was small each time, the quotes in the following text boxes have been included for illustration purposes only.

Text Box 4.8: Quotes from victims about the modi operandi for cyber defamation/slander
Defamation slander (n = 10)
- *'Fake reports on third party websites'.*
- *'Bad reviews spread on the Internet'.*
- *'Review containing lies'.*
- *'Telling lies on a website'.*

- *'Displeasure about people within the organisation posted on the 'oordeelzelf.nl' (Dutch for 'judge for yourself') website'.*
- *'Posting defamatory statements on forums by a former employee (whose job was system administrator) who was summarily dismissed after embezzlement, fraud and threats. The member of staff still had company information and software licence codes. These were presumably traded online'.*
- *'Deliberately spreading false information via a forum'.*
- *'Putting a defamatory, offensive and false message on the Internet'.*
- *'By writing a review of our company on Google that was not true. It is not possible to remove that review'.*
- *'By feeding a website with incriminating statements about our organisation. It was a kind of forum'.*

The internet offers cyber criminals an (anonymous) platform to deliberately attack the honour or reputation of a business. The quotes in Text Box 4.8 make clear that, among others, online forums and review websites are used for this.

Text Box 4.9: Quotes from victims about the modi operandi for skimming, defacing, identity abuse and a DoS attack

Skimming (card) (n = 6)
- *'Skimming of cards at a pay machine for parking in the centre of Amsterdam'.*
- *'PIN code stolen'.*
- *'Operation carried out in a group whereby person number 1 caused a distraction so that person number 2 could trace the PIN code during payment, after which person number 3 stole the card'.*
- *'Skimmed at a fuel station'.*
- *'Credit card number taken from an online sale and misused by third party. The credit card company sorted out the credit card fraud. The damage amounted to EUR 569'.*
- *'Skimmed at the fuel station!'*

Defacing (n = 4)
- *'They try to get attention for their websites via my guestbook so that they move up in search engines probably. This is automatic I reckon because, when it happens, it is often in large numbers. There is a filter so I only post what I think is suitable'.*
- *'Web server hacked'.*
- *'They enjoy hacking badly protected websites'.*
- *'Our (former) website administrator had an extremely simple password. Website administrator has gone. All passwords are now extremely difficult'.*

Identity abuse (n = 3)
- *'Used information from the website to masquerade as someone who worked for our company'.*
- *'Copied parts of the website'.*
- *'The website was hacked because we didn't do an update. A lot of spam was sent from the website'.*

> DoS attack (n = 1)
> - *'By using the Anonymous network'.*

Text Box 4.9 shows that bankcards are skimmed using fraudulent PIN machines. In addition, one of the quotes shows that bankcard details can also be copied online and then misused.

The quotes about defacing make it clear that defacing a website is not an isolated offence. Often it is necessary to first hack a computerised work before a website can be changed.

Identity abuse is done in various ways: cyber criminals pretend to be companies, copy parts of websites or companies perceive sending spam in the organisation's name as identity abuse.

Finally, one of the victims claimed to have fallen victim to a DoS attack carried out by 'Anonymous'.

Summary of the ways in which cybercrime is committed
This section described the extent to which companies know how the most recent cybercrime they experienced had been committed. Often entrepreneurs lack insight into the modi operandi of perpetrators. In most of the cases, the offender is unknown; companies generally do not know from which country the cybercrime was committed and normally it is not clear how the cybercrime was committed. For malware in particular, few companies indicated that they knew how the cybercrime was committed. For e-fraud, on the other hand, more companies knew how the offence was committed. That presumably has to do with the fact that there had been some kind of interaction between perpetrator and victim in cases involving e-fraud scams.

If they knew how it had happened, companies described how the cybercrime had been committed. Even though the number of descriptions per cybercrime was too small to make generalisable statements about the modi operandi of cyber criminals, quotes from the entrepreneurs give an impression of how cybercrime is committed. From the case descriptions of the most common types of cybercrime, it is apparent:

- that malware infections are mainly due to the own companies' or their employees' own internet behaviour, be it consciously high risk or not, and that cyber criminals try to spread malware via seemingly trustworthy parties;
- that phishing generally focusses on manipulating electronic payment traffic;
- that e-fraud comes in many forms and, of these, entrepreneurs mainly recognise and describe advertising fraud and fraud related to buying and selling;
- that hacking generally serves a underlying objective, for example, hacking is done to then steal company information or to send spam via the company network. Hackers use various methods, for instance, copying from login websites, in order to gain unauthorised access to the company network; and
- that tarnishing the honour or reputation of a company can be done by, for instance, simply posting messages on review websites.

4.2.3 Severity and damage

We also asked questions about the severity and damage incurred as a consequence of the most recent cybercrime incidents to which companies had fallen victim. It is worth noting that companies do not always categorise the most recent cyber incident that they were victims of as serious (Table 4.6).

Table 4.6   The extent to which companies view being confronted with cybercrime as serious

	N	Serious	Normal	Not serious
Total number of victims (n = 335)	335	26.3	40.9	32.8
Malware (n = 155)**	155	18.1	44.5	37.4
Phishing (n = 49)	49	24.5	28.6	46.9
E-fraud (n = 34)*	34	47.1	32.4	20.6
Hacking (n = 27)	27	40.7	33.3	25.9

*Difference with 'all other victims than those in this category' ** ($p < 0.01$), * ($p < 0.05$).*

Generally, respondents indicated that they found the most recent incident with which the company had been confronted to be 'not serious' or 'normal' (73.7%). More than a quarter felt it was 'serious' (26.3%). Malware incidents are perceived to be less serious than other cybercrimes. On the other hand, SMEs consider e-fraud to be a serious kind of cybercrime.

This finding may be explained by the fact that companies do not always suffer damage from cybercrime. For instance, if a company is confronted with malware but does not incur damage because the antivirus software detects the malware in time and removes it, the company has been confronted with cybercrime but did not incur any damage. Supplementary analyses show that the extent to which companies find it serious to be confronted with cybercrime is associated with the damage suffered by the cybercrime. Companies which fell victim to cybercrime and incurred damage are significantly more likely to report the most recent incident as serious compared to companies who experienced cybercrime but which did not suffer any damage from it. Figure 4.12 shows the extent to which and what kind of damage companies experience from cybercrime.

By their own account, almost 45 per cent of the companies said that they had not suffered any damage as a consequence of the most recent cyber incident. Loss of time and financial damages were the types of damage reported most: nearly 36 per cent reported loss of time and more than 1 in 5 companies suffered financial damage a consequence of cybercrime. Although they can only be compared to a limited extent, these results are echoed in other research into the damage from cybercrime among companies. The IT Barometer, for instance, also discovered that most of the companies did not incur damage from cybercrime and that one in five incurred financial damages (Ernst & Young, 2011). Based on the Norwegian Computer Crime Survey conducted in 2006, Hagen et al. (2008) state moreover that 'additional work' (loss of time) is the principle damage caused by cybercrime.

Figure 4.12   Damage suffered as a consequence of the most recent incident (n = 335)

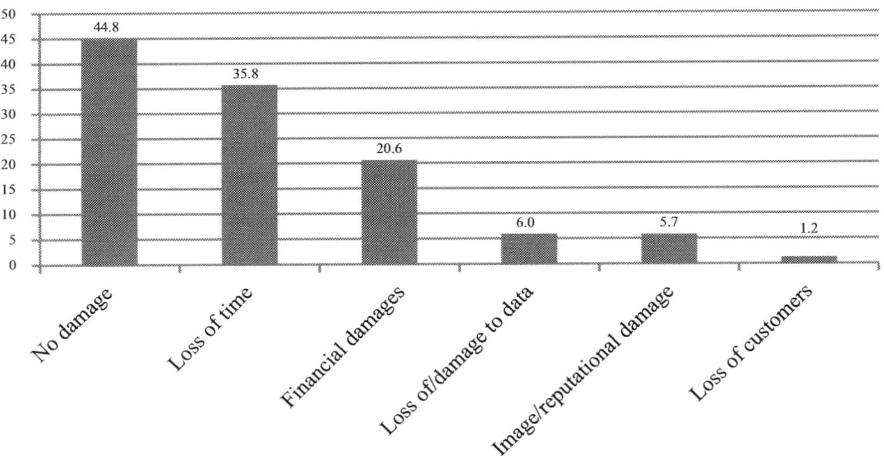

Malware – loss of time and powerlessness

When Mr Veldhuizen got malware on his company computer, he could not use it and he spent a lot of time calling and consulting with the virus scanner company. He had to do most of the work for his shop by phone and fax. The incident cost him a great deal of time, but there was no other damage. Looking back on the incident, Mr Veldhuizen was not even particularly annoyed that he had lost a week of his time trying to solve the problem. The worst thing for him was the feeling of powerlessness: 'The worst thing was that there was nothing I could do about it. That's when I get really angry, but especially because of the powerlessness of not being able to do anything. It's also so cowardly, of course, that you can't find out who did it. That feeling is even worse than the inconvenience it causes.'

Damage is partially specific to types of cybercrime (see Table 4.7). Damage from malware mainly has to do with loss of time: malware infections have to be remedied. Damage from fraud is generally financial. Phishing is a form of cybercrime that leads to damage in a relatively small amount of cases.

Table 4.7   Types of damage from the most recent incident reported by victims

	Total victimisation (n = 335)	Malware (n = 155)	Phishing (n = 49)	E-fraud (n = 34)	Hacking (n = 27)
No damage	44.8	43.2	**69.4	29.4	33.3
Loss of time	35.8	**46.5	*22.4	20.6	40.7
Financial damages	20.6	*15.5	**6.1	**61.8	33.3
Loss of/damage to data	6.0	7.1	4.1	0.0	11.1
Image/reputational damage	5.7	**0.6	0.0	5.9	7.4
Loss of customers	1.2	0.0	2.0	2.9	3.7

*Difference with 'all other victims than those in this category' ** (p < 0.01), * (p < 0.05).*

In cases involving financial damages, respondents were asked about the approximate extent of the damage. For this, respondents were asked to round off amounts to whole numbers. Financial damages were reported by 20.6 per cent (n = 69) of the companies. However, nine of the respondents who reported financial damages as a consequence of the most recently encountered incident did not know the extent of the damage. One entrepreneur indicated that he or she preferred not to mention the extent of the damage. Fifty-nine entrepreneurs did give an indication of the extent of the financial damages (that equates to 85.5% of all victims with financial damages). Together these 59 businesses suffered 442,953 euro worth of damage. This relates to damage as a consequence of the most recently cyber incidents experienced by these businesses. It is also possible that companies fell victim to cybercrime more than once, as shown in Table 4.1. If this is the case, it is possible that damage was also incurred from cybercrimes other than the most recent incident reported on here. So, the total amount of damage among the companies in our research is in fact probably higher. Furthermore, it should be noted that the reported damages vary considerably and range from 15 to 240,000 euro. That means that one of the reported damages accounts for more than half (54.2%) of the total amount of damage. This renders it impossible to justify any extrapolation of the findings.

A comparison with the damage mentioned in previous research is also pointless given the limited generalisability of the findings. Moreover, the results from previous studies are limited in terms of comparability and the damages vary widely, rendering it impossible to sketch a clear picture of the damage due to cybercrime incurred by companies (see Ernst & Young, 2011; FSB, 2013; PwC, 2013).

> **Hacking - anxiety felt on a daily basis**
> *Mrs Bijker owns a hairdressing salon and has fallen victim to cybercrime three times already. The last time she was the victim of a hacker who had gained access to her computer system. The hacker watched while Mrs Bijker made payments via internet banking and made sure that some payments were made several times. But the hacker didn't manage to siphon off money away. It took Mrs Bijker a great deal of effort to get the undue payments refunded. The incident made Mrs Bijker much more aware of cybercrime and resulted in her protecting her network as best she could. Yet she is still afraid of falling victim again and so she switches off her computer as soon as she sees anything 'strange'. She finds it quite scary that her business operations depend on IT: 'Twice I've had an intruder in my home, that was awful. But this is difficult to explain [...]. When you're dealing with an intruder you know whether someone has been in your home and among your things. But as soon as you switch on your computer, you don't know if someone is watching you or whether you're going to be ripped off again. And you simply have to deal with it on a daily basis.'*

Respondents were also offered the opportunity to report other kinds of damage. Many took this opportunity. Sometimes respondents used it to clarify what kind of damage they had suffered. In some cases, respondents also described the consequences of cybercrimes other than the most recent one they had experienced. Text Box 4.10 gives the damages described. Even though some of the companies did not mind becoming victims, some of the quotes confirm that cybercrime can indeed be serious. Victims of malware and hacking, for instance, could not use their e-mail accounts or the company network, and some were forced to replace the entire company network. In addition to technical and financial consequences, cybercrime can also have a personal, psychosocial impact on victims. For instance, one hacking victim reported experiencing 'a lot of anxiety and stomach pain' as a consequence of cybercrime and one victim has become 'more anxious about using' IT because of phishing. These are findings that were underscored by the results of the in-depth interviews.

Text Box 4.10: Types of damage described by respondents as a consequence of the most recent cybercrime experienced

Consequences of malware
- *'Not being able to work on the computers'.*
- *'Additional costs incurred to have the problems solved by third parties'.*
- *'Financial damages in the form of hours charged by our IT partner'.*
- *'Difficult to measure'.*
- *'New computer'.*
- *'Could not use the computer for a few days because of repairs'.*
- *'Couldn't take any bookings temporarily via the website'.*
- *'Had to replace the entire network'.*

Consequences of hacking
- *'No e-mail contact possible'.*
- *'A whole lot of anxiety and stomach pain'.*

Consequences of phishing
- *'More anxious about using [computer]'.*
- *'Damage for one of the members of staff'.*

Consequences of defamation/slander
- *'Loss of trust in our own members of staff'.*
- *'Cannot be measured: we don't know which customers have left us because of this'.*

Other consequences
- *'Could not use the network temporarily'.(victim of a DoS attack)*
- *'Loss of trust through customer'. (victim of ID abuse)*

Summary of the severity and damage from the most recently experienced incident
Businesses were not always inclined to categorise the most recently experienced cybercrime as 'serious'. A quarter of the companies did, however, feel that falling victim to cybercrime was serious. That counts for e-fraud incidents in particular. The severity of cybercrime is related to the damage suffered: the more damage suffered, the more serious companies consider the most recent incident to be. The fact that

many businesses did not suffer any damage from cybercrime explains why cyber incidents are not necessarily considered to be serious. It is principally financial damages and damage due to loss of time that companies experienced as a consequence of the most recent cybercrime encountered.

Damages were partially specific to types of cybercrime. For malware, the damage was mainly associated with the time it costs to remove the infection, while damage due to e-fraud was mainly financial in nature. The findings do not allow us to make general statements about the (average) level of financial damages from cybercrime among businesses. The information also does not offer an adequate basis to justify calculating a national amount for cybercrime damages or to calculate an average amount of financial damage per cybercrime.

It is clear, however, that cybercrime can have unpleasant consequences, despite the fact that a considerable proportion of the companies did not view the most recent incidents they had experienced as serious. In addition to financial implications, many victims indicated that they were temporarily unable to use their company's IT as a consequence of cybercrime and/or that they had experienced psychosocial consequences, such as becoming more anxious about using IT and experiencing anxiety and stomach pain.

4.3   REACTIONS FROM VICTIMS AND TACKLING CYBERCRIME

This section focusses on the reactions of SMEs who fell victim to cybercrime. In particular, we pay attention to the role that SMEs assign to the police in tackling cybercrime. Section 4.3.1 describes the actions that SMEs undertake as a consequence of the most recent cybercrime that they encountered. In Section 4.3.2, we describe how SMEs expect they will act if they become victims of cybercrime in the future. In addition, we discuss the extent to which SMEs have confidence in the police and who is responsible for the online security of companies according to the SME sector.

4.3.1   *Actions taken as a consequence of victimisation*

We asked companies who had fallen victim to cybercrime which actions they had taken as a consequence of the most recent incident that the company had experienced (see Figure 4.13). A quarter of the companies said that they had not taken any measures as a consequence of the most recent incident (24.5%).[10]

Companies that do take action are largely self-reliant: 37.9 per cent solved the problem themselves, for example, by getting their own IT specialists to investigate the problem. More than 1 in 5 learnt from the incident and took steps to prevent victimisation in the future (23.6%).

---

10. However, it is apparent from questions posed earlier about measures taken (see Section 4.1.3) that this does not mean that the company had not protected itself against online risks. Of these companies, 22.6, 24.3 and 19.0 per cent had taken at least one physical, technical or policy measure, respectively. Incidentally, these percentages are considerably lower than the overall percentages (see Figures 4.7 to 4.9).

Figure 4.13   Actions taken as a consequence of victimisation (n = 335)

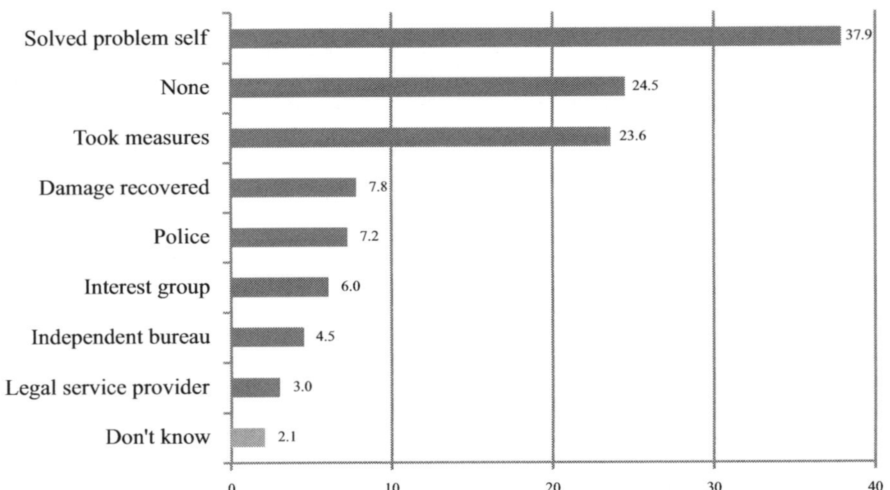

Self-reliance
Mr Delhaize created his company website himself. When his website was hacked, he was able to solve the problems himself. He had his password changed by the hosting company and he removed the piece of code that had been placed on his website. 'I am what you'd call an autodidact. Teach yourself and do it yourself, and [learn through] play.' Moreover, he can always turn to his friends for advice: 'I had a technical training myself and my group of friends is virtually only made up of techies.'

In almost 8 per cent of the cases, the company managed to recover the damage or tried to recover the damage. For instance, the damage was reimbursed by the insurance company or the bank, or the perpetrator returned the goods that had not been paid for. Twenty businesses got in touch with an interest group (6.0%). They mainly got in touch with the Fraud Help Desk (n = 7), the Chamber of Commerce (n = 6) and/or the Dutch Advertising Fraud Support Centre (n = 5).

Compared to other victims, companies who fell victim to malware were more inclined to solve the problems that had arisen themselves (51.0%; see Table 4.8). Also, malware victims took fewer measures to prevent future victimisation and they were less likely to seek compensation for damages. In addition, they were less inclined to contact the police or an interest group. These results are not altogether unexpected given that malware is a relatively mild form of cybercrime (entrepreneurs mainly experienced malware as 'normal' or 'not serious'; see Table 4.6).

Table 4.8   Actions taken by victims

Action	Total (n = 335)	Malware (n = 155)	Phishing (n = 49)	E-fraud (n = 34)	Hacking (n = 27)
None	24.5	28.4	32.7	8.8	14.8
Damage recovered[a]	7.8	**0.6	10.2	14.7	14.8
Solved the problem ourselves in some other way[b]	37.9	**51.0	**18.4	**11.8	44.4
Independent bureau	4.5	7.1	2.0	0	3.7
Took measures[c]	23.6	**16.8	20.4	**47.1	29.6
Police	7.2	**1.9	4.1	14.7	**25.9
Interest group	6.0	**0.6	14.3	23.5	0
Legal service provider	3.0	0	0	14.7	3.7
Do not know	2.1	1.9	4.1	2.9	0
Other	4.8	2.6	4.1	8.8	3.7

*Difference with 'all other victims than those in this category' ** ($p < 0.01$), * ($p < 0.05$).*
[a] Response option in the questionnaire: "My organisation tried to compensate for the damage itself/was compensated for damage: for instance, the damage was reimbursed by the insurance company/the bank, the website/webshop or the perpetrator returned the stolen goods".
[b] Response option in the questionnaire: "My organisation solved the problem itself, for example, by getting our own IT department to investigate (getting rid of the virus infection/plugging the leak)".
[c] Response option in the questionnaire: "My organisation took measures (learnt from the incident) to prevent future victimisation".

Phishing and e-fraud victims were less likely to solve the problems themselves compared to victims of malware. In addition, e-fraud victims were more inclined to take steps to prevent falling victim again (47.1%).

Contacted the police
In 7.2 per cent of the cases, the victims contacted the police (n = 24). This percentage is lower in comparison with other research findings. The most recent Corporate Sector Crime Monitor shows that around 60 per cent of companies notified the police of crime and in 26 per cent of cases they actually made a report (WODC, 2011). According to the IT Barometer, 16 per cent of companies *filed a report* as a consequence of cybercrime victimisation (Ernst & Young, 2011). Among individuals who fell victim to traditional crime, the reporting rate was around 35 per cent and the percentage of people who filed a report was 25 to 27 per cent (CBS, 2012a, 2012b). For cybercrime cases, 14.9 per cent of the individuals contacted the police (Domenie et al., 2013). Of these reporting rates and percentage of people who filed an official report, the 7.2 per cent for SME cybercrime victims who contacted the police is by far the lowest. More than any other kind of victimisation, cybercrime victimisation stays out of the police statistics: SMEs do not make this phenomenon visible to the police.
Businesses that have become victims of hacking are significantly more likely to contact the police than businesses which have fallen victim to other cybercrimes (Table 4.8).[11] It is noteworthy that victims of hacking are the ones more inclined to contact the

---

11. We used the Fisher's exact test for the analysis on hacking.

police and not victims of e-fraud. A study into the police's cybercrime workload, based on a sample of police files, showed that of the 142 randomly selected cybercrime police files, 71 related to e-fraud (50.0%) and 8 to hacking (5.6%; Leukfeldt et al., 2010). Police records therefore contain significantly more e-fraud cases than hacking cases. Also given the fact that the victimisation rate for e-fraud is higher than hacking (see Table 4.1), it could be expected that reports are mainly filed for e-fraud and not especially for hacking. Contrary to this expectation, companies are apparently more inclined to file official reports for hacking. We cannot find an explanation for this inconsistency in the research findings.

The companies that contacted the police were asked various questions so that more information could be obtained about why and how this took place, what the response from the police was and how the police response could be improved. To interpret these findings, an overview has been included in Table 4.9 about the cybercrimes for which the police were contacted.

Table 4.9   Victims who contacted the police (n = 24)

Cybercrime	Number of victims
Hacking	7
E-fraud	5
Identity abuse	3
Malware	3
Phishing	2
Cyber defamation/slander	2
Bankcard skimming	1
Cyber extortion	1

The first follow-up question about contact with the police was about the reasons for contacting the police (see Figure 4.14). The reason mentioned most often for contacting the police is that the companies wanted to file a report or notify the police that an offence had been committed (n = 14). In addition, companies considered it their duty to contact the police (n = 13). Half of the companies (also) gave as a reason that the perpetrator should be caught (n = 12). 'For insurance purposes' was mentioned least often, while this was the reason given most frequently (among members of the public) for reporting traditional crimes to the police: 'In 2011, the reasons mentioned most frequently for filing a report were for insurance purposes and that the respondents felt that the police should know about it (both 24 per cent)' (CBS, 2012a, p. 91). These findings reflect the fact that damage due to cybercrime is often not covered by insurance while traditional crimes (like bicycle theft, house burglaries and car theft) often are.

An in-depth analysis also showed that willingness to involve the police depends on the amount of financial damages suffered by the companies. Companies who contact the police are significantly more likely to have suffered financial damages from cybercrime than companies who did not contact the police (respectively, 45.8% and 18.6%).[12]

Figure 4.14 Why the police were contacted (n = 24)

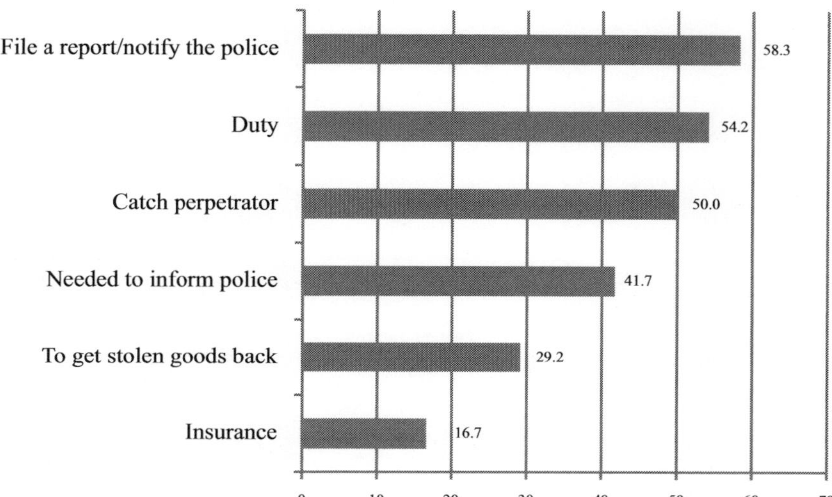

Figure 4.15 gives the results of the question about how the contact took place. Most companies went to the police station in person (n = 13). A quarter of the companies who contacted the police did so digitally (1.8% of all victims). Of these six companies, two companies contacted the Internet Fraud Hotline. In addition, respondents contacted the police digitally by filing a report online (n = 2) and via a police e-mail address (n = 2).

Statistics Netherlands wrote the following about the way in which traditional crime is reported to the police (by members of the public; CBS, 2012a, p. 84):

In 2011, 34 per cent [of the crimes] were reported over the phone; 30 per cent were reported at the police station (…). More than a quarter of the reports (28%) were done online (…). The way of reporting did not differ fundamentally from the way it was done in 2010. However, the proportion of reports made at the police station was lower than it was in 2008, while the proportion of reports made online was higher than in that year. In this research, the emphasis in comparison with traditional crime is therefore somewhat more on reporting at the police station and somewhat less on reporting by telephone. Perhaps the complexity of cybercrime that entrepreneurs experience means that they are more inclined to make a personal visit to the police station. Another explanation could be that companies (as opposed to individuals) prefer another method of reporting than the one chosen by members of the public surveyed by Statistics Netherlands.

---

12. We used the Fisher's exact test for this analysis.

Figure 4.15 Ways of contacting the police (n = 24)

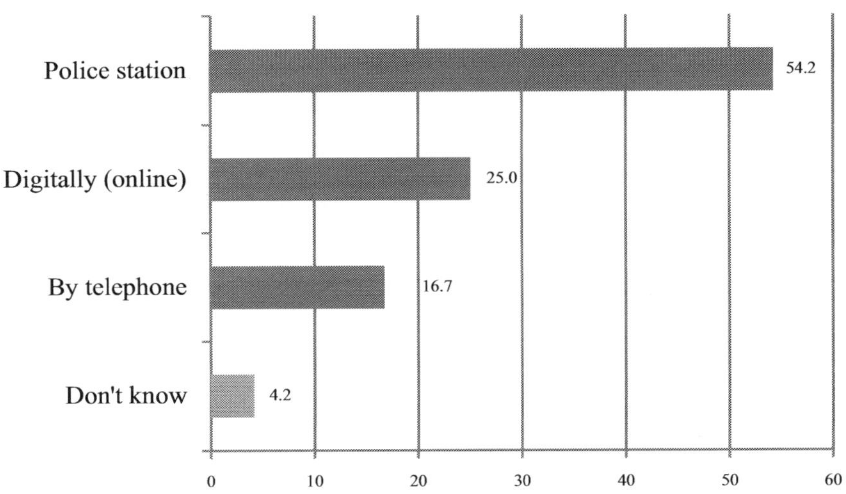

Contacting the police does not automatically mean that an official report was actually filed, although this was done for half of the reported cybercrimes. A notification in police registers was made for 12.5 per cent (n = 3) of the companies, and advice was given to the same number. Two of the companies did not know how the police responded; the police told one company that it involved a civil case. Finally, three companies reported other responses from the police (see Text Box 4.11).

> **Text Box 4.11: Other police responses**
> - *'They said that they had other priorities'.*
> - *'Nothing'.*
> - *'Filing a report was too much hassle. After a while the website closed down and the information I had filled in was gone. It took a lot of time and nothing was achieved'.*

Of the victims who contacted the police, 37.5 per cent (n = 9) was satisfied or very satisfied with the police response to their cybercrime case. Slightly fewer companies were dissatisfied or very dissatisfied (n = 7). This shows that some of those surveyed felt that the police's response was not appropriate. However, the group is too small to make generalising statements. Furthermore, it is not possible to verify whether or not the police acted correctly. Of the companies for whom an official report was filed (n = 12), three of those surveyed were dissatisfied and five were satisfied or very satisfied. So, filing a report does not always lead to a positive or more positive assessment of the police response.

Those companies whose assessment of the police response ranged from neutral to dissatisfied or very dissatisfied (n = 13) were asked about the ways in which their levels of satisfaction could be improved (Figure 4.16). All of these companies indicated that they would like to see feedback from the police about what happened with their report. Many of them also need certainty that the police would deal with the case (n = 12). Furthermore, the speed at which the police and the judicial authorities work can be improved according to SMEs (n = 11). In addition, companies would like to see the police paying more attention to victims and that it should be clear where companies can turn to report cybercrime (n = 9).

Figure 4.16 Improving satisfaction with the police response (n = 13)

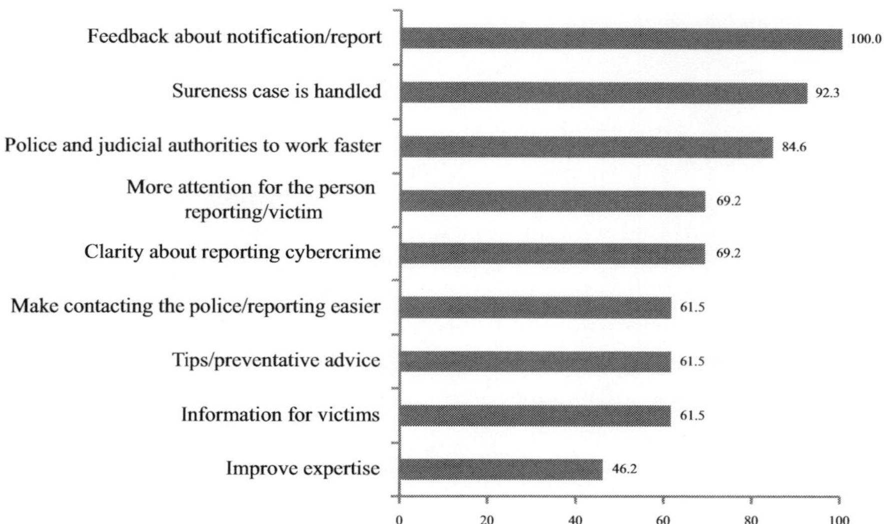

The businesses which were dissatisfied or very dissatisfied with the police expect the police to take various, far-reaching measures to fight cybercrime more effectively. Nevertheless, tackling cybercrime is not only the responsibility of the police; the web is too complex and extensive for this (Jewkes & Yar, 2008; Stol, 2008; see also Figure 4.25). In this regard, we would like to remind the reader that most SME victims (92.8%) did not contact the police about their victimisation but instead dealt with the issue in some other way, whether or not after contacting institutions other than the police.

Cybercrime as complex and far-reaching

Mr Alberda's company and staff have been confronted with a far-reaching cybercrime. A former employee who knows about IT has tarnished the company's honour and reputation, has made threats and stalked members of staff, both online and offline. As a consequence of the cybercrime, Mr Alberda has had to engage a wide range of parties: a corporate investigations firm, a lawyer, the police, an IT firm and a security company. All in all, Mr Alberda estimates that hiring external support and the loss of time has cost him some tens of thousands of euros. Mr Alberda made an appointment with the police to file an official report at the police station. 'We asked whether a officer with a bit more knowledge about computers could take down the report, but it didn't happen. It was just an officer in

> *training who took down the report.' According to Mr Alberda, the police then did nothing about the report. The case was brought before the courts, but the suspect was acquitted due to lack of evidence. Mr Alberda was extremely disappointed about this: 'Because the police hardly did any investigating, it was in fact our word against his' [the suspect]. The former employee has not stopped his cybercrime activities and, out of anxiety for a continuation of the problems, Mr Alberda is hardly, if at all, visible on the internet.*

Views of companies who did not contact the police
We asked companies who were victims but despite this did not contact the police (n = 311), about their motives for not taking action. It was possible for respondents to give several reasons (Figure 4.17). The reason mentioned most often for not contacting the police was an absence of damages or other negative consequences. Almost half of the respondents said that this was the reason for not contacting the police (49.5%). This seems to be the logical consequence of the fact that 72.9 per cent of SMEs who fell victim to cybercrime claimed that they did not suffer any damage.

Almost a quarter of the companies did not contact the police because they expected that the police would not do anything about the notification or report. Other police-related motives for not contacting the police were that the companies did not consider the police to be capable of investigating the cases (12.9%) and/or because companies held the view that it did not involve cases that were relevant to the police (17.4%).

> **Not going to the police – ignorance**
> *Mrs Bijker fell victim to a hacker who tried to transfer money using her details. She did not go to the police and is not really sure why she did not. She recognised the incident as a criminal activity, 'but who are you meant to turn to?' She did not think of contacting the police: 'I contacted my bank and my computer firm and cried "Boys, help!"'*

Figure 4.17   Reasons for not contacting the police (n = 311)

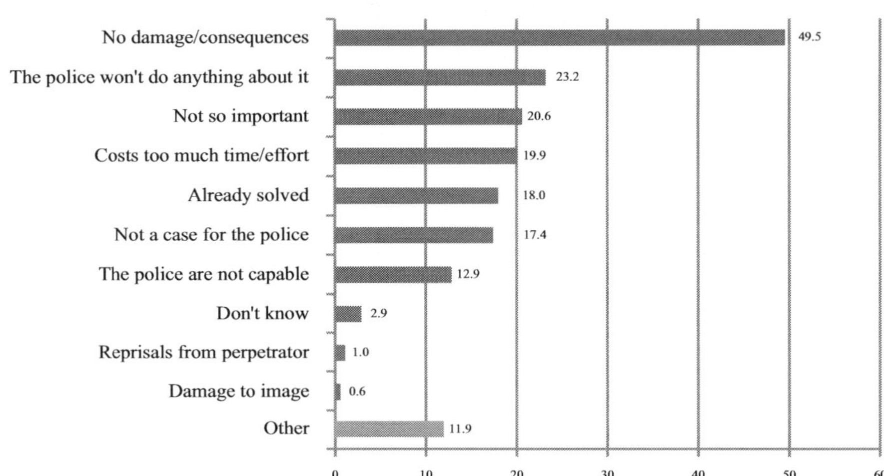

That filing a report costs too much time/effort (19.9%), that the incident is not considered important enough to contact the police (20.6%) and/or that the problems arising from cybercrime had already been solved (18.0%) may also have been factors that played a role when the companies decided not to contact the police. Respondents were far less inclined to mention fear of reprisals from the perpetrator and damage to their image as motives. Having said that, studies conducted by Ernst and Young (2011) and PwC (2011) show that, when asked about the aspects of cybercrime that companies are most concerned about, the response from 2 out of 5 was that they were particularly afraid that the company's image may be tarnished. That is not confirmed in this research. Perhaps this can be explained by the fact that this research was limited to the SME sector (2 to 50 employees).

Table 4.10 shows that significantly fewer victims of e-fraud compared to other victims gave no damage and/or negative consequences as reasons for not contacting the police. On the other hand, not calling in the police because taking action costs too much time/effort is a reason that e-fraud victims were more likely to give.

Just like victims of phishing, malware victims were more inclined to mention a lack of damage/consequences as a reason for not contacting the police than other victims were. This is not an unexpected result given that the previous section showed that the vast majority of malware and phishing victims did not suffer any damage or only lost time as a consequence (see Table 4.7). Finally, malware victims were more inclined not to consider their incident as a case for the police.

Table 4.10   Reasons for not contacting the police

Action	Total (n = 311)	Malware (n = 152)	Phishing (n = 47)	E-fraud (n = 29)	Hacking (n = 20)
No damage/consequences	49.5	*55.9	**70.2	**17.2	40.0
Not so important	20.6	23.7	17.0	3.4	10.0
Not a case for the police	17.4	*22.4	8.5	3.4	10.0
The police will not do anything about it	23.2	24.3	19.1	24.1	20.0
The police are not capable	12.9	13.2	14.9	6.9	15.0
Already solved	18.0	19.7	8.5	13.8	15.0
Reprisals from perpetrator	1.0	0.0	0.0	3.4	0.0
Damage to image	0.6	0.7	0.0	0.0	0.0
Costs too much time/effort	19.9	16.4	8.5	**44.8	15.0
Do not know	2.9	2.6	4.3	3.4	0.0
Other	11.9	7.2	10.6	20.7	10.0

*Difference with 'all other victims than those in this category' ** (p < 0.01), * (p < 0.05).*

Text Box 4.12 shows other reasons given by companies for not contacting the police.

Text Box 4.12: Other reasons for not contacting the police
- *'This is something that is our own responsibility'.*
- *'Didn't see it as a cybercrime, not aware that it was possible to take action'.*

> - *'It is a continuation, conducted by the same perpetrator, of a cybercrime committed in 2008. Because at the time the police did virtually nothing at all after filing a report, the perpetrator was acquitted due to lack of evidence. Also after appeal proceedings'.*
> - *'I had signed it myself so I thought I had no case'.*
> - *'I really have no idea why not. It has actually become too commonplace'.*
> - *'The bank is the first designated organisation. Perhaps the bank reports it to the police'.*

We then asked the group of companies who had not contacted the police which factors would ensure that they would decide to contact the police (see Figure 4.18). The factor that was mentioned by more companies than any other was that there would have to incur more (financial) damage (49.2%).

Almost one third of the companies indicated that they would want to be certain that their case would be handled (32.5%) and would like clarification about who they can turn to for reporting cybercrime (29.6%). More than a quarter said that they would like to see feedback from the police about what happened to their notification/official report (26.7%). Compared to the other victims, (even) more victims of e-fraud said that they require this feedback (44.8%; see Table 4.11).

Eighteen per cent of the companies said that the way in which the police can be contacted/official reports can be filed should be made easier. Apparently, these companies feel that too little is known about where one should report to and/or the process of contacting the police is still too difficult. Of those surveyed, 15.1 per cent would like to see the speed at which the police and the judicial authorities work accelerated. Fewer malware victims named this as a factor that would result in them contacting the police than victims of other types of cybercrime.

Figure 4.18   Factors that would lead to companies contacting the police (n = 158)

It should once again be pointed out when considering these results that the police are not the only designated party when it comes to fighting cybercrime. Furthermore, the focus of the police is not only on initiating a criminal investigation as a consequence of a single report. The police also have a service-related task which involves, for instance, advising victims of cybercrime about the steps to be taken. Referring victims on is then an option. The police can also use the information that companies provide them for analysis purposes. In this way, police operations are not aimed at taking action based on one report only. Instead, police efforts focus on mapping crime patterns so that they can then take action at a higher level of abstraction.

Table 4.11   Factors that would lead to companies contacting the police, divided according to the various cybercrimes (n = 158)

Action	Total (n = 311)	Malware (n = 152)	Phishing (n = 47)	E-fraud (n = 29)	Hacking (n = 20)
Nothing	8.0	11.2	4.3	0	10.0
More damage/more financial damages	49.2	52.0	57.4	31.0	35.0
If it is not possible to sort it out ourselves	25.4	25.7	25.5	31.0	15.0
Clarification about reporting cybercrime	29.6	34.2	29.8	27.6	15.0
Making it easier to contact/make a report	18.0	17.1	12.8	24.1	15.0
Certainty that the case would be handled	32.5	30.9	36.2	37.9	35.0
Certainty that the police have knowledge/expertise	20.6	21.1	21.3	27.6	20.0
Feedback about notification/report	26.7	23.7	27.7	*44.8	30.0
Tips/advice on prevention	11.3	11.2	10.6	6.9	20.0
Information when victimised	11.9	10.5	8.5	20.7	25.0
Police/judicial authorities to work faster	15.1	*9.9	12.8	27.6	25.0
Other	5.1	4.6	2.1	6.9	10.0

*Difference with 'all other victims than those in this category' ** (p < 0.01), * (p < 0.05).*

Respondents were also offered the opportunity to describe factors that would lead to them contacting the police other than those presented on the questionnaire. Text Box 4.13 offers insight into the answers they gave.

Text Box 4.13: Other factors that would lead to companies contacting the police (n = 158)
- *'Police should set up an e-mail address where [reports] related to false e-mails can be sent'.*
- *'When it clearly involves offences'.*
- *'If I was under the impression that the cybercrime was directed at me personally'.*
- *'Sending spam by e-mail doesn't strike me as a matter for the police, but where do you draw the line? When is it time to call the police instead of my IT firm?*

4.3.2   *Willingness to report in the future and confidence in the police*

Bearing in mind the information from the previous section, it is important to know whether businesses that fall victim to cybercrime in the future would file an official report. As opposed to the results already discussed in this section, we asked all companies about their willingness to report cybercrime incidents in the future (n = 1,203). Almost two thirds of the companies answered in the affirmative when asked whether they would file an official report should the organisation fall victim to cybercrime in the future (65.3%; see Figure 4.19). One third were not sure and only 1.5 per cent definitely would not report such incidents to the police. Even though not more than 7.2 per cent of the businesses contacted the police when they became victims of cybercrime this time, 65.3 per cent said they would in the future. It is questionable whether this is true; there may well be a discrepancy between intention and actual behaviour.

Figure 4.19   Willingness to report in the future (n = 1,203)

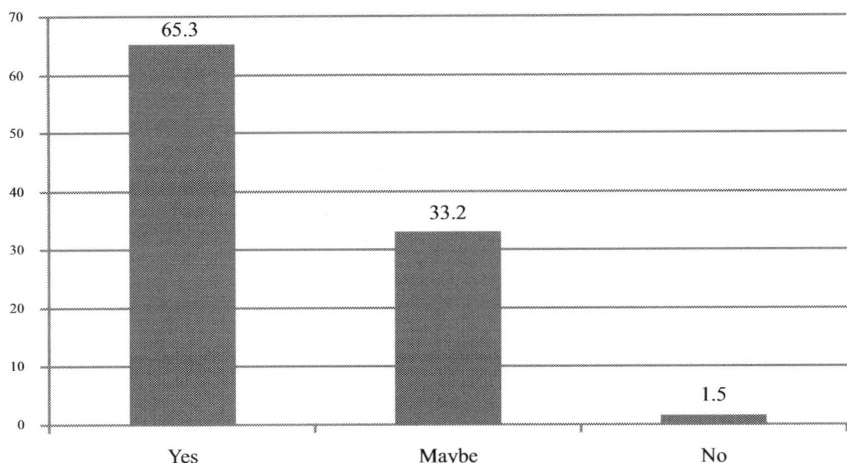

Those companies that said that they would (maybe) not file an official report then went on to give their reasons for deciding this. It was possible for respondents to give several reasons. The reasons are presented in Figure 4.20. By far the largest group of respondents would let this option depend on the damage that could arise from a future incident (64.7%). More than one third would not file a report because it is too much trouble (33.8%).

When we focussed on the role of the police, 57.5 per cent of the answers indicated that respondents expect that the police would not act on the report, the police are not capable of catching the perpetrators and/or that these offences are not a matter for the police. Almost 15.0 per cent of those surveyed expect that they will be able to solve the problem themselves. That contacting the police could possibly lead to reprisals from the perpetrator or damage to their image were reasons which were mentioned far less often. Text Box 4.14 contains a few other reasons.

Figure 4.20 Reasons for (maybe) not filing a report (n = 417)

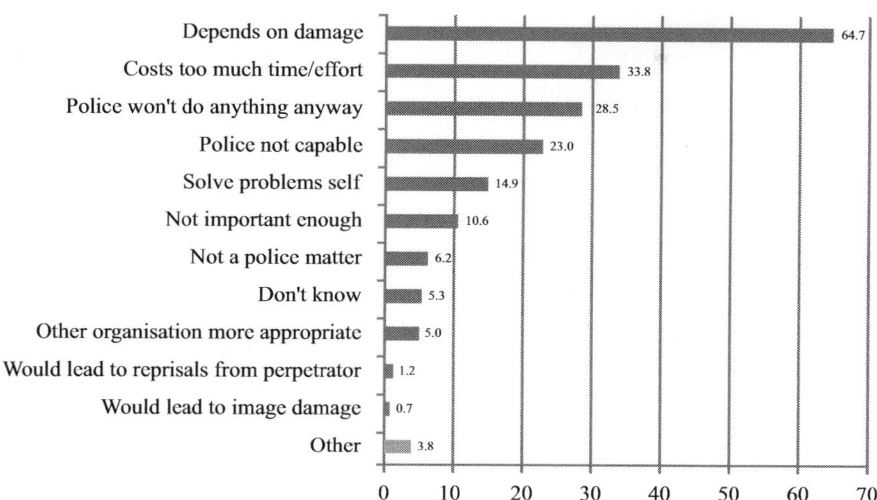

Text Box 4.14: Other reasons for perhaps or not filing a report
- *'Depends on the problem'.*
- *'It depends on whether personal details are being compromised: then I would involve the criminal justice system. You won't get anything back from financial damages/being unreachable'.*
- *'Often filing a report is a difficult, time-consuming, frustrating, pointless activity'.*
- *'Not sure exactly what I should do and to whom and how to make a report'.*

Those businesses that indicated that they would file a report were asked which method they would then choose. Figure 4.21 shows that, in the event of cybercrime victimisation, businesses would prefer to file a report digitally or by telephone (50.0% and 24.5%, respectively). As it stands now, cybercrime victims from the SME sector are mainly inclined to opt to visit the police station (see Figure 4.15). The question that these findings raise is whether SMEs which are now saying that they would prefer to file a report digitally would actually choose to do so when they do fall victim. This is an important matter for the police. Were they to gear their organisation according to the requirements of the SME sector, namely their expressed intention to file an official report digitally, then they would be on the wrong track if companies prefer to go to the police station in the event that they do actually become victims. It is therefore important for the police not to base their actions completely on what the SME sector says it intends to do. It would also be prudent to look closely at the actual behaviour of SMEs that were victims of cybercrime: in 92.8 per cent of the cases they did not contact the police and in 1.8 per cent of the cases they did, and then using digital channels.

Figure 4.21   Preference for type of reporting in the event of future victimisation (n = 1,203)

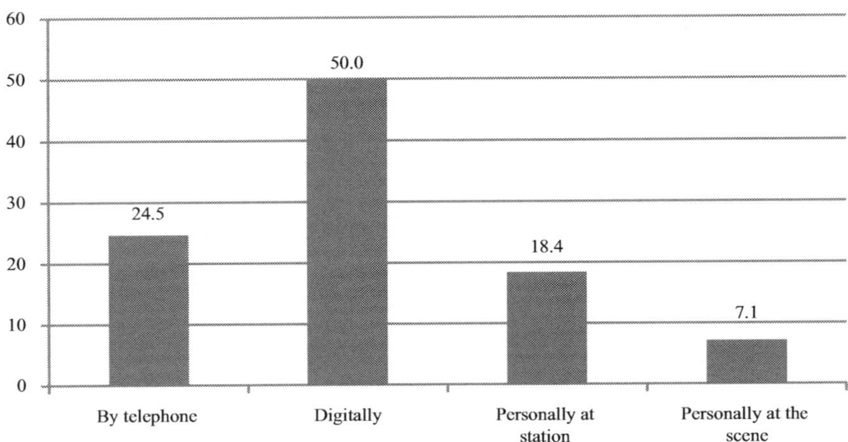

We went on to ask respondents about whether they would like to have a digital help desk which their organisation could turn to. A total of 38.4 per cent of those surveyed said they had no need for such a desk. The majority, however, did not share this opinion and stipulated moreover that the service desk itself would need to focus on registering notifications and filing official reports as well as on giving advice about cybercrime (42.4%). A digital service desk that only focusses on providing advice is in any event not the preferred option (see Figure 4.22).

Figure 4.22   Demand for a digital service desk (n = 1,203)

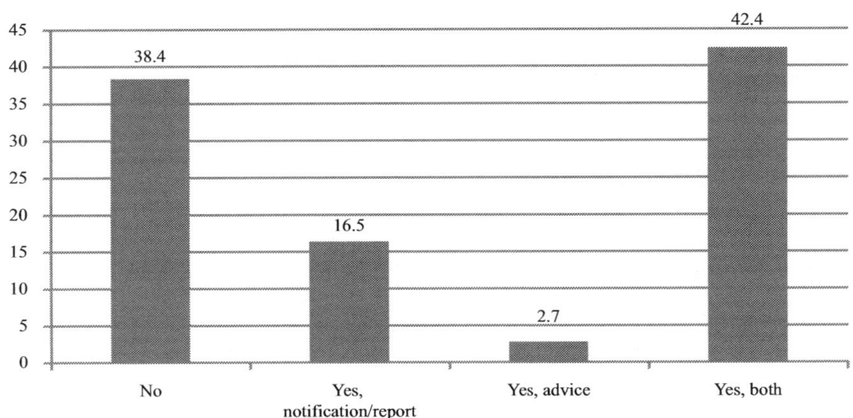

Whether or not a digital service desk would work is, however, a good question. Research into the functioning of the Digital Cybercrime Desk for Businesses (DBC) showed that this desk is only used to a limited extent. A possible explanation for this is that companies tend to forget that the service desk exists after a while. So, should a digital service desk be set up, then it would be advisable to inform companies about it regularly (Jansen et al., 2013a).

> **Digital company service desk**
> *Mr Veldhuizen sees the service desk as 'a kind of automobile association'. It could "point the way for people who have fallen victim – so not solve the problem itself, but instead point the way – to where and how the problem can be solved". He gives as an example his own experiences with an infected computer. According to Mr Veldhuizen, the police should be able to specify who he should turn to – an IT company, the webhost – to solve these kinds of problems. Mr Alberda, who experienced a whole series of incidents, claimed that he definitely needs such a service desk. He also has certain expectations in this regard. "The police should be more aware that these things can have a profound impact and can cost a lot of money. And I hope that this leads them to giving these cases a higher priority".*

Confidence

Finally, all respondents were asked a number of questions about the confidence they have in the police. Figure 4.23 shows the confidence in the police in general and the confidence in the police concerning cybercrime. Taken together, 32.7 per cent of the respondents had confidence or a great deal of confidence in the police in general, as opposed to only 21.0 per cent in terms of cybercrime. The IT Barometer produced similar results: 28 per cent of companies are relatively confident in the police as far as cybercrime is concerned; none of the companies chose 'a great deal of confidence' in response to this question (Ernst & Young, 2011). It emerged from the results discussed previously that some had doubts about the police's knowledge and expertise in the field of cybercrime. One respondent gave the following clarification as a

Figure 4.23   Confidence in the police (n = 1,203)

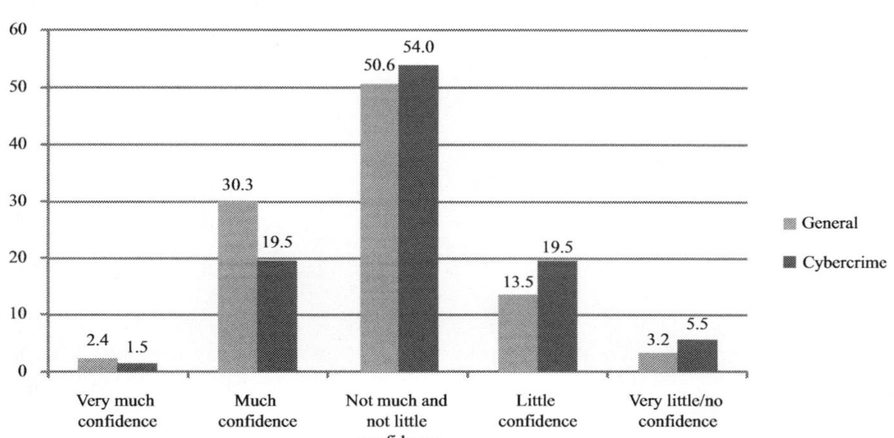

response to a question asked earlier: '[Filing a report] is completely pointless with the current level of knowledge that the police have'.

For SMEs that were victims of cybercrime, the question of whether or not the police are capable of dealing with such cases properly is not a primary consideration (see Figure 4.17). Their principal concern is whether the case is serious enough, in terms of damage, to contact the police. The police thus need to take into account that increasing confidence in their ability to deal with cybercrime cases is not a guarantee that SMEs will then start reporting cybercrimes en masse. Furthermore, it should be noted that, when it comes to having less confidence in the police in issues involving cybercrime, the SME sector also do not consider the police to be the organisation principally responsible for security on the internet. We will return to this later.

In order to take a closer look at confidence in the police, and because confidence is difficult to measure, two statements were included from the report entitled *100 per cent* by Van Dijk (2007) about the confidence that members of the public have in the police. These statements which measure confidence in the police are: 'When it really comes down to it, the police will do their utmost to help you' (Statement 1) and 'When it really comes down to it, the police will be there for you' (Statement 2). Of the companies surveyed, 54.5 and 55.0 per cent, respectively, agreed or completely agreed with these statements. These percentages are substantially higher when compared to the results in Figure 4.23 above.

Figure 4.24   Confidence in the police: Statements 1 and 2 (Van Dijk, 2007; n = 1,203)

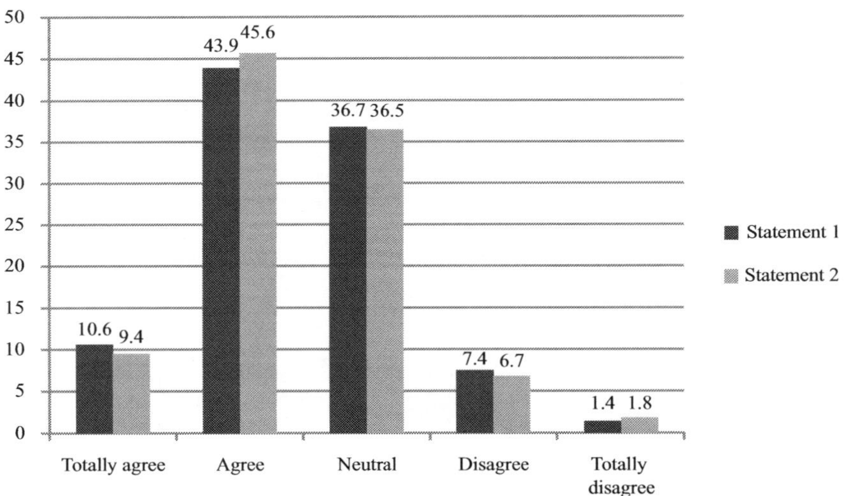

Finally, companies were asked who they consider to be responsible for their organisation's security on the internet (see Figure 4.25). Companies mainly consider themselves to be responsible for their online security (90.1%). This is followed by 83.7 per cent of companies who lay the responsibility at the door of internet service providers. In addition, companies view financial institutions (81.7%), software manufacturers for businesses (81.4%) and website owners (81.1%) as the ones responsible for internet security. According to two thirds of those surveyed, national authorities are the responsible party (65.1%).

Entrepreneurs are not IT experts

A member of staff at a consultancy firm holds the opinion that companies have a duty to protect themselves as best they can against cybercrime, for instance, by encrypting files and by using good usernames and passwords. According to him, IT firms should provide information so that companies know what they are dealing with. 'I think that specialised IT companies have a lot of expertise, more than the police.' Mr Veldhuizen, owner of a furniture shop, also feels that entrepreneurs should be careful when e-mails come in and every entrepreneur ought to have a virus scanner. At the same time, he holds the opinion that knowledge about cybercrime among companies is limited and so they will have to use the expertise of others: "Computers are tools and not our business, [...] I wouldn't be able to climb into a plane and fly it".

The responsibility is not often assigned to the police in comparison to how often it is assigned to other parties. Slightly more than 2 out of 5 companies believe that the police are responsible for the online security of companies (41.6%). Research into the assessment of the DBC showed that 33.6 per cent of companies said that the police are the responsible party, compared to 93.2 per cent who lay the responsibility at the door of the company itself (Jansen et al., 2013a). This research therefore confirms that companies do not view fighting cybercrime as exclusively a responsibility of the police.

Figure 4.25 Responsibility for security on the internet according to members of the public (n = 1,203)

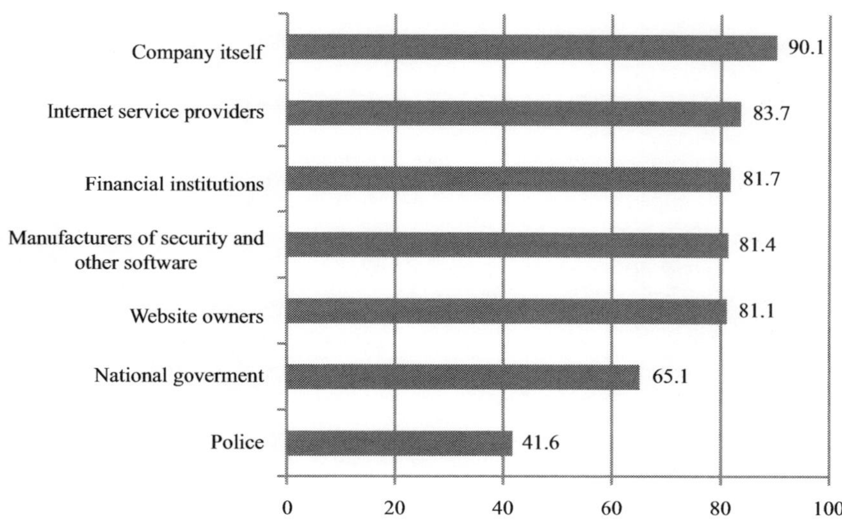

Summary
Businesses that fall victim to cybercrime are generally self-reliant. A significant proportion of companies are able to solve the problems themselves, especially in the case of malware. If the problem cannot be solved by the company, then action is taken, such as taking steps to prevent future victimisation or engaging external private parties.
Only 7.2 per cent of cybercrime victims contacted the police as a consequence of the most recent incident. So, the SME sector is not making the police aware of the issue of cybercrime. Not more than 1.8 per cent of the victims contacted the police using digital means. Deciding to involve the police is mainly based on the fact that companies wanted to file a report. In addition to this, it is considered a duty and SMEs want the perpetrator to be caught. It is also mainly companies who had incurred damage as a consequence of cybercrime who turned to the police.
Despite the fact that it is possible to file a report online, most companies opt to use the 'old-fashioned' option of going to the police station. Yet they also know how to find the police using digital means: a quarter of the companies contacted the police digitally. It is not possible to draw firm conclusions about satisfaction with the police based on the contact that respondents had with them. Dissatisfied businesses would in any event like the police to keep them informed about developments in their case to a larger extent. Companies also attach importance to being certain that their cases are being handled.
From responses from companies which did not contact the police as a consequence of victimisation, it can be concluded that the underlying reason for this is mainly a lack of damage/negative consequences. Moreover, people do not expect that the police will do anything about it and/or they do not consider the incident to be important enough.
Companies said that they would contact the police if they were certain that their case would be handled and/or it was made clear who they could turn to for filing a report about cybercrime. Furthermore, victims would like feedback about what had happened to their notification/report, particularly victims of e-fraud.
Even though not more than 7.2 per cent of the businesses contacted the police when they became victims of cybercrime this time, 65.3 per cent said they would in the future. Those companies that doubt whether they would, mainly let their decision depend on the amount of damage. No reasons were found in this research to explain why the SME sector currently does not contact the police in large numbers, but many of them claimed that they would involve the police in the event of future victimisation. Presumably, there is a discrepancy between intentions and actual behaviour.
The answers to the question of whether companies would not or probably not file a report when they became victims of cybercrime show that there is uncertainty about the competence of the police: businesses question whether the police are capable of fighting cybercrime and/or what is done with the report. However, in light of the

other findings, this is not the main reason for not contacting the police en masse (92.8%). Instead, the reason that they do not go to the police is more likely to be that they do not consider the case to be serious enough (due to a lack of damage) and that they consider security on the internet to be more a responsibility of others rather than the police.

<table><tr><td>5</td><td>

Cybercrime among one-man businesses and the comparison with SMEs

</td></tr></table>

In this chapter, we discuss the results of the research among one-man businesses in the Netherlands. Where possible, these results are compared to the results from the study among SMEs. As was the case in Chapter 4, the main and sub-questions are the basis for the subdivision of this chapter (see Table 2.4 on page 29). In Section 5.1, we describe the extent to which one-man businesses separate work and private use of IT and which activities they carry out on the internet. Section 5.2 discusses awareness of cybercrime victimisation and the protective measures taken by one-man businesses against cybercrime. In Section 5.3, we provide an insight into the nature and extent of victimisation among one-man businesses. In addition to prevalence rates, we also discuss the impact, financial and otherwise, of cybercrime. Furthermore, risk factors for cybercrime victimisation, the ways in which cybercrime is committed and the actions that victims take against cybercrime are examined. Finally, in Section 5.4, we answer the question of what role one-man business people assign to public and private parties when it comes to tackling cybercrime.

5.1 IT use and online activities

5.1.1 *Separating IT use for work and private purposes*

We asked one-man businesses about their use of computers and internet access for private or business purposes. Virtually all one-man businesses (95.3%) use their computers with internet access for business as well as private purposes. This confirms the suspicion that use of the internet for work and private purposes is intertwined at one-man businesses. The division between work and private use differs significantly from internet use among SMEs. SMEs are more likely to use different computers with internet access exclusively for business purposes (see Figure 5.1).

It also emerged during the in-depth interviews that private and business internet use among most one-man businesses are intertwined. The reason mentioned most often for this was convenience: occasionally private affairs also need to be investigated during work and vice versa. Starting up a separate computer is not convenient. In addition, financial reasons play a role given that buying an additional computer is not cheap. Several one-man business people also pointed out that they cannot see the point of separating private and business use in this regard.

Figure 5.1   Uses of computers with internet access (n = 1,622 one-man businesses, 1,203 SMEs)**

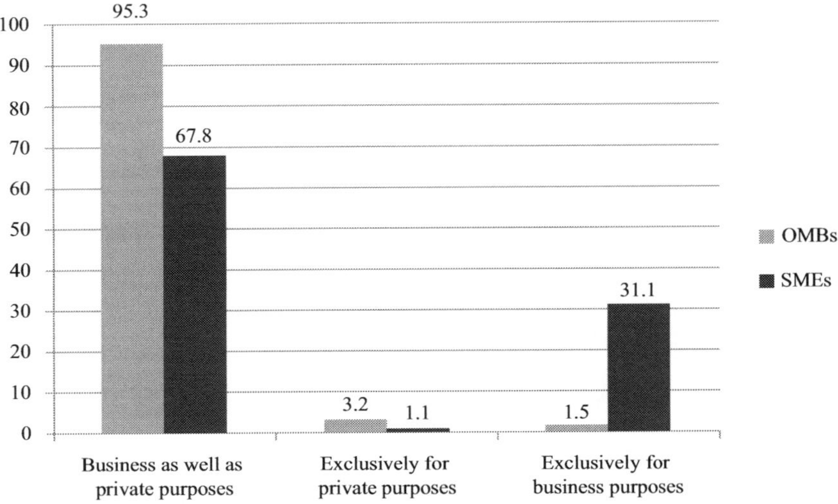

To gain more understanding about the interconnectedness of business and private use, we went on to ask one-man business people how the division between private and business use of computers and the internet worked exactly (see Figure 5.2).

Figure 5.2   Relationship business/private use of computers with internet access (n = 1,546)

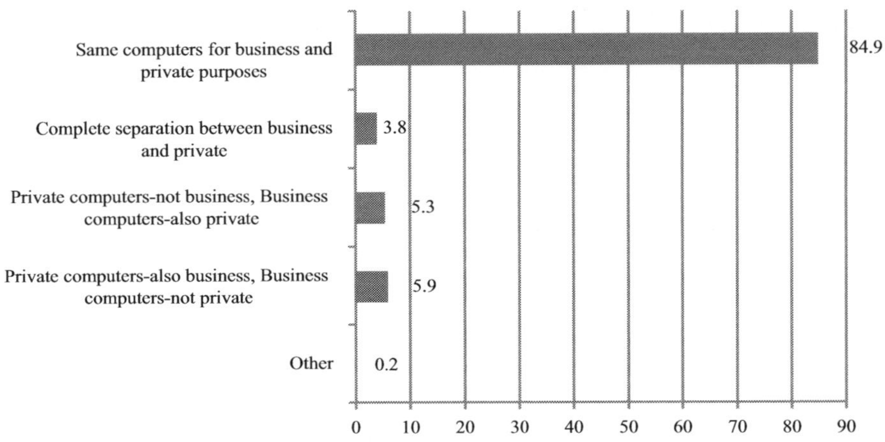

Figure 5.2 shows that the majority of one-man businesses use the same computer for business and private purposes (84.9%). Some respondents (11.2%) partly separated their use: of these, 5.9 per cent also used computers that are intended for private

matters for business purposes. Computers that are used by this group of respondents for business purposes are not, however, used for private purposes. Conversely, 5.3 per cent of one-man businesses did not use computers that are intended for private purposes for business purposes, while company computers were also used for private purposes. Only 3.8 per cent separated business and private use completely. Respondents were given the opportunity to give answers other than the ones on the questionnaire. Text Box 5.1 contains the other answers.

> **Text Box 5.1: Other answers to the questions about business or private use of computers**
> - *'One separate computer for payment traffic'.*
> - *'The PC that administrations are on is not connected to the internet'.*
> - *'I separate the equipment using software. Effectively I use the same equipment for private and business use but then using different profiles, settings and security measures'.*
> - *'For my business use I work in a secure Virtual PC'.*

Separating private and business internet use

Mr Visscher is a journalist, publisher and copywriter and does not separate his work on his computers. He has two Apple laptops. He uses the one often and the other serves more as a backup for when the other one does not work properly. He does, however, separate the files: private files are kept on the laptop and business documents are all in the cloud. Not separating computers is therefore a conscious choice, because the documents are online but they are still available everywhere. At the same time, business files can also be opened on his iPad and smartphone. Mr Visscher is busy on the internet the entire day, from when he gets up until it's time to go to bed.

We went on to ask how many hours one-man businesses spent on the internet on average each day (see Figure 5.3). More than a third of the one-man businesses surveyed go online for two hours at most each day (34.8%). This section of one-man businesses apparently do not do work that requires them to be continuously online. A further 28.5 per cent of one-man businesses said that they spend between two and four hours each day on the internet. Almost a fifth of one-man businesses spend the entire working day on the internet: 9.6 per cent are online between six to eight hours per day and 10.0 per cent can be found in cyberspace for even more than eight hours per day.

Busy on the internet

Mr Stoel is a programmer and has a software development company. He has six company computers. In his private capacity, he hardly does anything on the internet; occasionally he'll look something up or read an e-mail, but that is rare. Because Mr Stoel writes customised software for his clients, the number of hours he spends online differs per client. It could be 3 hours for one client, and then 10 for another. On average he spends around 8 hours a day online.

Figure 5.3   Number of hours on average per day on the internet (n = 1,622)

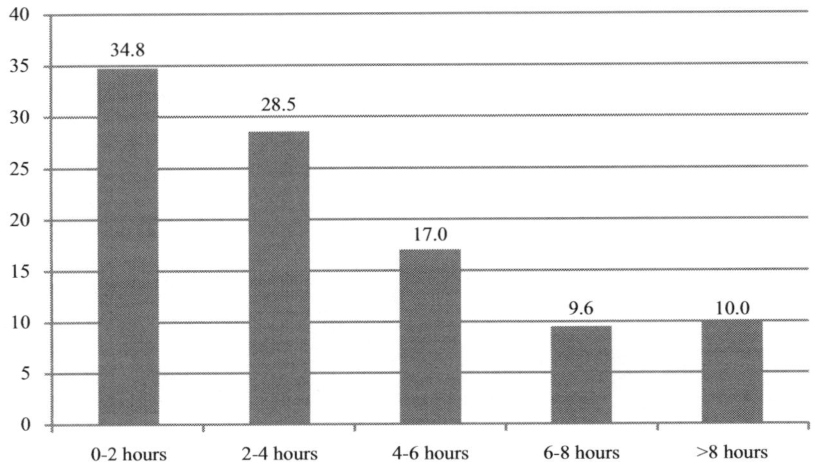

5.1.2   *Online operations*

One-man businesses were then asked which operations they carry out online (private and business internet use combined). It was possible for respondents to give several answers. Figure 5.4 indicates the extent to which one-man businesses perform various internet activities. Each bar gives the total percentage of one-man businesses that carries out that internet activity, regardless of the frequency of doing so. The colours inside each bar give insight into the intensity with which certain activities are carried

Figure 5.4   General online activities (n = 1,622)[1]

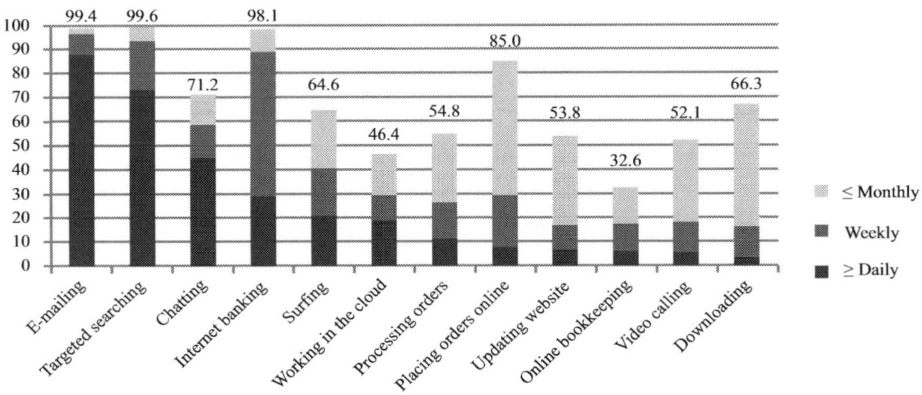

---

1. The response categories were: continuously (24/7) – daily – weekly – monthly – less frequently than monthly – not at all. In Figure 5.4 'continuously' and 'daily' are combined as '≥daily', and 'monthly' and 'less frequently than monthly' as '≤monthly'.

out. As an example, virtually all one-man businesses search for specific information on the internet (targeted searches) (99.6% in total). Three quarters do so every day to continuously. Targeted searching is something that the rest do weekly or less often. According to Statistics Netherlands, 88 per cent of the Dutch population use the internet daily and for a variety of purposes (CBS, 2014). One-man businesses, too, are active internet users. Almost all one-man businesses use e-mail facilities (99.4%),[2] search specifically for information on the internet (99.6%) and/or do internet banking (98.1%). In addition to this, 85.0 per cent use the internet to place orders and more than 71 per cent chat online, for instance, via a website or using WhatsApp. Approximately two thirds surf without a specific objective (64.6%) and/or use the internet to download (66.3%). More than half also process orders online (54.8%), have a website (53.8%) and/or make video calls (52.1%). The online activities mentioned least often were working in the cloud and doing bookkeeping (respectively 46.4% and 32.6%). Even though one-man businesses are active and use the internet for a variety of purposes, not every online activity is undertaken as frequently by everyone. E-mailing, targeted searching for information and internet banking are activities which one-man businesses mainly engage in on a weekly basis or more frequently. Chatting online is also an internet activity that more than half of one-man businesses undertake frequently. The remaining internet activities are undertaken on a weekly basis or more frequently by fewer than half of one-man businesses.

Figure 5.5 compares the online activities carried out by one-man businesses with those undertaken by SMEs. The graph shows the percentages for the proportion of companies that carry out an activity daily or continuously, not the overall

Figure 5.5   General online activities: ≥daily (n = 1,622 one-man businesses, 1,203 SMEs)

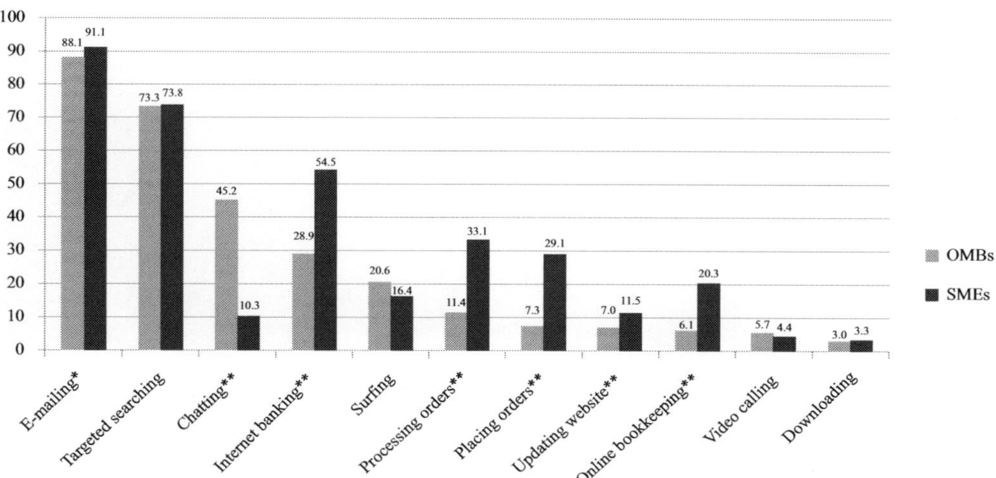

2. See also the One-Man Business Barometer (ZZP Barometer, 2014).

percentages. This has been done because these results give the most important insight into the daily practices of these companies on the internet.

Typical business activities, for instance, online placement and processing of orders and online bookkeeping, are activities which SMEs are more likely to undertake daily or continuously. SMEs also e-mail and do internet banking more frequently. Chatting online, on the other hand, is an activity that one-man businesses are more likely or much more likely to carry out on a daily basis. This result may be explained by the rise of chat services like WhatsApp (the one-man business research was conducted 12 months later than the SME research) and it may be related to the interconnectedness between private and business internet use among one-man businesses. Another factor may be that one-man businesses do not have colleagues in their immediate vicinity.

Finally, we investigated the extent to which one-man businesses had their own company website. In 2013, 84 per cent of Dutch companies with ten or more members of staff had a company website (CBS, 2014). To all intents and purposes, that percentage is the same as the percentage of SMEs who have their own website (83.5%, see Chapter 4). One-man businesses are less likely to have a company website (61.9%). They also spend significantly less time on updating their website than SMEs do (7.0% versus 11.5%).

Social media
The Netherlands is among the top three European countries in terms of social media users. Seven out of ten members of the public and half of companies with a workforce of at least ten people use social media (Bighelaar & Akkermans, 2013; CBS, 2014). We also asked one-man businesses about the extent to which they use social media (private and business use combined). In total, 89.1 per cent of one-man businesses said

Figure 5.6   Social media activities (n = 1,622)

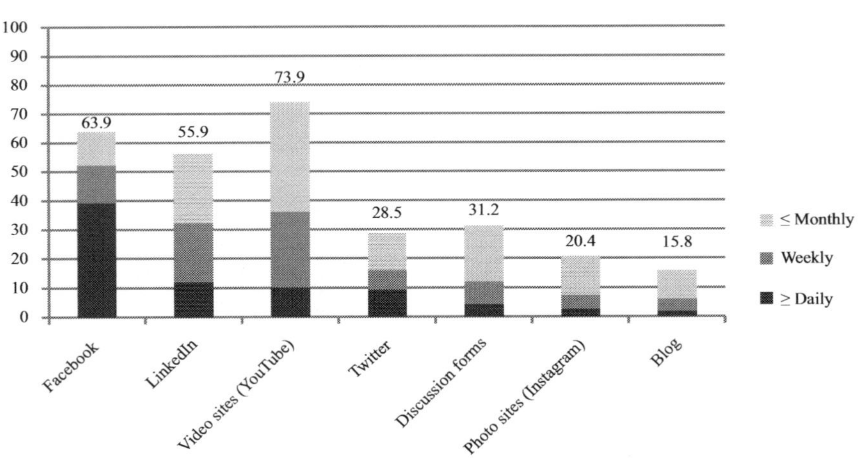

that they use one or more social networks (n = 1,446).[3] Almost 46 per cent (45.9%) have one or more company profiles on social media.

As was the case in Figure 5.4, the intensity of using social media is illustrated by the colour: the darker the colour, the higher the frequency of the activity.

Although video sites like YouTube are visited by the largest group of one-man business people (73.9%), Facebook is used most intensively. Almost 40 per cent of one-man businesses use Facebook daily or continuously. More than half use LinkedIn (55.9%), mainly on a weekly to monthly basis. Twitter is used by 28.5 per cent of one-man businesses. Photographic websites, like Instagram and Pinterest, and keeping blogs are less popular activities, relatively speaking. These social media are used by 20.4 and 15.8 per cent of one-man businesses, respectively.

We also investigated the extent to which social media usage among one-man businesses differed to social media usage among SMEs (see Figure 5.7). Once again, the graph shows the percentages for the proportion of companies that carries out an activity daily or continuously.

Figure 5.7   Social media activities: ≥daily (n = 1,622 one-man businesses, 1,203 SMEs)

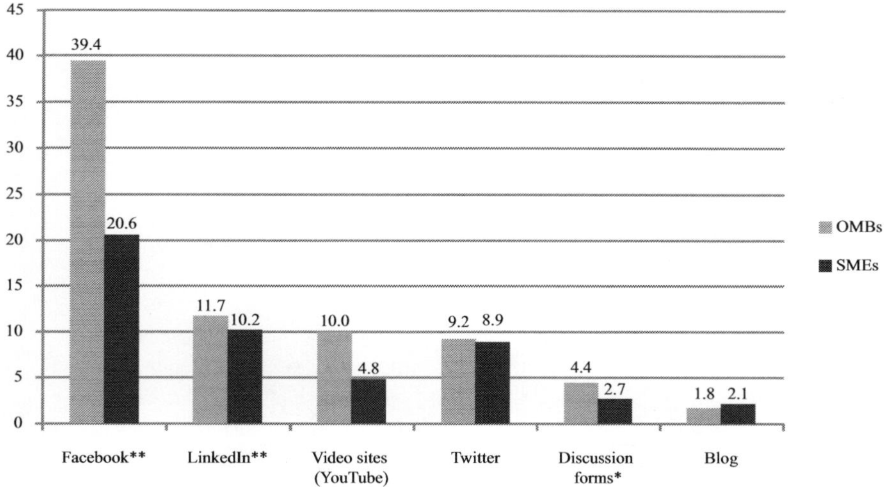

Facebook is used significantly more frequently on a daily basis to continuously by one-man businesses than by SMEs. This difference may be explained by the fact that business and private use among one-man businesses is intertwined and that Facebook is also used for private purposes.

Moreover, one-man businesses use LinkedIn more than SMEs do. This may be because LinkedIn plays an important role among one-man businesses in the recruitment of clients. It emerged from the One-Man Business Barometer that one-man

---

3. This percentage only refers to the social media included in the questionnaire.

businesses that use LinkedIn and who published their profile for business purposes online, recruited 44 per cent of their clients via this platform (ZZP Barometer, 2014). Finally, one-man businesses use community and/or discussion forums more than SMEs do. Online forums can be used to hold discussions on the internet about a variety of subjects, and knowledge and experience can be shared. The fact that one-man business owners are inclined to use it more may be explained by the fact that they do not have any colleagues. After all, those in the SME sector have the option of consulting their colleagues and to acquire the necessary knowledge in this way. One-man business owners probably use the internet for this.

Delivery via webshops
The last question that we asked one-man businesses about their online activities is whether they deliver their products and/or services via a webshop. The results are presented in Figure 5.8. The majority of one-man businesses said that they do not supply any products and/or services via a webshop (89.8%). Of the 10.3 per cent that do, not more than 2.5 per cent supply *exclusively* via a webshop; 7.8 per cent *also* supply via a webshop, but not exclusively. For comparison purposes: 18 per cent of Dutch companies with more than ten members of staff sold goods or services via a website in 2012 (CBS, 2014). So one-man businesses use webshops to a lesser degree than larger companies. Perhaps the nature of the work that one-man businesses do or a lack of resources (money, expertise) may offer an explanation.

Figure 5.8   Supplying products and/or services via a webshop (n = 1,622)

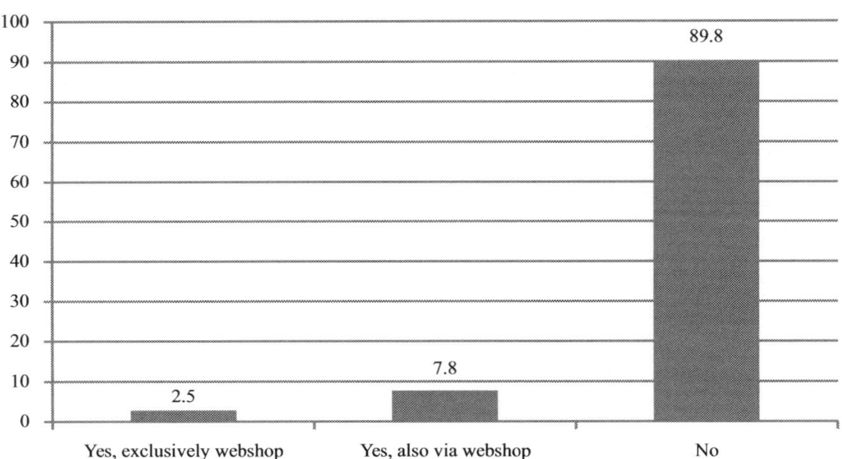

Summary
Work-related and private use of the internet among people operating one-man businesses are interwoven. The majority of people operating one-man businesses use the same computers for business and private purposes. This as opposed to SMEs which are more likely to use separate computers for business purposes.

Most one-man business owners are online for up to four hours a day. For them it is not necessary to be online continuously. That said, almost a fifth of one-man businesses spend six or more hours on the internet.

Just like SMEs, people operating one-man businesses are active internet users. Almost all one-man business people e-mail, carry out targeted searches for information and/or use online banking facilities on the internet. Chatting online is also popular: three quarters chat online, for instance, on WhatsApp. Working in the cloud and doing bookkeeping online is less popular among people operating one-man businesses.

People operating one-man businesses are also active social media users. Virtually all of them use one or more social networks. Facebook is the social media site used most intensively. SMEs use Facebook less often. LinkedIn and online forums are also used more frequently by people operating one-man businesses than by SMEs. Yet only around half of one-man businesses had one or more company profiles.

5.2   PROTECTION AGAINST CYBERCRIME

Protection against cybercrime is the focus of this section. We first give insight into dependency on IT and the extent to which one-man businesses store confidential information on computers. We go on to discuss the protective measures taken by one-man businesses to fight cybercrime and the confidence that they have in these measures. Finally, we discuss how great one-man business people estimate the chances to be that they themselves and other one-man businesses will fall victim to cybercrime.

5.2.1   *Data storage and protection*

Dependency on IT
We have already noted that one-man business people are active internet users. In order to map the significance of IT to one-man businesses in greater detail, we asked them about the extent to which they are dependent on IT (see Figure 5.9).

Figure 5.9   Dependency on IT (n = 1,622 one-man businesses, 1,203 SMEs)**

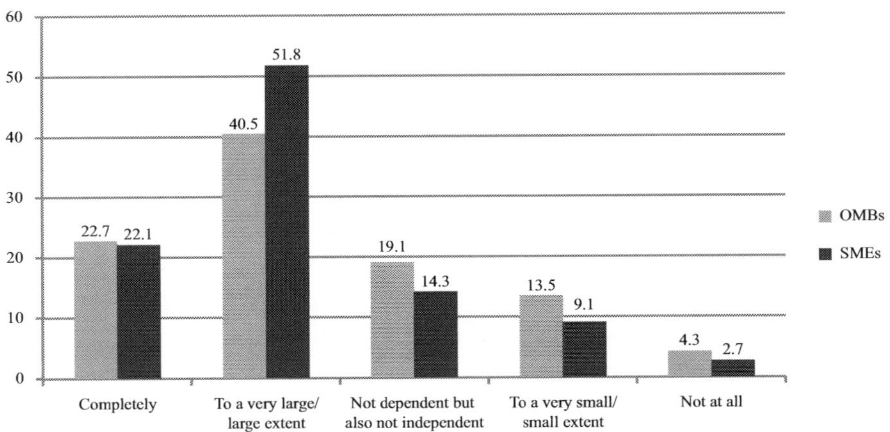

As Figure 5.9 shows, almost two thirds of one-man business people consider themselves to be dependent to a large or very large extent or to be entirely dependent
on IT (63.2%). SMEs were asked a similar question. A comparison of the results shows
that more SMEs than one-man businesses consider themselves to be dependent to a
large or very large extent on IT for their business operations. So when IT lets entrepreneurs down, this could mean that a significant group of entrepreneurs can no longer do their work. The group of one-man businesses that consider themselves to be
dependent on IT to a minor or very minor extent comprises 17.8 per cent.

Confidential information
We went on to ask about the extent to which one-man businesses store confidential
information on one or more computers (see Figure 5.10). Confidential information is,
for instance, customer information or information about product development.[4] Of
those in the one-man business sector, 45.1 per cent said that they stored confidential
information on their computers to a large or very large extent. More than a third of the
people operating one-man businesses said that they stored confidential information
on their computers to a minor or very minor extent or not at all (34.6%).

---

4.   The question was formulated as follows in the questionnaire: To what extent do you store confidential
     company information, such as customer and administrative information and/or information about
     product development, on your computer(s)?

Figure 5.10   Extent to which confidential information is stored on computers (n = 1,622 one-man businesses, 1,203 SMEs)**

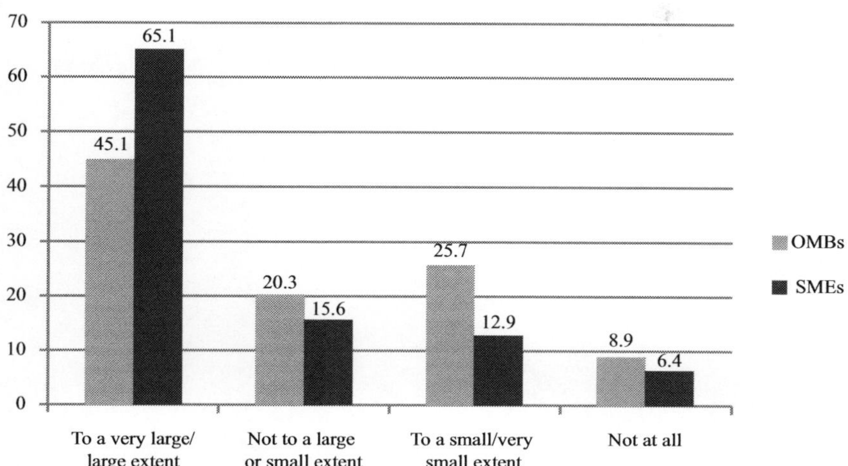

One-man businesses differ significantly from SMEs when it comes to storing confidential information on one or more computers. The percentage of SMEs who said that they store confidential information to a large or very large degree is significantly higher than the percentage of one-man businesses that said the same (65.1% versus 45.1%) (p < 0.01).

Data protection

According to one-man businesses, they are heavily dependent on IT and the majority said that they keep confidential company and other information on their work computers. This means that the demand for data protection is important. As Figure 5.11 shows, 67.7 per cent of one-man businesses consider data protection to be important or very important to their companies. Only 5.6 per cent are of the opinion that it is unimportant or very unimportant. Once again, the percentages of one-man businesses differ from those of the SME sector. A larger proportion of SMEs consider data protection to be important or very important (83.7%).

Figure 5.11   Importance of data protection (n = 1,622 one-man businesses, 1,203 SMEs)**

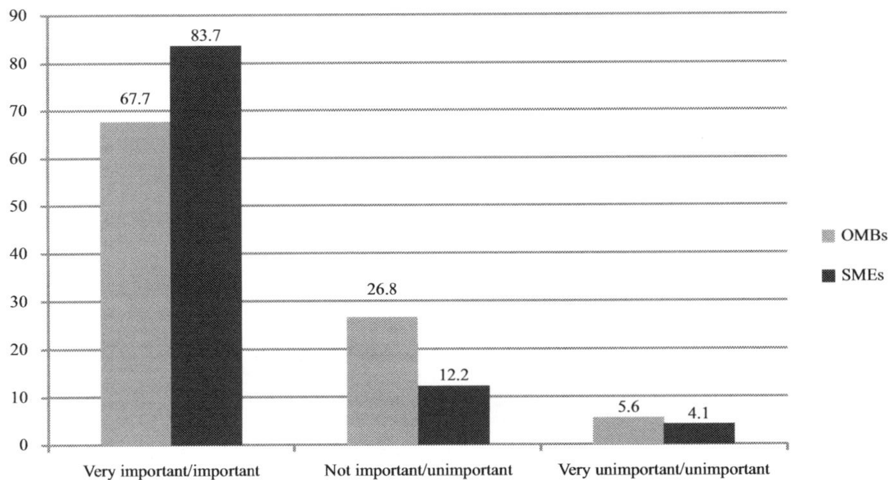

The extent to which one-man business owners consider protection of information important to their companies depends significantly on the degree to which confidential information is stored on the computer (Figure 5.10).[5] Of the one-man businesses that indicated that they store confidential company information to a large or very large degree, 86.6 per cent said that they consider data protection on computers to be important or very important. Only four people operating one-man businesses (0.6%) from this group consider protecting their information to be unimportant or very unimportant. Generally, one-man businesses tend to take care of the security of their computers themselves (see Figure 5.12). No less than 80.0 per cent of one-man businesses did not feel that it was necessary to outsource information security. Even when they store confidential company information on their computers to a large or very large degree, the majority of one-man businesses do not opt to outsource security: only 18.6 per cent of this group leave it to external parties. Almost half of SMEs, on the other hand, outsource the protection of digital, company-related information to a third party (47.4%). This means that SMEs are more likely to engage external parties to protect their computers.

5.2.2   *Protection against cybercrime*

Various research publications claim that it is important to take steps to counteract cybercrime, but that it is a challenge for small companies due to a lack of resources (Cresanti, 2014; Dimopoulos, Furnell, Jennex & Kritharas, 2004; Gunderson Hunt, 2013; Gupta & Hammond, 2005; Schaper & Weber, 2012). So the question is whether one-man businesses take measures and whether the extent to which they do so differs from the extent to which SMEs defend themselves against cybercrime. As was the case with SMEs, one-man businesses were therefore asked which measures they take to

---

5. $r = 0.45$, p < 0.01.

deter cybercrime. The measures have been subdivided into physical, technical and other measures and are discussed in succession in that order.

Figure 5.12   Protecting computers (n = 1,622 one-man businesses, 1,203 SMEs)**

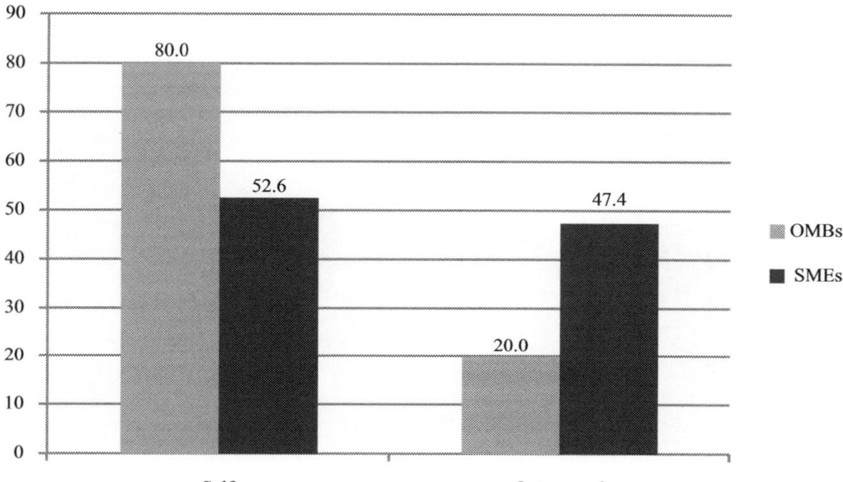

Physical measures
All in all, 59.6 per cent of one-man businesses took at least one physical measure to protect their computers (see Figure 5.13). The computers of almost two fifths of one-man businesses are kept in a protected room (39.3%). Almost a third had marked their IT equipment so that they can ascertain who the owner of the computer is (29.7%). A further 23.2 per cent had made sure that their IT equipment is protected against calamities, like fire. Only 3.9 per cent had attached their computers to a cable lock. Compared to SMEs, one-man businesses were more likely to have marked their IT equipment. That said, SMEs were significantly more likely to have taken other physical measures. This finding may be explained by the fact that SMEs were more likely than one-man businesses to be of the opinion that they have confidential information stored on their computers (Figure 5.10).

Figure 5.13   Physical measures (n = 1,622 one-man businesses, 1,203 SMEs)

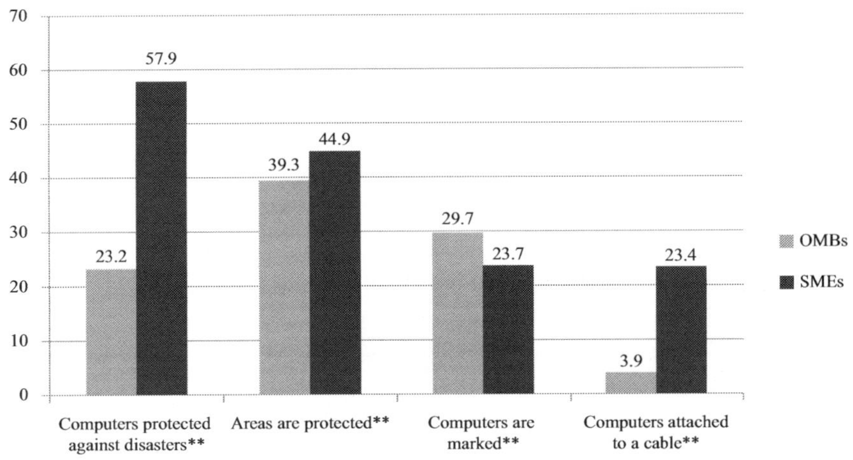

Technical measures

Virtually all one-man businesses had taken one or more technical measures (99.6%) (see Figure 5.14). Using a virus scanner (92.7%), up-to-date software (91.2%), a secure network (91.0%) and a firewall (89.5%) are measures that had been applied by many one-man businesses. The same impression emerged in the in-depth interviews. Backing up files regularly is also a measure taken by a large group of one-man businesses (81.5%). Relatively speaking, storing files in an encrypted format is less popular among this group. Nearly a quarter of one-man businesses use encryption (23.6%). It emerged from the interviews with one-man businesses that this may be explained by the fact that one-man businesses either do not know what encryption entails or that they

Figure 5.14   Technical measures (n = 1,622 one-man businesses, 1,203 SMEs)

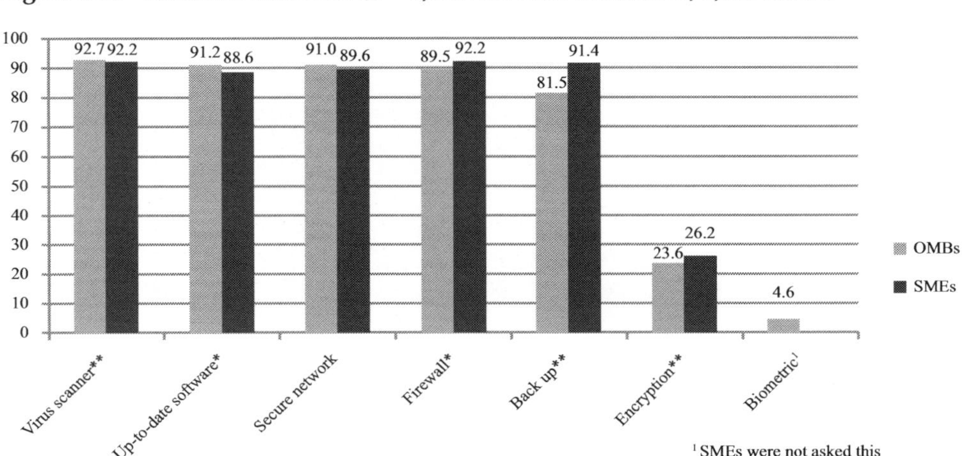

¹ SMEs were not asked this

are familiar with it but find it too complicated and/or cumbersome to use. In addition, they mentioned that they do not keep any confidential files on their computers and so storing encrypted files is therefore, in their opinion, not necessary.

Using biometric security methods, for instance fingerprint readers, are technical measures that were hardly taken at all. Only 4.6 per cent of one-man businesses protected their computers in this way.

Installing a virus scanner and keeping software up to date were technical measures that one-man businesses were more inclined to apply than SMEs were.[6] Using firewalls and making back-ups were, however, measures that SMEs were more likely to take. SMEs were also significantly more likely to use encryption. Once again, this can probably be linked to the fact that SMEs were more likely to say that they had confidential information stored on their computers.

> **Measures taken against cybercrime**
> *Mrs Volkersma works on her computer a lot, which is why she has virus scanners on it. For the rest, she reckons all she can do is pay attention and keep her wits about her, despite the fact that she has become less vigilant thanks to work-related pressure. She's well aware of what encryption is, but she doesn't use it because all her files are simple Word files. For the rest, Mrs Volkersma has all her work on an external hard drive and she takes this drive with her, for instance, when she goes away for a day or on longer holidays. Along with the hard drive, she also takes her little book in which she has written down all her passwords.*

Other measures

A total of 96.5 per cent of one-man businesses took at least one of the other measures to exclude cybercrime from their computers as much as possible (see Figure 5.15). More than 90 per cent apply rules for opening potentially unsafe files and for disclosing information. The same emerged from the interviews: 'I am discerning when it comes to opening attachments and links in e-mail messages. I always check them before I open them'. Moreover, most one-man businesses (also) apply rules for dealing with confidential information and making online payments (respectively 82.6% and 81.8%). More than half of one-man businesses apply rules for periodically changing passwords (55.3%).

One-man business people are less familiar with how they should act if they fall victim to cybercrime (22.6%). Also, relatively speaking, not many one-man businesses have investigated how they could fall victim to cybercrime (27.7%). This means that one-man businesses are less likely to recognise cybercrime and that they are not immediately sure which steps they should take if they become victims of cybercrime.

6.　This does, however, raise the question of whether a difference between 92.7 and 92.2 per cent (for the installation of a virus scanner) is a relevant and significant difference given that the group of one-man businesses that had a virus scanner is only 0.5% larger than the group of SMEs. From a statistical point of view, a factor when establishing a significant difference is that these are percentages that border on 100% (or 0%). Small differences here are more likely to be significant. The probability of a significant difference between 50.0 and 50.5 per cent, for example, is much smaller.

Figure 5.15 Other measures (n = 1,622)

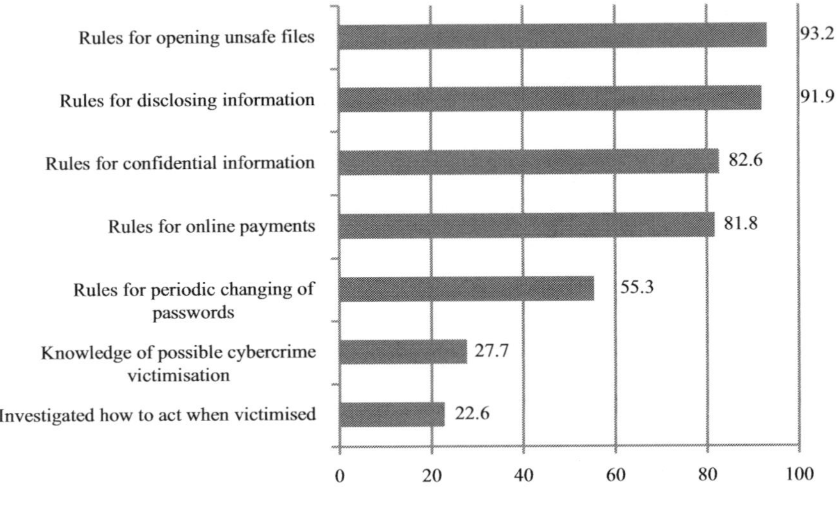

Confidence in measures taken

We have established that one-man businesses undertake a variety of measures to protect themselves against cybercrime. We asked one-man businesses how much confidence they have in the measures they have taken to avoid online risks. The results are given in Figure 5.16. More than half of one-man businesses surveyed said that they have confidence or a great deal of confidence in the measures they have taken (53.7%). Only 4.0 per cent said that they have little, very little or no confidence in these measures. These percentages did not differ from those of SMEs.

Figure 5.16 Confidence in measures taken (n = 1,622 one-man businesses, 1,203 SMEs)

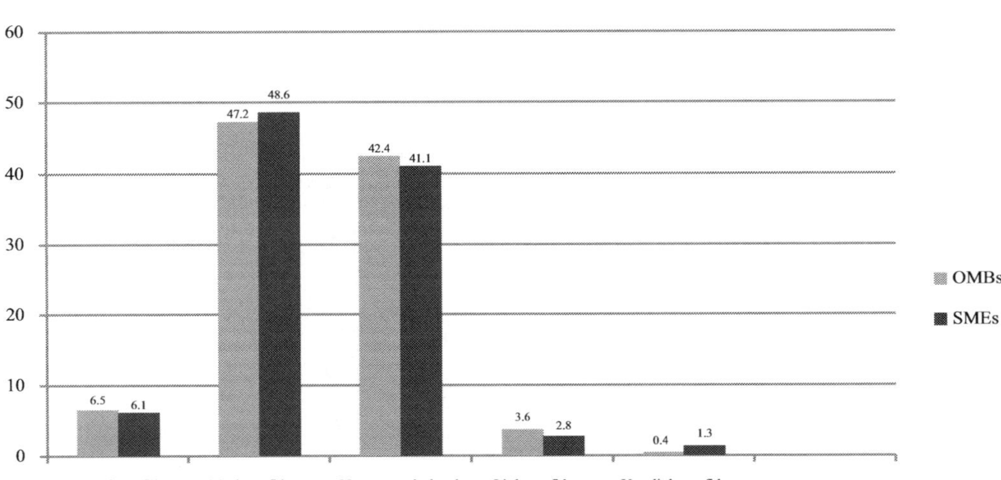

5.2.3   *Estimated probability of victimisation*

One-man business people were asked to estimate – in the form of a percentage – the likelihood that Dutch one-man businesses would fall victim to cybercrime in a 12-month period. They were then asked to estimate how significant they thought the risk is that they themselves would fall victim to cybercrime in the same period of time. Figure 5.17 shows the averages of the percentages they mentioned.

Figure 5.17   Estimated probability of cybercrime victimisation in one year (n = 1,622)*

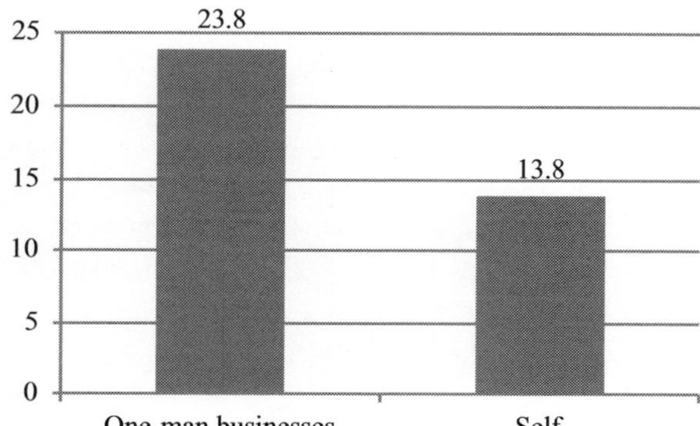

People operating one-man businesses estimated that almost a quarter of one-man businesses in the Netherlands would fall victim to cybercrime in a period of one year (23.8%). As we will see (in Section 5.3), that is quite a good estimate. However, their estimates of their own chances of victimisation was significantly lower (13.8%). The difference between the average percentages (10, 95% confidence interval [9.2, 10.7]) is significant (t(1621) = 24.2, p < 0.001).[7]
An in-depth analysis[8] shows that respondents who did not become victims to cybercrime in the previous year (see Section 5.3) not only estimated the probability that one-man businesses would fall victim (22.5%), but also that they themselves would fall victim (12.8%), to be lower than the respondents who did fall victim in the previous year (respectively 27.0% and 16.4%).[9] Recent experiences with cybercrime therefore result in the probability of future victimisation being estimated to be higher.

---

7.   Paired sample t-test.
8.   Independent samples t-test.
9.   Probability of victimisation among one-man businesses: Victims estimated the probability on average to be higher (M = 27.0, SE = 1.03) than non-victims (M = 22.5, SE = 0.55). The difference of –4.51, BCa 95% CI [–6.76, –2.39] is significant t(1620) = –3.858, p = 0.001. The likelihood of own victimisation: Victims estimated the probability on average to be higher (M = 16.4, SE = 0.94) than non-victims did (M = 12.8, SE = 0.47). The difference of –3.598, BCa 95% CI [–5.84, –1.63] is significant t(1620) = –3.426, p = 0.001.

In the in-depth interviews, we asked people operating one-man businesses whether they were aware of online risks and on what this risk awareness was based. Practically all respondents said they were very much aware of online risks. According to them, they became aware of the risk through their own experiences: knowledge about IT, cybercrime victimisation or attempts at it ('learned the hard way'), reports in the media, but also the experiences of other people had raised their risk awareness: 'I keep a close eye on the stories about all the things that can go wrong on the internet via the media and my son who is studying IT. But I am very well aware that a mistake on the internet can happen just like that and it can happen to anyone'.

Probability of victimisation
Mr Maas is aware of online risks, but doesn't worry about them. As a journalist, he writes a lot about subjects like data usage and working in the cloud. So he is well informed. He does not open suspicious websites and he checks to see that 'https' is in the bar when there should be additional encryption. Because of his background knowledge, he estimates his own chances of falling victim to cybercrime to be smaller than those of other people. Moreover, he has never fallen victim to cybercrime, despite being online a lot, being active on Marktplaats and visiting webshops often.

Summary
By their own account, the majority of one-man businesses are dependent on IT. In addition, most said that they keep confidential company information and other information on their computers. Consequently, one-man businesses generally felt it is important to protect information. This is reflected in the finding that most one-man businesses take various measures to prevent cybercrime. Virtually all of them have a virus scanner, firewall, up-to-date software and a secure network. Furthermore, most apply rules for opening potentially unsafe files and for disclosing information. Nevertheless, there are also measures which are important for IT protection but which are not taken by all one-man businesses. Encryption, attaching computers to a cable lock and protecting computers against calamities are measures that are not taken by many. One-man business people were also less familiar with how they should act if they fall victim to cybercrime and they had hardly done anything to find out how they could fall victim to cybercrime. Previous research among members of the public in the United Kingdom led to similar observations (Intomart GfK, 2013; Hernandez-Castro, Boiten & Barnoux, 2013; McGuire & Dowling, 2013). McGuire and Dowling claim: 'Internet security software is commonly used, but other "good practices" are less well adopted' (2013, p. 24). Despite this, more than half of one-man businesses surveyed said that they have confidence or a great deal of confidence in the measures they had taken. Whether this confidence is justified is the question. To begin with, one-man businesses estimated the probability of themselves falling victim to cybercrime in the coming year at almost 14 per cent. One-man businesses that had fallen victim to cybercrime themselves in the previous year were inclined to think the likelihood would be higher (16.4%). Those running the most risk of falling victim to cybercrime,

according to one-man business people, were their fellows in the one-man business sector: they estimate the probability of victimisation among one-man businesses in general at almost 24 per cent. The next section is about the actual probability of victimisation.

5.3　Cybercrime victimisation

5.3.1　*The nature and extent of cybercrime*

In the same way that we determined the extent to which Dutch SMEs fall victim to cybercrime, we also established the nature and extent of victimisation among one-man businesses. Table 5.1 shows the extent to which one-man businesses were confronted with the various kinds of cybercrime in the year prior to the research.

Table 5.1　Types of cybercrime and the extent to which one-man businesses were confronted with these in the previous 12 months (in %) (n = 1,622)

	Don't know	Not at all	≥1 failed attempt (s)	Once	>Once	Total number of victims
Malware	7.0	51.4	27.8	8.1	6.2	14.3
E-fraud	1.4	79.7	13.6	4.3	1.2	5.5
Phishing	5.8	46.4	43.2	1.4	3.4	4.8
Hacking	10.8	78.5	6.8	3.3	0.6	3.9
Skimming – bankcard	2.8	91.5	1.8	3.7	0.2	3.9
DoS attack	4.7	87.4	4.1	2.8	0.9	3.7
Defacing	2.3	94.2	1.2	1.6	0.7	2.3
Identity abuse	6.9	88.3	2.7	1.6	0.6	2.2
Unauthorised use of company network	9.7	85.9	2.5	1.4	0.6	2.0
Cyberstalking	2.1	94.5	1.5	1.4	0.5	1.9
Theft of data	8.1	88.6	1.4	1.7	0.1	1.8
Theft of data carriers	2.0	96.0	0.4	1.5	0.1	1.6
Cyber defamation/slander	2.9	94.6	0.9	1.0	0.5	1.5
Destruction of data	2.4	95.6	0.9	0.8	0.3	1.2
Cyber blackmail	1.4	95.3	2.5	0.5	0.4	0.9
Cyber extortion	1.7	94.1	3.5	0.4	0.2	0.6
Espionage	8.3	91.1	0.4	0.1	0.2	0.3
Skimming – payment system	1.7	98.1	0.1	0.1	-	0.1

Victims were defined as one-man businesses that had been the victim of forms of cybercrime once or more in the year prior to the research. Failed attempts were not included in this. We did not take theft of data carriers into consideration when calculating the nature and extent of victimisation because it is not a cybercrime (see note b in Table 2.1 on page 26). The research showed that 27.9 per cent of one-man businesses were victims. This victimisation rate does not differ significantly from the corresponding rate for the SME sector (28.5%). So cybercrime occurs to a similar extent among these two target populations.

Comment on phishing victimisation

What is noticeable in Table 5.1 is that people operating one-man businesses that had fallen victim to one type of cybercrime generally only fell victim once. Only for phishing the percentage of one-man businesses that fell victim more than once is higher than the percentage who said that they had only fallen victim once. An explanation for this is that some of the respondents may have incorrectly reported receiving a phishing e-mail as victimisation even though they did not subsequently fall for it or actually have information extracted. According to the law, disclosing information is, however, essential to be able to speak of fraud, the offence for which phishing was made punishable (Section 326 of the Dutch Criminal Code). This means that the victimisation rate for phishing may be lower in reality than has been reported here. We checked what effect this potential bias would have on the overall cybercrime victimisation rate among one-man businesses: if phishing is not taken into consideration when calculating the total victimisation rate, 26.8 per cent of one-man businesses fell victim to cybercrime. The impact of a possible bias from phishing on the overall cybercrime victimisation rate is therefore marginal. Phishing victimisation has not been excluded from the follow-up analyses: firstly, because doubts about the accuracy in the way the victimisation for this offence was measured were based on only a few answers given to open questions. Secondly, because many of the analyses relate to individual kinds of offences (malware, phishing, e-fraud, skimming, hacking and DoS attacks), which means that phishing can be assessed separately.

In the research among SMEs, malware (17.9%), phishing (7.2%), e-fraud (4.1%), hacking (3.4%) and DoS attacks (3.0%) turned out to be the most common kinds of cybercrime. Even though the order of prevalence is different, one-man businesses are most likely to fall victim to these same kinds of cybercrime (see Figure 5.18). What is remarkable is that bankcard skimming was not one of the most common kinds of cybercrime among SMEs, while it was among one-man businesses. One-man businesses were significantly more likely than SMEs to fall victim to skimming. Indeed, the victimisation rate for skimming was as high as it was for hacking (3.9%). The fact that one-man businesses not only report about their business experiences, but also their private experiences, may well explain this relatively high victimisation rate. It is, however, not possible to determine this based on this data.

SMEs were significantly more likely to fall victim to malware and phishing than one-man businesses. Given that one-man businesses reported about their private as well as business affairs, while SMEs only reported about business-related confrontations with cybercrime, it is to be expected that the victimisation rate for these offences would be higher among one-man businesses. Having said that, various factors may explain the higher victimisation rates for malware and phishing among SMEs.

Figure 5.18   Cybercrime victimisation (n = 452 one-man businesses, n = 343 SMEs)

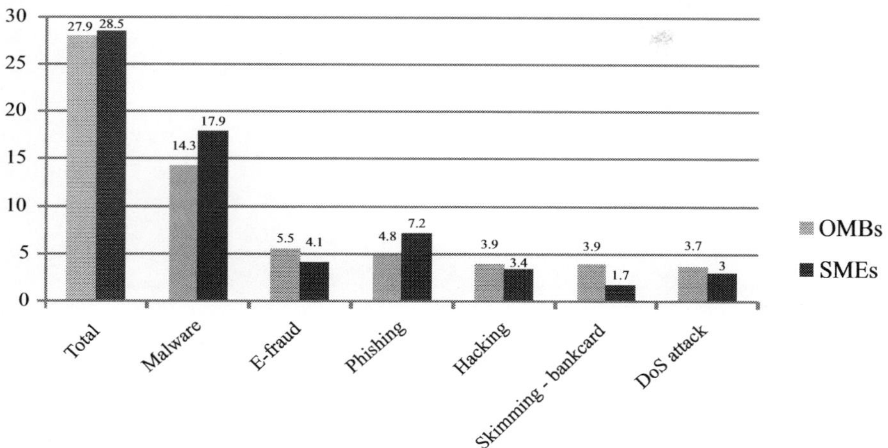

First, one could assume that cyber criminals use malware and phishing to launch targeted attacks against larger companies (2 to 50 members of staff in our case), probably because there is more to be gained from targeting SMEs than one-man businesses. Brewer (2014), for example, claims that cyber criminals launch targeted attacks against businesses, particularly larger ones.

An alternative possibility could be that the larger online attack surface that SMEs offer explains why SMEs fall victim to phishing and malware more frequently. It is more difficult to form a united front and keep attacks outside the organisation in places where several people work. Phishing and malware are crimes that use victims who are unintentionally 'cooperating' (disclosing codes, opening attachments and so on). The attack surface at SMEs, where by definition more than one people work, all of whom may potentially 'cooperate' in the offence, is larger than the online attack surface at one-man businesses. It is also possible that employees at SMEs are less cautious with company IT than one-man business owners would be with their own systems. An additional analysis partly confirmed that the attack surface at SMEs influences the likelihood of falling victim to cybercrime. Malware victimisation has a significant correlation with the size of the company ($p < 0.01$): the more employees an SME has, the more likely it is to fall victim to malware. This correlation was not, however, established in the case of phishing. Furthermore, it still does not explain why the overall cybercrime victimisation rate among SMEs is the same as that for one-man businesses. There are apparently mechanisms at work that neutralise SMEs' additional vulnerability due to their larger attack surface.

The conclusion has to be that our research does not provide an unequivocal explanation for the discrepancies we found in victimisation, nor for the finding that victimisation rates for SMEs and one-man businesses do not differ overall.

A closer examination of e-fraud

Because e-fraud is a catch-all term, we asked one-man businesses about the type of fraud they had been confronted with. Figure 5.19 gives the responses to this question. Half of the fraud victims bought and paid for a product which was ultimately never delivered. 35.2 per cent fell victim to advertising fraud (phantom invoices). Approximately one fifth received a product or service that failed to meet the promised standard in terms of quality (20.5%) or were landed with a subscription that they did not want (19.3%). Less common kinds of fraudulent activities included internet banking fraud (13.6%), sales fraud (8.0%) and advance fee fraud (1.1%).

Figure 5.19   Victimisation: types of e-fraud (n = 88 one-man businesses, n = 45 SMEs)

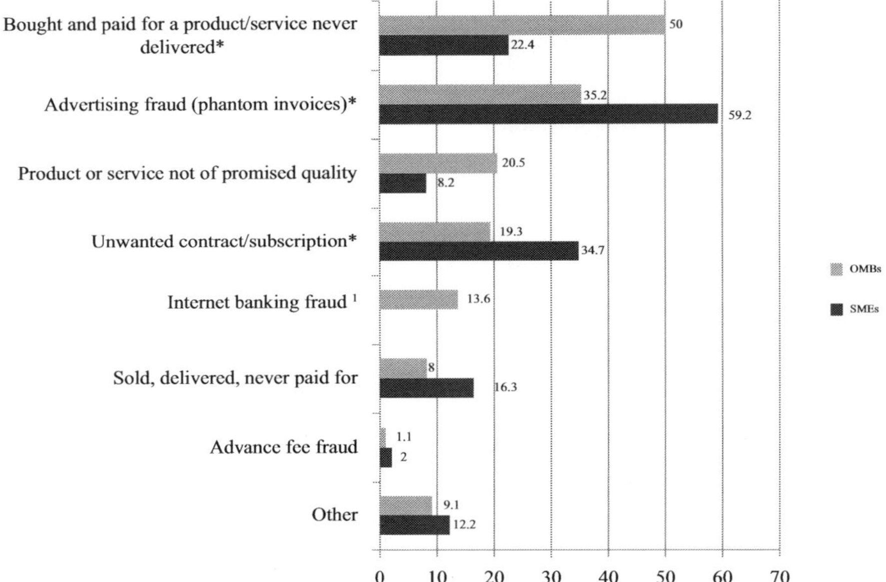

[1] SMEs were not asked this.

There are significant differences compared to the SME sector research: twice as many one-man businesses were confronted with purchasing fraud (50.0%) as SMEs (22.4%). A possible explanation for this significant difference is that private and business victimisations among one-man businesses are intertwined. The opposite is true for advertising fraud: even though it is also a common kind of fraud among one-man businesses (35.2%), significantly more SMEs (59.2%) fell victim to it. The percentage of SMEs who were stuck with a subscription that they did not want is significantly higher than the percentage of one-man businesses in the same position (34.7% versus 19.3%).

Respondents who stated that they had fallen victim to another kind of fraud (9.1%) were offered the opportunity to explain what had happened to them in an open answer field. What is noticeable is that four out of a total of eight explanations involved credit card fraud. The open answers are cited in Text Box 5.2.

> **Text Box 5.2: Quotes from entrepreneurs who fell victim to fraud**
> - *'The fraud involved my credit card number, presumably via the site that did not deliver the services'.*
> - *'Credit card fraud'.*
> - *'Withdrawal using credit card'.*
> - *'Credit card details which a third party'.*
> - *'Orders were made in my name but I didn't want the products'.*
> - *'Customers who use Paypal to pay, don't want a registered dispatch and then report that the product never arrived. Paypal then transfers the amount back to the customer. In some cases the report could be considered "suspicious"'.*
> - *'Booked a market, never got the money back when the booking was cancelled'.*

Compared to members of the public

Now that we know the extent to which entrepreneurs are the target of cybercrime, it is interesting to compare these findings with the nature and extent of cybercrime among members of the public. Based on available literature on the subject, we mapped the extent to which cybercrime is something that affects society as a whole as opposed to it being a phenomenon that is directed at entrepreneurs specifically (see below).

At first glance, it seems as though there is a difference between the extent to which companies as opposed to members of the public are confronted with cybercrime: 27.9 per cent of one-man businesses and 28.5 of the Dutch SME sector were cybercrime victims, while the most recent Victim Survey in Holland (the Security Monitor) shows that one in eight of the Dutch population (11.2%) aged 15 years and above fell victim to cybercrime. However, studies into cybercrime among SMEs and one-man businesses asked about more and different types of cybercrime than those surveyed by the Security Monitor conducted by Statistics Netherlands. For this reason, prevalence rates are not comparable and so it is not possible to state with certainty that cybercrime occurs to a greater extent among companies than it does among members of the public. Indeed, further analysis gives the impression that cybercrime affects the whole of society and that various groups within society are confronted with the same kinds of cybercrime.

The most common types of cybercrime among the corporate sector are the same types of cybercrime with which members of the public are most frequently confronted. Members of the public are mainly confronted with malware, hacking and e-fraud (CBS, 2015; Domenie et al., 2013). These cybercrimes are also among the four most common kinds of cybercrime that affect companies. It is not known whether members of the public fall victim to the other most common kinds of cybercrime that affect businesses to the same extent as well. Members of the public were not asked about phishing, skimming and DoS attacks (in a similar fashion).

Even though members of the public and corporate sector are – to the best of our knowledge – mainly confronted with the same cybercrimes, there are differences in the prevalence rates. Table 5.2 shows the prevalence rates for the most common kinds of cybercrime divided according to the target populations.

Table 5.2   Prevalence rates for the most common kinds of cybercrime divided according to target populations

	SME (n = 1,203)	One-man businesses (n = 1,622)	Members of the public $n_{(malware)}$ = 9,163 [2011] $n_{(hacking/fraud)}$ = 86,382 [2014]
Malware	17.9	*14.3	16.7 (Domenie et al., 2013)
Hacking	3.4	3.8	*5.2 (CBS, 2015)
Buying and selling fraud[1]	*1.5	3.0	3.5 (CBS, 2015)

[Year] the years between square brackets are the years that the data was collected.

[1] Given that Statistics Netherlands understands fraud to only mean buying and selling fraud, we used this same restriction in the SME and one-man businesses columns; these percentages are therefore lower than the percentages for 'fraud' in Figure 5.18.

* Significant difference with both other percentages – which do not differ significantly from each other. Each time $p < 0.01$ applies, except for the difference between 14.3 and 16.7 for malware rates for one-man businesses and members of the public, respectively; and the difference between 3.8 and 5.2 per cent for the hacking rates for one-man businesses and members of the public, respectively. For these, $p < 0.05$ applies (Z-score for proportions; Loether & McTavish, 1980, p. 556).

To start with, we can see that the order of the three offences is the same in each group: malware victimisation occurs most frequently, followed by hacking and then buying and selling fraud. For each of the three offences, there is one group with a percentage that differs significantly from the other two (see the legend in Table 5.2).

Malware victimisation is significantly less common among one-man businesses (14.3%) than among SMEs (17.9%) and members of the public (16.7%). There is a different pattern for hacking: members of the public are significantly more likely to be victims (5.2%) than one-man businesses (3.8%) and SMEs (3.4%). For buying and selling fraud, the victimisation rate is significantly lower for SMEs (1.5%) than the corresponding rate for one-man businesses (3.0%) and members of the public (3.5%).

In succession, the questions that these findings raise are:

a. Why do one-man businesses report malware victimisation less frequently, relatively speaking?
b. Why do members of the public report hacking victimisation more frequently, relatively speaking?
c. Why do SMEs report buying and selling fraud victimisation less frequently, relatively speaking?

Empirically tested answers to these questions are not available based on our data. We can, however, put forward some suggestions for further research.

- (Re a) Malware victimisation may be linked to security measures. Assuming that the average internet surfer (members of the public) may have less protection on their computer than the average one-man business, this may explain why members of the public are more likely to fall victim to malware than one-man businesses are. It does not, however, explain why SMEs are confronted most frequently, i.e. more frequently than members of the public, with malicious software. The larger attack surface that SMEs have may weigh more heavily than the protective measures they take. Based on this reasoning, SMEs fall victim to malware more frequently than members of the public and one-man businesses because the likelihood of victimisation increases in proportion to the number of employees a company has. As soon as one member of staff opens the wrong file, the SME in question falls victim to malware. This explanation is consistent with the previously established correlation between malware victimisation and the size of the company.

- (Re b) Hacking victimisation may also be linked to taking security measures, assuming that the protection on the average business computer will be better than that on computers owned by members of the public.
- (Re c) Buying and selling fraud may be linked to online purchasing done by private individuals. A factor in this may be that buying and selling fraud mainly takes place in the market for private individuals, and one-man businesses and members of the public report on this type of fraud, while SMEs were asked to report on business-related experiences.

As can be deduced from the aforementioned analysis, cybercrime is a problem that affects the whole of society. It confronts members of the public as well as entrepreneurs. Even though prevalence rates may sometimes differ, the most common types of cybercrime are the same for all the groups and occur in the same order in terms of prevalence. More research is required to clarify the differences in the extent to which the various target populations are confronted with common types of cybercrime.

Do one-man businesses view cybercrime as a business-specific problem?
In connection with this, we asked one-man businesses whether they thought that they had fallen victim to cybercrime because of their internet activities as entrepreneurs. Figure 5.20 shows that 64.0 per cent of one-man business people who fell victim to cybercrime thought that cybercrime is not related to business activities per se.

Figure 5.20   Did you fall victim because of your internet activities as an entrepreneur? (n = 452)

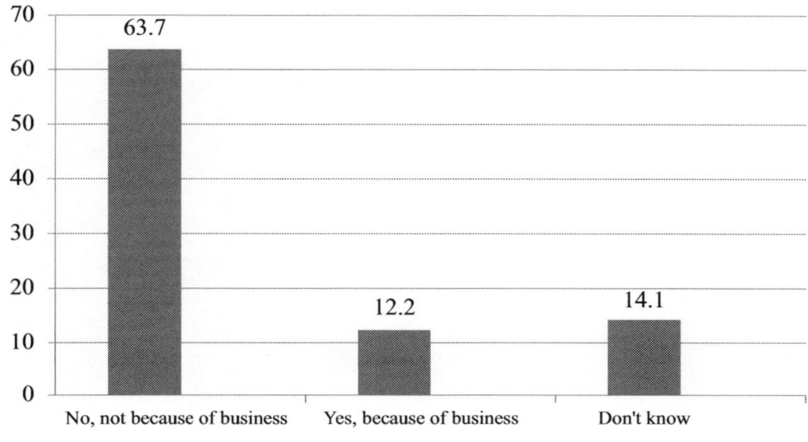

One out of eight entrepreneurs thought that they fell victim to cybercrime as a consequence of their business internet activities and quarter indicated that they did not know whether victimisation was linked to doing business.
Respondents were given the opportunity to clarify why they thought that their online business operations may or may not have led to cybercrime victimisation. The explanations they gave contributed to interpreting the findings (see Text Box 5.3).

> **Text Box 5.3: Quotes from entrepreneurs who fell victim to fraud**
> Cybercrime does not target specific victims
> - *'The criminals don't necessarily know in advance whether they are dealing with an entrepreneur or not'.*
> - *'If I had been the focus of a targeted attack, the attacks would probably have been more successful'.*
> - *'The attempts always targeted the company e-mail accounts as well as private accounts'.*
> - *'I think that private individuals are scammed in the same way, so there's no difference'.*
> - *'I cannot imagine that my twitter account was hacked because I am a one-man business. I think it's more likely to be coincidence'.*
> - *'It's a shotgun approach and I happened to be hit'.*
> - *'I think it was a coincidence'.*
> - *'Everyone gets to deals with it'.*
> - *'Malware and phishing are sent as bulk mail. Not targeted as far as I know'.*
> - *'Private and business bank details were traced'.*
>
> Examples of personal targeting
> - *'The attacks were directed at me as a person, not at the company'.*
> - *'It was a private purchase via marktplaats'.*
> - *'Someone was jealous of the fact that I had been given a job (alongside my one-man business) so they made a fake profile on a social media site to harass me, and to tarnish my good name'.*
>
> Examples of the business being targeted
> - *'The phantom invoices targeted my company. For years I had no idea that they were phantom invoices until my accountant warned me'.*
> - *'I suspect that they buy up addresses at the Chamber of Commerce and then write to companies or send fake invoices based on this information so that they can extract money'.*
> - *'[It involved] DoS attacks and bad link building from Russia, it must have been carried out by a competitor'.*

Although certain cyber attacks seem to be specifically directed at entrepreneurs (such as advertising fraud) or indeed at private individuals (such as buying or selling fraud and defamation/slander), the respondents explained that cybercrime is generally not targeted. The attacks are not specifically directed against companies or private individuals: cybercrime is – in the words of one of the respondents – like shotgun fire that can hit everyone who is online. This finding is consistent with the previous observation that the most common kinds of cybercrime are a problem that affects society as a whole.

> **Victimisation as an entrepreneur**
> *Mr Koenraads does not think that the chances of victimisation are bigger because he is an entrepreneur. Nevertheless, as a person running a one-man business, the chances of targeted victimisation can never be ruled out. If hackers who are active on the internet are interested in his business specifically, then they will always be able to find what they are looking for. However, because he has a small company, he does not think that he is interesting enough for them to crack his website, for instance. But maybe they would if he had a large and well-known company. Mr Koenraads thinks that victimisation among entrepreneurs depends on this.*

Summary
In the 12 months prior to the research, 27.9 per cent of one-man businesses fell victim to cybercrime. Cybercrime prevalence is the same among SMEs. The extent of cybercrime is therefore similar to the extent of traditional crime among the corporate sector (WODC, 2011). The most common types of cybercrime among one-man businesses as well as among SMEs are malware, phishing, e-fraud, hacking and DoS attacks. Moreover, victimisation does not seem to be the consequence of doing business per se: the most common types of cybercrime that confront entrepreneurs are also the ones that members of the public fall victim to most frequently, insofar as the prevalence rates are comparable. In this light, it is not an entrepreneur-specific problem: cybercrime can affect anyone. This finding confirms the findings of earlier research (Jansen et al., 2013b). Advertising fraud is perhaps the only exception to this rule: it is the most common kind of e-fraud among SMEs and the second most common kind among one-man businesses. How often members of the public have to contend with phantom invoices is not known, rendering a straight comparison impossible.

Furthermore, it is striking that, although SMEs, the one-man business sector and members of the public face the same common kinds of cybercrime, prevalence rates differ. An empirically tested explanation for the differences is not available; more research is required for this.

5.3.2   Risk factors for victimisation

This section provides insight into risk factors for cybercrime victimisation. We conducted analyses to see which factors influence the probability of falling victim to cybercrime. In the process, we assessed whether there were links between victimisation and:

- personal attributes;
- company attributes;
- internet activities;

- the extent to which protective measures are taken against cybercrime and
- the extent to which people operating one-man businesses are familiar with and/or use government measures.

Various considerations underlie our choice of these factors. Firstly, there is a lack of knowledge about risk factors for cybercrime victimisation among companies. So we investigated, where possible, whether company attributes help explain cybercrime victimisation. Secondly, previous victim research conducted among other target populations, such as members of the public and young people, showed that some of the aforementioned factors offer an explanation for victimisation: young people, people with relatively low self-control and people who are more active and/or visible on the internet than on average are more likely to be cybercrime victims (Domenie et al., 2013; Hernandez-Castro & Boiten, 2014; Jansen et al., 2013b; Van Wilsem, 2010). Based on such findings, it can be assumed that personal attributes (like age and self-control) and internet activities may also explain why one-man businesses fall victim. Furthermore, it is relevant to investigate whether protective measures influence the probability of victimisation, although previous research suggests that their impact is limited (Bosler & Holt, 2009; Hutchings & Hayes, 2009; Leukfeldt, 2014). Investigating the influence of protective measure may, after all, provide insight into action strategies against cybercrime.

Bivariate correlations with victimisation
27.9 per cent of one-man businesses were victims of cybercrime. This group of victims is diverse: it includes respondents who have been confronted with at least one of the 17 types of cybercrime surveyed in this research. Because victims of the various offences may have various attributes, we first assessed at a bivariate level the extent to which the attributes of respondents who only fell victim to one of the crimes, like malware or hacking, influenced the probability of victimisation. This means that we tested separately whether there was a correlation between victimisation for a specific type of cybercrime and each possible risk factor, like age. The exploratory analyses showed that the number of victims per offence was too small to determine correlations in a statistically reliable manner. For this reason, we did not conduct further analyses on offence-specific victim attributes. We then carried out exploratory bivariate analyses to map correlations between risk factors and the total group of victims (being 27.9 per cent). The analysis shows that, in comparison with non-victims, cybercrime victims:
- operate internationally as businesses to a greater extent;
- are younger;
- are more computer literate;
- are more active on the internet: victims spend more time on the internet; are more likely to have their own company website (with a webshop); search specifically for information (targeted searching) more frequently; download, chat online, make video calls and e-mail more frequently; are more likely to use cloud services and are more likely to place and process orders online and

- are more active on social media: victims are more likely to use Twitter, Facebook, LinkedIn, photographic sites like Pinterest, video sites like YouTube, online forums and blogs.

Furthermore, the analysis shows that taking protective measures and the extent to which government initiatives to protect companies against cybercrime are known and used by one-man businesses do not reduce the probability of victimisation.[10]
So one-man businesses that fell victim to cybercrime differ from respondents who did not fall victim to cybercrime. These are familiar correlations: just as previous research has shown, victims tend to be younger, prove to be active internet users and that protective measures do not contribute to the prevention of victimisation. Based on these findings, we decided to take the entire group of victims as the basis for further victim analyses.

Multivariate analysis
So far we have presented the results of bivariate analyses. For this, we tested whether there was a correlation between cybercrime victimisation and each possible risk factor separately, such as personal or company attributes. The literature and the bivariate analyses both show that various factors influence the probability of falling victim to cybercrime. For this reason, we also carried out multivariate analyses: this analysis provides insight into the combined impact of various risk factors, controlled against one another, on the probability of falling victim to cybercrime (see also Section 3.2.6).

Profiling victims
We first carried out a binomial logistic regression. Using this multivariate analysis method, it is possible to compare two groups – in this case victims versus non-victims. The outcome of the analysis provides insight into victimisation risk factors. The risk factors included in the analysis account for 8.1 per cent (Nagelkerke R^2) of the reasons why one-man businesses fall victim to cybercrime (see Table 5.3).
Although the analysis does not account for as much as 10 per cent of the reason why one-man businesses fall victim, the results confirm the findings of previous research: victims are on average younger (entrepreneurs up to and including 45 years of age are significantly likely to run more risk) and have lower levels of self-control than non-victims. In addition to this, they distinguish themselves with their above-average internet activity. Company attributes and protective measures do not affect the likelihood of becoming a victim of cybercrime.
Some of the bivariate correlations demonstrated in previous analysis were no longer significant in this multivariate analysis. Being more likely to be operating internationally for business purposes; being more computer literate and having more knowledge

---

10. With the exception of the National Internet Fraud Reporting Centre [*Landelijk Meldpunt Internet Oplichting* in Dutch (LMIO)]: victims of cybercrime are more likely to know this hotline. A possible explanation for this is that a significant proportion of the victims were confronted with e-fraud, and consequently became aware of the existence of the LMIO.

about computers and being active on social media are no longer correlated with victimisation when the influence of various risk factors are weighed against one another.

Given the results of this analysis, reducing the likelihood of falling victim to cybercrime based on practicable recommendations is no simple task. After all, it is difficult to give practical advice that can be applied based on a person's age and degree of self-control. The recommendation to simply not go on the web as much is not sustainable in an increasingly digital society.

Table 5.3   Regression model for one-man businesses that fell victim to cybercrime (n = 1,543)

	Cybercrime victimisation (compared to non-victims)	
	B	OR
***Personal attributes*[a]**		
Male	0.183	1.201
Age	****-0.168**	0.845
Level of education	-0.012	0.988
Self-control	***-0.397**	0.672
Awareness of online risk	0.280	1.323
Computer/internet skills	0.003	1.003
***Company attributes*[b]**		
Separating business and private use of computers and the internet	0.103	1.108
Operating in the corporate market	-0.323	0.724
Operating in the consumer and corporate market	-0.184	0.832
Operating regionally	-0.042	0.959
Operating nationally	0.038	1.039
Operating internationally	0151	1.163
Internet and social media activities		
Number of hours on the internet per day	0.062	1.064
Has a company website	-0.017	0.983
Has a webshop	0.203	1.226
Frequency of internet activities	***0.257**	1.293
Has a company profile on social media	0.225	1.252
Frequency of social media activities	0.150	1.162
Protective measures		
Physical measures	0.030	1.030
Technical measures	0.048	1.050
Apply rules for safe internet behaviour	-0.060	0.942
Awareness and use of government measures	-0.478	0.620
Nagelkerke R^2		**8.1%**

[a] The results for men were compared to the results for women (reference group).

[b] The results for one-man businesses which separated private and business use of computers and the internet were compared to the results for one-man businesses that did not separate these uses. The results for companies that were operating either in the corporate market or in the consumer and corporate market were compared to the results for companies which were only operating in the consumer market.

Opportunities for preventing cybercrime victimisation
We also carried out a multinomial logistic regression to gain more insight into starting points for prevention and intervention strategies. This multivariate analysis method makes it possible to compare the attributes of more than two groups with one another. In the analysis we carried out, we distinguished between three groups:

- a group of respondents who did not fall victim to cybercrime and did not encounter any attempts at cybercrime;
- a group of respondents who were confronted with at least one cybercrime attempt, but did not fall victim and
- a group of respondents who did fall victim to cybercrime.

Respondents who fell victim to cybercrime were compared to one-man businesses that had not fallen victim to cybercrime and also did not encounter any attempts at cybercrime. By doing so, the analysis provides insight into the risk factors involved in cybercrime victimisation. The attributes of respondents who were confronted with at least one cybercrime attempt but did not fall victim were also compared to the attributes of victims. This comparison provides insight into the factors that lead to some one-man businesses becoming victims, while other one-man businesses – despite being confronted with cybercrime attempts – managed to avoid victimisation. This analysis may provide insight into action strategies for preventing cybercrime victimisation. The results of this multivariate analysis account for 15.0 per cent (Nagelkerke R^2) of the reasons why some one-man businesses have an increased risk of being confronted with cybercrime. Table 5.4 presents the results of analysis.

The correlation between victimisation and being more active on the internet stands. One-man businesses that became victims of cybercrime are more active on the web than one-man businesses that did not fall victim to cybercrime and who were also not confronted with an attempt at cybercrime. At the same time, victims are more likely than non-victims to have profile on social media which they use for business purposes. In short, the more frequently that internet activities are performed, the greater the likelihood of falling victim to cybercrime.

On the one hand, that active internet behaviour leads to an increased probability of cybercrime victimisation is not surprising. On the other hand, however, the finding is surprising because it means that internet experience does not protect users. For prevention policy, this finding means that it is important to make one-man business owners aware of the risks that accompany their own internet behaviour so that they can be cautious when using the internet.

Table 5.4   The influence of risk factors in confrontations with cybercrime (n = 1,543)[11]

	Cybercrime victimisation (compared to non-victims, no attempts)		Attempt, not a victim (compared to respondents that were victims)	
	B	**OR**	**B**	**OR**
Personal attributes[a]				
Male	0.117	1.125	-0.258	0.772
Age	-0.047	0.954	****0.249**	1.283
Level of education	0.034	1.034	-0.063	1.065
Self-control	-0.272	0.762	***0.478**	1.613
Awareness of online risk	0.284	1.329	-0.272	0.762
Computer/internet skills	0.254	1.289	-0.197	1.218
Company attributes[b]				
Separating business and private use of computers and the internet	0.167	1.182	-0.069	0.934
Operating in the corporate market	-0.217	0.805	0.084	1.088
Operating in the consumer market	-0.033	0.968	-0.341	0.711
Operating regionally	0.080	1.084	0.099	1.104
Operating nationally	0.086	1.089	-0.020	0.980
Operating internationally	0.178	1.195	-0.140	0.869
Internet and social media activities				
Number of hours on the internet per day	0.054	1.056	-0.076	0.927
Has a company website	0.205	1.228	0.198	1.219
Has a webshop	0.148	1.160	-0.237	0.789
Frequency of internet activities	***0.370**	1.448	-0.176	0.838
Has a company profile on social media	***0.350**	1.418	-0.139	0.870
Frequency of social media activities	0.155	1.168	-0.164	0.848
Protective measures				
Physical measures	-0.063	0.939	-0.092	0.912
Technical measures	0.083	1.087	-0.012	0.988
Apply rules for safe internet behaviour	0.020	1.021	***0.117**	1.124
Awareness and use of government measures	-0.428	0.651	0.472	1.603
Nagelkerke R[2]				***15.0%***

[a] The results for men were compared to the results for women (reference group).

[b] The results for one-man businesses which separated private and business use of computers and the internet were compared to the results for one-man businesses that did not separate these uses. The results for companies who were either operating in the corporate market or in the consumer market were compared to the results for companies which were operating in the consumer market as well as in the corporate market.

---

11. The multivariate analysis was based on the responses from 1,543 instead of 1,622 one-man businesses because only those respondents who used computers with an internet connection for private and business purposes were included. Seventy-nine respondents said that they only use computers linked to the internet for either private purposes or business purposes.

It may be possible to find more reference points for prevention by comparing the profiles of victims to those of one-man business owners that avoided falling victim to cybercrime despite having been confronted with at least one cybercrime attempt. Since there are no significant differences between the internet behaviour of respondents who only reported attempts and the internet behaviour of victims, both groups can therefore be classified as active internet users. Apparently one-man business owners who did not fall victim despite having been confronted with cybercrime attempts – and despite their active internet behaviour – managed to avoided falling victim. The question this raises is: which factors distinguish this group of respondents from victims?

Table 5.4 shows that respondents who only reported attempts, as opposed to victimisation, are significantly older than victims. Despite this, they are just as active on the web, as noted above. Perhaps the life experience concomitant with age of the group of respondents who are only confronted with cybercrime attempts enables them to recognise cybercrime more effectively.

Self-control, too, is a factor in preventing victimisation: respondents who were confronted with cybercrime attempts but avoided victimisation have more self-control than victims. It may well be that this is the reason why these respondents are less impulsive and more cautious when confronted with cybercrime attempts, thus avoiding victimisation.

As previously noted, with a view to suggesting prevention strategies for other one-man businesses, age and self-control are difficult to influence as modifiable risk factors. However, these findings do point to target populations at which prevention can primarily be aimed. A finding which allows itself to be converted into recommendations on how to avoid falling victim to cybercrime more effectively is that respondents who were just confronted with attempts at cybercrime tended to apply rules for safe internet practices to a greater extent than victims. This involves, for instance, rules which one-man business owners apply for themselves about opening potentially unsafe file, rules about disclosing information online or rules about making online payments. This finding gives direction to previous recommendations on how to safely use the internet.

A recommendation along the lines of 'do not act impulsively' may thus be too vague. Specific recommendations, provided they are converted into specific rules for conduct on the internet, may well provide a degree of protection against victimisation.

Summary
Victims of cybercrime mainly distinguish themselves from non-victims in that the former are more active on the internet. In addition, victims are younger (45 years and younger) and have less self-control. These findings are widely supported by the literature (see inter alia Domenie et al., 2013; Hutchings & Hayes, 2009; Jansen et al., 2013b; Van Wilsem, 2010). With a view to formulating action strategies to prevent cybercrime, age and self-control are difficult to influence as modifiable factors. The analysis does show, however, that in order to prevent cybercrime victimisation, it is important to be cautious when using the internet. In addition, self-imposed rules, like abiding by rules when disclosing information online or making online payments, can contribute to the prevention of victimisation. Other protective measures (physical or technical) hardly contribute at all to preventing victimisation. This finding also confirms previous research (Bosler Holt, 2009; Hutchings & Hayes, 2009; Leukfeldt, 2014).

5.3.3   *The way in which cybercrime is committed*

This section is about how cybercrimes are committed. All respondents were asked in-depth questions about this, but only about the *most recent* incident that the respondent fell victim to, because otherwise the questionnaire would have been to long. We also opted for this strategy because we assumed that victims would remember the most recent incident more clearly than the others. A disadvantage of this method was that it was not uncommon for respondents to have fallen victim to cybercrime more than once (see Table 5.1). That means that the results related to the most recent incident may be limited in terms of generalisability for all cybercrimes experienced by one-man businesses.
The responses from respondents who reported on theft of data carriers as their most recently experienced incident have been not taken into consideration. In this research, theft of data carriers is not considered to be cybercrime (see note b in Table 2.1 on page 26). Of the total of 452 victims (27.9%), five reported 'theft of data carriers' as the most recently experienced incident. The analyses presented below which concern one-man businesses are therefore based on the answers from a maximum of 447 respondents.

Victimisation rates and perceived severity of the most recently experienced incidents
Table 5.5 presents the victimisation rates for the most recently experienced cybercrimes. The most reported recently experienced types of cybercrime were malware, e-fraud, skimming, phishing and hacking. This is hardly an unexpected finding given that these kinds of cybercrime are the most common across the board (see Table 5.1).

Table 5.5   Victimisation most recent incident (n = 447)

	Victimisation rate	n
Malware	33.6	150
E-fraud	13.4	60
Skimming – bankcard	10.5	47
Phishing	8.5	38
Hacking	7.4	33
DoS attack	7.2	32
Identity abuse	4.0	18
Cyber defamation/slander	3.6	16
Unauthorised use of company network	3.1	14
Defacing	2.5	11
Cyberstalking	2.2	10
Cyber blackmail	1.3	6
Theft of data	0.9	4
Destruction of data	0.9	4
Skimming – payment system	0.4	2
Cyber extortion	0.2	1
Espionage	0.2	1

Knowing the perpetrator

As was the case in the research among SMEs, one-man business owners were asked whether they knew the identity of the person who committed the most recent incident. The majority of the victims did not know who committed the cybercrime (76.5%); a significantly smaller group were aware of the identity of the perpetrator (14.5%) and a still smaller group had a suspicion about the perpetrator's identity (8.9%).

The findings from the research among one-man businesses broadly correspond to the findings from the research among SMEs (see Figure 5.21). Despite this, there is a significant difference between one-man businesses and the SME sector when it comes to whether they know the identity of the perpetrator. One-man business owners were significantly more likely to know who committed the cybercrime or at least have a suspicion who the culprit is. Given that the private and business lives of people running one-man businesses are intertwined, and that these people also reported on their private experiences of cybercrime, it may well be that they are more likely to be victims of offences in their private capacity. This may also explain why they are more likely to be aware of the perpetrator's identity.

Figure 5.21   Do you know who committed the cybercrime? (n = 447 one-man businesses, 335 SMEs)*

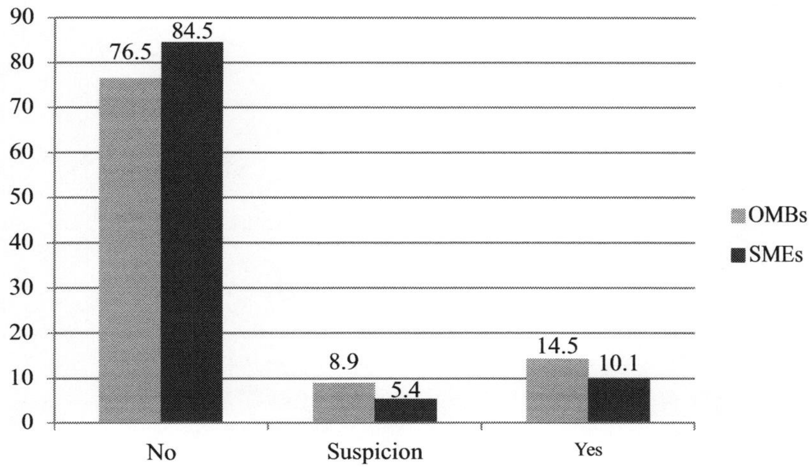

An in-depth analysis demonstrates that the extent to which one-man business owners are aware of the identity of the perpetrator of the most recent incident depends on the types of offence (Table 5.6). Victims of malware and phishing are significantly less likely to have a suspicion about or to know the identity of the perpetrator than victims of other cybercrimes. E-fraud victims were significantly more likely to have a suspicion about or to know the identity of the perpetrator than victims of other offences. This finding is to be expected given that e-fraud, as opposed to malware and phishing, involves personal contact, for instance, when buying or selling a product.

Table 5.6   Knowing the perpetrator per offence

	Yes	Suspicion	No
Total number of victims (n = 447)	14.5	8.9	76.5
Malware (n = 150)**	2.7	7.3	90.0
E-fraud (n = 60)**	40.0	18.3	41.7
Bankcard skimming (n = 47)	8.5	6.4	85.1
Phishing (n = 38)*	2.6	2.6	*94.7
Hacking (n = 33)	9.1	12.1	78.8
DoS attack (n = 32)	3.1	3.1	93.8

*Difference with 'all other victims than those in this category' ** (p < 0.01), * (p < 0.05).*

We asked respondents who said that they knew or had a suspicion about the identity of the perpetrator who it was that they thought had committed the cybercrime. Figure 5.22 shows who the victims thought had committed the most recent cybercrime that they had experienced.

Figure 5.22   Who committed the cybercrime? (n = 105 one-man businesses, 52 SMEs)

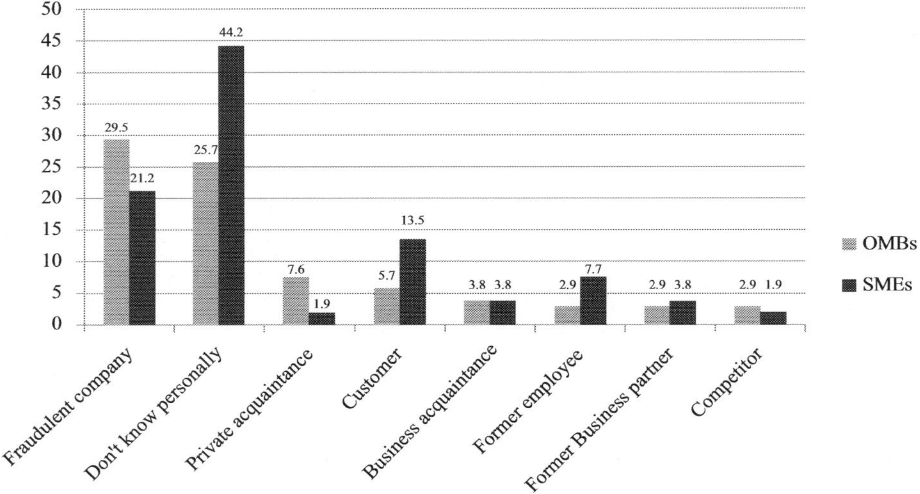

The analysis suggests that one-man businesses had to contend with victimisation on a business as well as private level. Other (fraudulent) companies and acquaintances from the business sector, but also people they knew in their private lives, were pointed to as the perpetrators of the most recently experienced incidents. Respondents gave clarifications in an open answer field about who they suspected the perpetrators of the cybercrime may have been. Some examples have been included in Text Box 5.4.

Text Box 5.4: Quotes from entrepreneurs about the perpetrators of cybercrime

- *'Partner's ex'.*
- *'A guest of a co-network user'.*
- *'An online casino'.*
- *'Catering employee at airport'.*
- *'Supplier'.*
- *'NSA and other security services'.*
- *'Someone who I knew from the past'.*
- *'A pupil'.*

The internationalisation of cyber and other types of crime

Cybercrime crosses national borders and so we also asked one-man businesses about whether the most recent cybercrime incident was committed from within the Netherlands. Most of the one-man business owners did not know whether the most recent offence to which they fell victim was committed from within the Netherlands. 22.6 per cent said that the perpetrator operated from within the Netherlands and 14.8 per cent knew for sure that the perpetrator was operating from abroad. Although the findings are broadly similar to the results of the research among SMEs, one-man businesses are significantly more likely to know where the crime was committed than SMEs (see Figure 5.23). As previously noted, 22.6 per cent of one-man businesses indicated that the offence was committed from within the Netherlands, as opposed to 19.1 per cent of SMEs who said the same. In addition to this, 14.8 per cent of one-man businesses said

Figure 5.23   Was the offence committed from within the Netherlands? (n = 447 one-man businesses, 335 SMEs)*

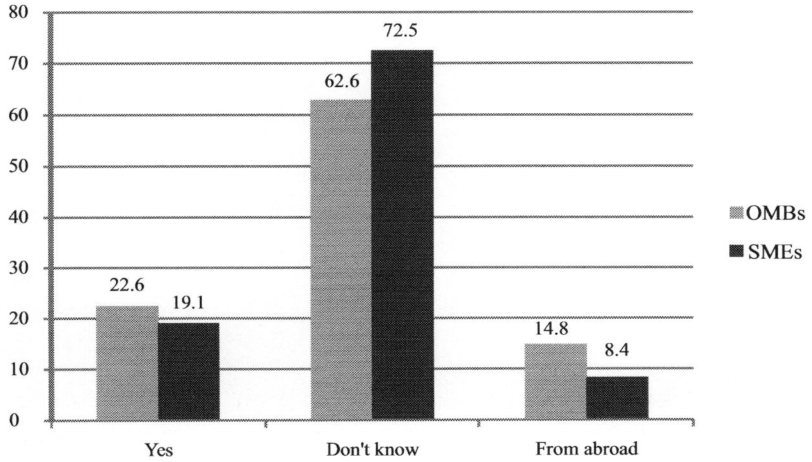

that the offence was committed from abroad, as opposed to 8.4 per cent of SMEs who said the same.

Almost 15 per cent of the offences most recently experienced by one-man businesses were committed from abroad. This means that cybercrime crosses national borders and that the police are confronted with suspects operating from abroad in a substantial proportion of cybercrime cases. Despite this, most of the cases have a national character.

An in-depth analysis demonstrates that the extent to which people with one-man businesses were aware of where the crime was committed depends on the type of offence (Table 5.7). Victims of malware, phishing and DoS attacks are significantly less likely to know where the offence was committed than other victims. This is not a strange finding given that there is often no direct contact between the victim and the perpetrator of these offences.

One-man businesses that reported e-fraud and bankcard skimming as the most recent incident were more likely to know where the crime was committed. E-fraud and skimming were offences which were mainly committed by perpetrators operating from within the Netherlands, as far as the victims were aware. Despite this, these offences were more likely than average to have been committed in a foreign country or from abroad – 20.0 per cent of the fraud offences and almost 32 per cent of the reported skimming cases were committed abroad. There is a logical explanation for this finding too: for e-fraud, contact between the perpetrator and the victim is not rare, for instance, because of the process of buying or selling a product, and victims who have their bankcards skimmed can easily find out where and when they were skimmed by checking their bank account statements.

Finally, hacking victims indicated more frequently than on average that the offence was committed from abroad.

Table 5.7   Was the offence committed from within the Netherlands?

	Yes	No	Do not know
Total number of victims (n = 447)	22.6	14.8	62.6
Malware (n = 150)**	3.3	6.0	90.7
E-fraud (n = 60)**	63.3	20.0	16.7
Bankcard skimming (n = 47)**	42.6	31.9	25.5
Phishing (n = 38)**	2.6	10.5	86.8
Hacking (n = 33)*	9.1	27.3	63.6
DoS attack (n = 32)**	0.0	9.4	90.6

*Difference with 'all other victims than those in this category' ** (p < 0.01), * (p < 0.05).*

American perpetrators
Mrs Thiemen uses her credit card to make transactions from abroad. She buys products from America online. When she checked her monthly statement, she discovered that her credit card details had been hacked and that money had been taken out of her account several times. A total of 2,300 euro had been deducted for vehicle parts, restaurants and hotels. Mrs Thiemen suspects that the perpetrators are from America given that the products were bought there.

The modi operandi of perpetrators

So far, the impression one gets is that one-man businesses that fall victim to cybercrime do not know much about the way in which cybercrime is committed: the majority do not know who the perpetrator is and from which country the most recently experienced cybercrime was committed. To gain an understanding of the modi operandi used by perpetrators, we asked one-man businesses whether they knew how cyber criminals set to work. Figure 5.24 shows that more than half of the one-man businesses did not know how the cybercrime was committed (52.8%); 29.1 per cent did know how the perpetrator set to work and 18.1 per cent had a suspicion. Although there is generally a similar pattern to be seen among victims of cybercrime in the SME sector, there is a significant difference between the extent to which one-man businesses know about the perpetrator's modi operandi and the extent to which SMEs know about it. One-man businesses are more likely to have a suspicion or know how the cybercrime was committed.

Figure 5.24 Do you know how the cybercrime was committed? (n = 447 one-man businesses, 335 SMEs)*

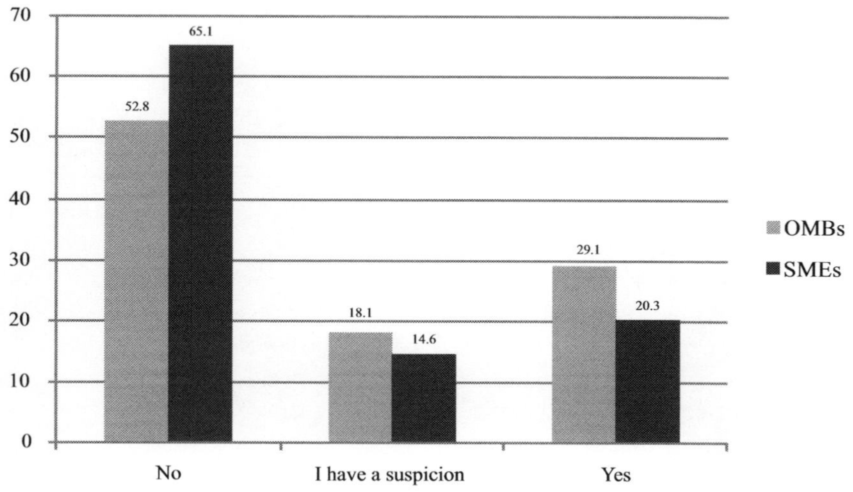

Victims of malware and phishing were significantly less likely to know how the cybercrime was committed than the other victims of cybercrime, while victims of e-fraud on

the other hand were more likely to know or have a suspicion about how the cybercrime was committed (see Table 5.8).

Table 5.8   Do you know how the cybercrime was committed?

	Yes	Suspicion	No
Total number of victims (n = 447)	29.1	18.1	52.8
Malware (n = 150)**	15.3	14.0	70.7
E-fraud (n = 60)**	56.7	23.3	20.0
Bankcard skimming (n = 47)	40.4	21.3	38.3
Phishing (n = 38)*	18.4	7.9	73.7
Hacking (n = 33)	18.2	24.2	57.6
DoS attack (n = 32)	15.6	15.6	68.8

*Difference with 'all other victims than those in this category' ** ($p < 0.01$), * ($p < 0.05$).*

We asked victims who knew or had a suspicion about how the most recent cybercrime
that they had experienced was committed to describe the perpetrator's modi operandi
(n = 211). Of these, 87.7 per cent (n = 185) gave a short description of the modi operandi. The descriptions of the most common kinds of cybercrime are presented below.
We have also included an overview of the descriptions of the modi operandi of the
other cybercrimes. It is not possible to make generalisable statements about the
methods that cyber criminals use per offence, because the number of descriptions
is too small. The quotes from the victims do, however, illustrate the way in which
cybercrimes are committed.

Note: the victims' descriptions of modi operandi have been quoted literally, i.e. grammatical and spelling errors have been incorporated.

Malware modi operandi
A total of 39 victims of malware described the (presumed) modi operandi of the perpetrators (see Text Box 5.5). Several patterns can be detected in these descriptions.
First, various quotes point to the fact that malware victimisation is linked to downloading files. It is not uncommon for victims to assume that they are downloading an
ostensibly reliable programme when in fact they are retrieving malware.
In addition to downloading infected files, opening infected e-mails and/or visiting
infected websites also leads to malware victimisation. Recognising infected e-mails
and/or websites is no easy feat. Malware may be hidden in banners, for instance,
or spread via websites or e-mails from seemingly reliable organisations.
Firewalls and/or virus scanners which are not functioning properly also seem to be a
factor in malware victimisation. A few respondents explicitly described that not all
malware infections are recognised as such. In addition, a respondent reported that
their virus scanner was mistakenly not turned on for a long time.
The descriptions of the ways in which one-man businesses became infected by malware are similar to the ways that SMEs claimed that they had been infected. The SME

sector study showed that the respondents' own (unwittingly high-risk) internet behaviour led to malware victimisation.

Text Box 5.5: Quotes from malware victims
Downloading
- *'When downloading via the internet when surfing and installing software online'.*
- *'Content download from unreliable source'.*
- *'By mistakenly downloading things that are not relevant for the actual programme to be downloaded'.*
- *'Downloaded freeware programme and that's where it was in'.*
- *'I downloaded a file myself where it turned out there was a Trojan. After I started up the software my PC was infected. It is not uncommon'.*
- *'Leaks in the webrowser and/or unintentional link downloads, like download assistants'.*
- *'Malware sent with a download'.*
- *'Malware via a download of a free utility app. Irritating enough to realise straight away and then to have to spend some time to try and work out how to remove it again'.*
- *'Installed with what used to be a reliable app'.*
- *'Piggybacking of malware with utilities, sometimes even with virus or malware scanners'.*
- *'With a banner advertisement which says DOWNLOAD. It has nothing to do with what you really want to download'.*
- *'Malware installed when downloading a file'.*
- *'Via software download'.*
- *'Via facebook. I thought it was a flash player download upgrade'.*

Visiting infected websites and opening infected e-mails
- *'Via an application by e-mail'.*
- *'A fake website had been copied that looked so real that I clicked on a banner that was on it. Afterwards it turned out that it was a pop-up menu that had been installed on top of the real website'.*
- *'E-mail'.*
- *'Via e-mail'. (Twice)*
- *'Got a virus by clicking on the website. But the antivirus blocked it'.*
- *'Malware on a website that my virus scanner and firewall did not recognise as unsafe. Despite the fact that this software is checked daily for updates'.*
- *'Executables from visiting website'.*
- *'Clicked on wrong link'.*
- *'Opening a site via e-mail'.*
- *'Opened the wrong e-mail. CryptoWall virus… Because I'm an IT expert myself, I knew what I had to do, so I quickly disconnected the internet and carried out several operations. Despite my professional knowledge, the virus still managed to be busy on my laptop for around 10 minutes. The result: of the approximately 600,000 files around 100,000 files were modified with an encryption. Obviously I didn't pay these blackmailers, instead I restored the files*

> *using a backup. Unfortunately a few files were still unusable and I lost a few hours of my sleep'.*
> - *'Suspect I was infected with malware via a website/blog'.*
> - *'Via visiting other websites'.*
> - *'Via a website (browsed from one of the children's PC). I don't know which website'.*
> - *'Via a website which was accessed unintentionally during a search'.*
> - *'Caught it from visiting a harmful website'.*
> - *'Via e-mail issued as an existing, reliable institution but it wasn't one'.*
> - *'From a PDF file by e-mail'.*
>
> Other quotes
> - *'Blocked the computer and then demanded money to unblock the computer again. I sorted out the problem myself'.*
> - *'Because the user licence for a security package had run out, it turned out that one of my systems was suddenly no longer protected. As a result, I got malware, solved it by doing a clean up. So I will never buy that programme again, it's an outrage'.*
> - *'Downloading information via a USB stick, with a pretext, "I want to show you something, but I first have to install some software"'.*
> - *'Via an infected USB stick'.*
> - *'Large-scale virus spreading [campaign]'.*
> - *'My malware bytes turned out not to have been switched on for a while. Not sure how that happened'.*
> - *'From hacking of information?'*
> - *'From part of a programme from the United States of America'.*

E-fraud modi operandi

In total, 60 victims indicated that they had been confronted with e-fraud. Forty-one of them described the (presumed) modi operandi of the perpetrators. As previously noted, e-fraud comes in various forms (see Section 5.3.1) and purchasing fraud is the most common type among one-man businesses. The same impression is given in the quotes from fraud victims (see Text Box 5.6). Offering a product or service, receiving money in advance for this and then not delivering the product or service is a method that fraudsters have tried and tested. As the quotes show, what also happens is that, although the product or service is delivered, it does not live up to the promised quality. There are not enough quotes from fraud victims to be able to gain insight into other methods. What these other quotes do emphasise, however, is that a whole range of fraudulent acts are possible: from social engineering to fraud using electronic payment traffic and identity abuse, as was the case in the SME research.

Text Box 5.6: Quotes from e-fraud victims
Buying and selling fraud
- *'Offer via Marktplaats, no more response after payment'.*
- *'Purchase via Marktplaats. Filed a report but it had no effect'.*
- *'Advertisement via Marktplaats'.*
- *'Was offered as article via E-bay. From a Chinese seller, for a very attractive rate. The delivered item was a fake peso coin. Supplier was then pursued by E-bay as a fraudster. Money deposited back [into my account]'.*
- *'Ordered, paid, but not delivered'.*
- *'The products paid for were not delivered, also not after demands'.*
- *'Deliberately not delivered after payment'.*
- *'Bought concert tickets, paid but not supplied'.*
- *'A Dutch website offers designer shoes, but after much insistence they deliver fakes. Also it turned out that I still had to pay a huge amount in import costs. They promised me that they would refund me some of my money, but they never did'.*
- *'[In] the rules for participating in Binairy Options they lie to you. Once you have deposited the money they don't live up to your expectations and they don't stick to the deal. The organisation wants to extract even more money from you through empty promises'.*
- *'I ordered a product from China but it was not delivered. It involved a small sum of 3 euro'.*
- *'Placed an order online and paid properly and received something completely different to what I had ordered'.*
- *'I bought something but it was not delivered, they pretended it had been lost in the post. After that they were suddenly no longer reachable'.*
- *'Bought a laptop via Marktplaats but never received it'.*
- *'As a consequence of an ad I had looked up on Marktplaats I was called by the fraudster. Never heard anything again after transferring the money'.*
- *'Goods not delivered which had been paid for'.*
- *'Paid item not delivered'.*
- *'Fraud via Marktplaats'. Sale of iPad for the normal amount but it was not delivered'.*
- *'Offer a product, receive payment and not delivered'.*
- *'The product that was offered was not delivered. Another, similar product was delivered'.*
- *'Website with items for sale, order, pay in advance and not delivered'.*
- *'Software ordered (38 euro) and received incomplete (no activation code) and lost the communication (e-mail). The bank could not give me any details because I wasn't a client of RABO'.*
- *'Paid in advance for a booking and then never delivered the service, no refund'.*
- *'Sale via a webshop, paid in advance via Ideal, confirmation of payment receipt e-mail, ordered goods have never been received to this day'.*
- *'Swindled out of 46.75 by someone who said they had a saddle for a motorbike. Blindly transferred the money without even googling his name first, probably called using a prepaid number so I couldn't find out who he was. That was the first time I was caught now I watch out and don't trust anyone anymore when I buy online, even if it's just for a few bucks. Fortunately I learnt a lot from it'.*

- *'Website which offered toys that you couldn't get anywhere else anymore. In this case it was a walking doll. Because it wasn't available anywhere else and your child really wants it, you take the chance and transfer the money'.*
- *'Invoice payable in arrears. The invoice was never paid and the order was delivered to a house that was up for sale. The real estate agent was not able to help me. Maybe he was involved. False name, fake telephone number, afterwards I saw the search term "jewellery payable in arrears" in my stats. Stupid of me'.*
- *'Webshop'.*

Social engineering, electronic payment traffic fraud and other kinds of fraud
- *'[Someone] called on behalf of Microsoft for a security issue, convinced me they would solve the security issue for a small sum of money, paid online and subsequently (much more) money was taken out of my account'.*
- *'You're called to find out whether you can open an e-mail. And then you have to print it and sign it and send it back. This is to not extend the contract to be in a booklet, but if you check the small print you're actually signing a contract'.*
- *'Bought all kinds of things with my CC. They probably broke into my PC and hacked the CC details. Address information details known to Police, didn't do anything about it'.*
- *'Unlawful use of credit card information'.*
- *'Paypal fraud'.*
- *'Via a bank transaction from the netherlands to england'.*
- *'Ordered goods via a (reliable) internet shop after which this shop was hacked and details were stolen'.*
- *'You want to do it for your company. Seems like fun, which is why I did it a couple of times, but you don't get anywhere with it. It cost me Euro 1,500 in 1 year. Now I don't take part in anything anymore as standard practice, so the good has to suffer alongside the bad. I am a member of the Advertising Fraud Support Centre. If I think something is dodgy or I have doubts, I get in touch with them'.*
- *'Someone visited my site and thought there's something up for grabs here'.*
- *'Phantom invoice'.*
- *'Front man, name and address known. Bank acct no. too. The police "closed" the case due to lack of evidence. Tens of thousands of euros. All the names were known to the group of victims within a week. In other words...'.*
- *'Via information from the Chamber of Commerce'.*
- *'Via e-mailing (fake mail) requested a new sim card (without me knowing)'.*

Bankcard skimming modi operandi
Twenty-seven of the 47 one-man businesses that had fallen victim to skimming described how their bankcards had presumably been skimmed. Given the nature of the offence, it is no surprise that most of the victims described that manipulated payment equipment had been used for the skimming. What is remarkable, however,

is that cyber criminals seem to focus on manipulating payment systems used at (unmanned) fuel stations. Nevertheless, PIN machines at other places are also manipulated, for instance, at restaurants, train stations or parking garages. Also, a few quotes raise the suspicion that card-related payment details are also extracted online, for instance, when buying products via webshops or when making reservations for hotels.

Text Box 5.7: Quotes from victims whose bankcards have been skimmed

Fuel stations, manned and unmanned

- *'POS terminal at station'.*
- *'POS terminals at fuel station'.*
- *'Copied my card details at an unmanned fuel station'.*
- *'Card copied when filling up [at petrol station] and they were sold on to china'.*
- *'Skimming equipment was installed at an unmanned fuel station'.*
- *'Card reader had been modified at a fuel station'.*
- *'PIN code was copied when filling up [at petrol station] without staff. After that money was withdrawn from my account from Mexico'.*
- *'Fuel card skimmed when filling up at an unmanned fuel station in the neighbourhood'.*
- *'Skimming at a petrol pump the bank drew my attention to it'.*
- *'Via a POS terminal at the petrol station'.*
- *'Via ATM at fuel station'.*
- *'DEBIT CARD details were copied when filling up with debit card in zoeterwoude'.*
- *'Skimming at the pump by foreigners I heard. The police also fill up there and they noticed it and the perpetrators were arrested. The money that had disappeared out of my account was refunded'.*

Manipulation of payment systems other than at fuel stations

- *'Credit card copied in a restaurant'.*
- *'Debit card skimmed at the train station'.*
- *'Card skimmed in supermarket or at ATM'.*
- *'ATM at parking garage'.*
- *'Credit card skimmed with payment in a restaurant/café in the United Kingdom'.*
- *'Someone skimmed my debit card while I was drawing money out of the ATM'.*

Other quotes

- *'I made a private purchase, with my credit card, I never got that product. A few weeks later 3,000 euro worth of gift vouchers were bought from Amazon.com, which I had not done. Incidentally, the credit card insurance company sorted everything out and the amount was refunded in full. Since then I've been a bit more careful ... but the sales website looked legitimate ... so yes, what can you do'.*
- *'Credit card details provided were extracted from a hotel that was booked'.*
- *'Credit card skimmed'.*

- *'Credit card details skimmed'.*
- *'I was sent a notification that my card had been invalidated because I had made a transaction at an ATM where someone had fallen victim to skimming'.*
- *'No, the ING dealt with it'.*
- *'Debit card skimming'.*
- *'Skimming from a POS terminal'.*

Phishing modi operandi

Eight of the victims who most recently experienced phishing described how the perpetrators set to work (Text Box 5.8). The quotes indicate that cyber criminals get their hands on the e-mail addresses of entrepreneurs. They then try to extract information, like passwords, from entrepreneurs by e-mail in which the criminals sometimes masquerade as trustworthy financial institutions.

Text Box 5.8: Quotes from phishing victims
- *'Sent an e-mail'.*
- *'E-mail in which the sender pretends to be a financial institution'.*
- *'Sending fake e-mail messages that encourage people to make online payments and/or disclose personal information. VB credit card, ING, CJIB, Ideal...'.*
- *'Try to find out business information (mainly Chamber of Commerce number and account number) by e-mail'.*
- *'Via an e-mail, with one of our names as sender, so that we opened the e-mail. After that our e-mail was hacked, after which we changed all our passwords'.*
- *'An e-mail was sent via a mobile phone which looked a lot like the bank in terms of layout etc. They then asked for my details'.*
- *'Password extracted using a fake e-mail'.*
- *'Phantom invoices after advertisements had been placed'.*

Hacking modi operandi

Ten of the hacking victims (n = 33) explained what the hackers' modi operandi (presumably) were. Hackers use various ways to gain unauthorised access to IT. The results show, for instance, that login information is discovered – sometimes obtained using scripts written for that purpose – and that hackers also look for security leaks. As was the case in previous research, including the research among Dutch SMEs, the quotes indicate that hacking is not a goal in itself. As a number of the quotes illustrate, hacking often has an underlying objective, like being able to send spam or disabling websites.

Text Box 5.9: Quotes from hacking victims
- *'They managed find out what the administrator login was by using password scripts'.*
- *'They posed as microsoft problem solvers'.*
- *'Broke into hosting server'.*
- *'It was done through an unprotected router which had just been connected and was searching around in the server and downloading info'.*
- *'Our (old) website was hacked and used to send spam'.*
- *'Via a leak in Joomla'.*
- *'Via scripts that test for security leaks in online software. After renaming a few folders we haven't had any more problems so far'.*
- *'Finding out passwords'*
- *'Hacked my passwords from my hosting firm and website and so everything went down'.*
- *'They got into the system via the login pages'.*

DoS modi operandi

Although no impression can be gained based on the nine quotes from DoS attacks victims about the working methods of these cyber criminals, the explanations that victims give suggest that DoS attacks are not always directed against entrepreneurs specifically. People operating one-man businesses repeatedly described how the DoS attacks were not directed against them specifically, but rather at the companies that host their websites, for instance.

Text Box 5.10: Quotes from DoS attack victims
- *'Attack on the servers of the internet firm that manages them and to whom I outsourced it'.*
- *'DDos'.*
- *'DDos attack on web server in hosting firm's data centre'.*
- *'A client of the company that hosts my website and stores my data on its server launched an unsafe website, after which the other clients had problems. I had problems with my e-mails, I could receive e-mails on my business address but couldn't send. Other e-mail addresses did work so I could still send my e-mails. Didn't encounter any noticeable problems with other applications, for instance internet banking'.*
- *'First twitter was hacked, and after that the website'.*
- *'Put a lot of messages on Wordpress website'.*
- *'A lot of requests from non-existent elements from a network which meant that the network wasted a lot of time finding out that the requested object didn't exist and so didn't get round to doing normal work'.*
- *'Via pop unders from visited websites'.*
- *'E-mail account password cracked hence spam was sent from my e-mail'.*

Modi operandi for other offences

In addition to the explanations from victims about the most common types of cyber-crime, we also listed the other descriptions of the modi operandi per offence. As far as other offences were concerned, most of the victims' explanations were about identity abuse, cyber defamation and unauthorised use of company networks. For this reason, these offences are mentioned separately in the text below.

Identity abuse

Fourteen of the 18 victims who were most recently confronted with identity abuse explained how the perpetrator set to work. The quotes illustrate that identity information is misused for a variety of objectives: criminals try to avoid bills by using other people's identities, the identity (e-mail addresses) of victims are used to send spam and identities are misused to create fake internet pages and/or to cast aspersions on a person's good name.

Text Box 5.11: Quotes from identity abuse victims

Identity abuse

- *'Orders were placed using my business details. The criminal created an e-mail address using my contact details my address and acct. number, tel no etc. Things were ordered and collected from a petrol station. And then the bill was sent to my address'.*
- *'They found out my personal details + bank account number and placed orders and took out subscriptions'.*
- *'A company had other personal details, but they linked my account number to them'.*
- *My business e-mail address was used by a spambot. It was possible because my e-mail address was not on my site as an image, but as a text. It has been changed and now I don't have problems anymore'.*
- *'E-mails were sent to other people with (non-existent) e-mail addresses from my domain. The domain registration was public and so everyone could see it. One of the e-mail recipients informed me of this. You can quite easily send e-mails on behalf of someone else using an SMTP. I informed the provider who manages the SMTP server of this'.*
- *'The name of one of my domains was used to send spam'.*
- *'An FB page was opened using the company name'.*
- *'Sending adverts from me via facebook'.*
- *'Put a film shot on a smartphone on youtube without asking'.*
- *'Stole a photo from the internet and published it under another name'.*
- *'I think via access to my laptop by the administrator of my site and software'.*
- *'Unprotected login at an airport in Africa ... that's where it must have happened'.*
- *'Randomly tried to break into twitter accounts'.*
- *'Trust betrayed and "stole" info'.*

Cyber defamation/slander

Cyber defamation occurs in various ways. It emerged from the 12 quotes from a total of 16 victims that the internet offers criminals the opportunity to make negative statements about victims or their companies in a relatively easy fashion. For instance, incriminating and/or false information is spread on review websites and/or via social media. The objective is to besmirch a person's honour or reputation.

> **Text Box 5.12: Quotes from victims of cyber defamation**
> Cyber defamation
> - *'Personal images of me were put on gay contact websites'.*
> - *'By giving incriminating and false information to the media who were looking for it and then through press releases'.*
> - *'Somebody put an undue negative reaction about my shop on Google'.*
> - *'Looked up my company online and checked out the portfolio. Then e-mailed me using very threatening language and tried to approach the clients in my portfolio about my "practices" in order to destroy me'.*
> - *'Spreading negative [information] via social media'.*
> - *'An acquaintance created a fake profile of me on a social media site'.*
> - *'Incorrect review via my business Facebook page when I don't know the person. But Facebook doesn't do anything about it?? I blocked the person because he was also doing things on my private page'.*
> - *'Twitter and facebook'.*
> - *'Providing false information online'.*
> - *'Spreading sensitive info and slander to private contacts'.*
> - *'Made very negative comments via the company page while the person in question was not known to my company, and then referring people to another company'.*
> - *'Accused of inappropriate conduct via e-mail and a blog. It was meant for someone else'.*

The question that the quotes about cyber defamation raise is whether criminal law is always the appropriate means for tackling the problems. Ultimately it depends on the case whether action can be taken based on criminal law against 'an (unjustified) negative reaction' on Google or on a company page.

Unauthorised use of company networks

The 7 descriptions from the 14 victims whose networks were used by people who did not have the authority to do so were not specific enough to be able to form a description of the method used by these cyber criminals. What the quotes did point to, however, was that company networks are misused for a variety of objectives, for instance, to send spam or to place orders.

> **Text Box 5.13: Quotes from victims about the unauthorised use of company networks**
> Unauthorised use of company networks
> - *'By a request via e-mail'.*
> - *'Fake telephone call from a so-called Microsoft help desk. Called several times a month, always hung up straight away because I didn't trust it. Eventually I had a computer problems after which I was called that same day. At first I gave them access but after a few minutes I didn't trust it, I broke the internet connection, hung up the phone and immediately took the laptop in question to a computer shop and had them format and install everything again so that I was sure that there was no malware or other software like "key logger" installed without my permission'.*
> - *'My domain provider did not protect me adequately'.*
> - *'Extracted personal details from the company website and used them to place an order, company account is/was used regularly to send spam'.*
> - *'Via the contact form on the website which was not protected with a CAPTCHA which meant that e-mails could be also be sent again from the e-mail address that was linked to the contact form'.*
> - *'Wifi network hacked'.*
> - *'Depends what the definition of cybercrime is. That person didn't do it deliberately. But the problem that arose was rather serious for a "mistake" like that'.*

Other offences

Text Box 5.14 contains descriptions of the way in which other offences were committed. There are not many descriptions of the modi operandi for each offence, but the quotes do illustrate – from the victims' perspectives – how the various offences were carried out.

> **Text Box 5.14: Quotes from victims about the perpetrators' modi operandi for cybercrime offences other than the most common**
> Cyberstalking
> - *'I once asked for information about a job, I then decided against it because the additional costs were too high. After that I was bombarded by e-mails for weeks (?!) full of payment notices and financial threats (bailiffs and so on)'.*
> - *'Not very special, but continuously being harassed by e-mails with strange texts and proposals to meet.'*
> - *'Stalking is being harassed on the internet. Especially on Twitter and forums'.*
> - *'It was based on Private circumstances but IJsselland Police never wanted to deal with it'.*
> - *'I was bothered with nasty texts via Facebook. When it didn't stop, I removed the contact'.*
>
> Defacing
> - *'Hacked from an outdated version of PhPBB'.*
> - *'Leak in the protection of web software that I used'.*

- *'Old system via Joomla which had a leak. I knew about it and I updated the site immediately'.*
- *'Outdated Joomla website'.*

Theft of data
- *'All my website pages were grabbed'.*
- *'Via phishing and identity theft'.*
- *'See the publications based on information from Edward Snowden'.*

Data destruction
- *'Scam software installed on the web server'.*
- *'My website was hacked to send spam. Webreus and Google blocked my website, I uploaded a new, clean website and changed the password, problem solved, now I change login details more often and use safe passwords'.*

Cyber extortion
- *'Registration in a kind of commercial register, later they wanted money for it'.*

Cyber blackmail
- *'They were looking for me in africa and I had to pay lots of money, or something like that. The FBI were looking for me, etc. Someone had a job for me. I didn't respond and got a fine of a million euro. Play the lottery'.*

Cyber espionage
- *'Intercepting internet traffic and from servers of SAAS providers'.*

Summary
Based on a summary of research into cybercrime conducted so far, McGuire and Dowling (2013) concluded that not much was known about cyber criminals and their methods. One-man business owners also do not know much about the way in which cybercrime is committed. Although one-man business owners generally knew more about the modi operandi of the perpetrators than SMEs, the research among SMEs led to the same conclusion. It was not generally known who the perpetrator is, from which country the most recent cybercrime that victims encountered was committed, and how the perpetrator set to work. There was a lack of knowledge in particular about the modi operandi for cybercrimes in the narrow sense, more so than about the way criminals set to work in the broader sense, such as e-fraud.
Although the majority of the cases were domestic as opposed to international in nature, almost 15 per cent of the offences encountered were suspected to have been committed from abroad. This means that cybercrime, including the relatively minor cases, crosses national borders and that the police are confronted with suspects operating from abroad in a substantial proportion of cases. That said, 80 per cent or more

of the offences were committed from within the Netherlands. Measures aimed at fighting cybercrime should therefore still primarily be aimed at the domestic situation.
The case descriptions suggest that cybercrime is not generally rooted in interpersonal conflicts. Cybercrime among one-man businesses is more inclined to be untargeted, as could once again be deduced from the descriptions of incidents put forward by the victims.

*5.3.4		Severity of and damage from the most recent incident*

This section describes the severity of and damage incurred by cybercrime based on the most recently experienced incident. The results from the research among one-man businesses are also compared to the research findings from the SME survey.

One-man business people generally rated the most recent cybercrime incident as not serious (21.3%) or neutral (44.5%) (see Figure 5.25). Nonetheless, more than a third were confronted with cybercrime and rated it as serious. Moreover, more one-man business owners judged falling victim to cybercrime to be serious than SMEs did: 34.2 per cent of one-man businesses rated the most recent incident as serious versus 26.3 per cent of SMEs.

Figure 5.25 The extent to which companies view being confronted with cybercrime as serious (n = 447 one-man businesses, 335 SMEs)*

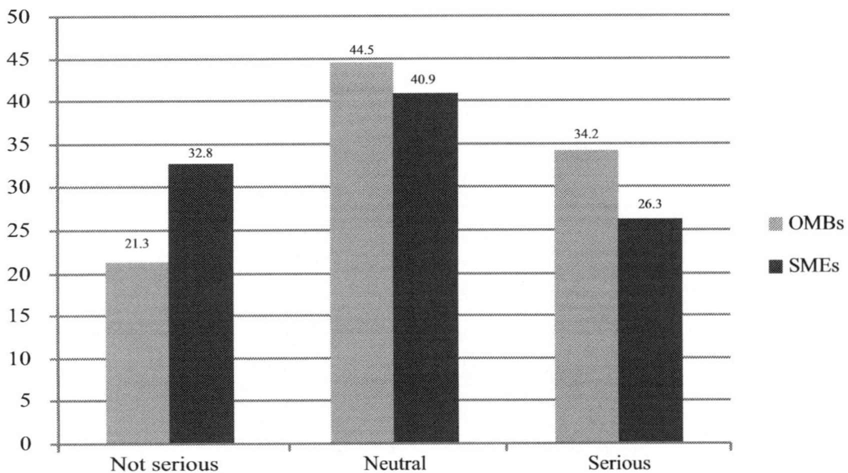

Table 5.9 offers additional insight into the severity of most common offences. The severity for each offence is compared with the experienced severity of the other offences.

Table 5.9   Perceived seriousness of the most recently experienced cybercrimes

	Not serious	Neutral	Serious
Total number of victims (n = 447)	21.3	44.5	34.2
Malware (n = 150)**	30.0	50.0	20.0
E-fraud (n = 60)**	11.7	38.3	50.0
Bankcard skimming (n = 47)**	19.1	25.5	55.3
Phishing (n = 38)*	34.2	50.0	15.8
Hacking (n = 33)	9.1	57.6	33.3
DoS attack (n = 32)	15.6	46.9	37.5

*Difference with 'all other victims than those in this category' ** ($p < 0.01$), * ($p < 0.05$).*

Victimisation due to malware and phishing were considered to be less serious than victimisation due to other offences. Additional analysis demonstrates that the absence of damage offers an explanation for this: the damage that victims reported for malware and phishing was significantly less extensive than for the other offences. The opposite applies to victims of e-fraud: they were more likely to view their victimisation as serious and they also experienced a higher level of damage than victims of other offences. The same also applies to victims whose bankcards were skimmed: they were significantly more likely to rate being a victim as serious than victims of the other offences were. There is, however, no correlation with damage suffered in this case: the extent to which skimming victims suffered damage as a consequence of the cybercrime they experienced did not differ from the extent to which other victims suffered damage. A possible explanation for this is that banks compensate financial damages suffered as a consequence of skimming. However, this still does not explain why skimming is considered to be relatively serious.

Embarrassed and angry
Mr Kolsteeg received an e-mail from someone he knew and opened the link in the e-mail. Malware was then installed on his computer and e-mails with the same link were sent from his address to his contacts. E-mails were also sent to his clients and that gives a bad impression: 'I was embarrassed and was furious with the perpetrator. The information that is extracted from you is not valuable, yet it is important to your sense of privacy.' Mr Kolsteeg compares it to the theft of a photograph album. The photos are much more valuable to you than they are to the thief.

In addition to the severity of cybercrime, we also analysed the associated damage (Figure 5.26). Two fifths of the one-man businesses (and almost 45% of SMEs) did not suffer any damage as a consequence of the most recent incident. That cybercrime does not normally result in damage is confirmed in research into cybercrime victimisation among members of the public (Hernandez-Castro et al., 2013). The most common kinds of damage are loss of time (24.8%) and financial damages (21.5%). These are also the kinds of damage reported most often by SMEs. SMEs, however, were significantly more likely to have to contend with loss of time than one-man businesses.

Figure 5.26   Damage suffered as a consequence of the most recent incident (n = 447 one-man businesses, n = 335 SMEs)

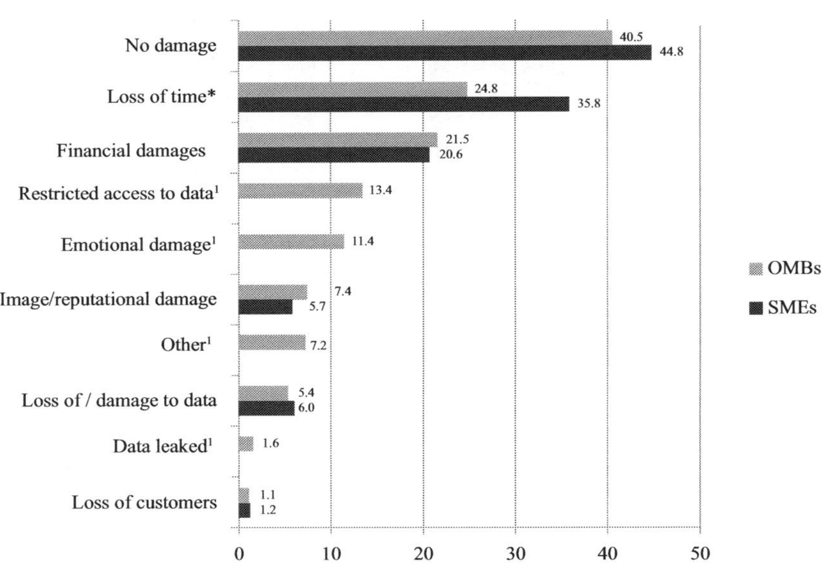

[1] SMEs were not asked this.

Respondents in the SME study were not asked whether they suffered damage due to restricted access to data and emotional damage. However, some of the open answers indicated that entrepreneurs did encounter these kinds of damage. Furthermore, it emerged in previous research among members of the public that cybercrime has an emotional impact on victims (Hernandez-Castro et al., 2013). Based on evolving insights, we gave one-man businesses the opportunity to indicate whether the most recent cyber incident led to restricted access to data and emotional damage. In response, 13.4 and 11.4 per cent of one-man businesses reported limited access to data and emotional damage respectively as damage. Other losses were experienced by less than 1 in 10 victims. Although respondents were given the opportunity, none of the victims said that they had 'gone bankrupt' as a consequence of cybercrime. The claim that a company had gone bankrupt was indeed partly a reason for conducting this research. This finding means that the number of bankruptcies as a consequence of cybercrime is probably small. Despite this, it should be noted that the possibility exists that one-man businesses that went bankrupt due to cybercrime would not have been part of our sample because they would have deregistered with the Chamber of Commerce or because they would have indicated at the beginning of the questionnaire that they had not been operating (and would have stopped completing the questionnaire, see Section 3.2.4.).

Respondents were given the opportunity to explain the damage incurred in an open answer field. Text Box 5.15 contains quotes regarding these explanations. The quotes illustrate the kind of emotional damage that cybercrime can lead to, for instance.

> **Text Box 5.15: Explanations of the damage incurred**
> - *'Damage to software. Web browser among other things'.*
> - *'…disquiet, because your know that someone else has your information. Login name, passwords and those kinds of things'.*
> - *'I got a huge fright when I saw myself on the screen through my webcam, you don't expect something like that. Then you immediately start thinking, who can see that??'*
> - *'Violation of your sense of security'.*
> - *'Irritation and damage to trust in digital possibilities'.*
> - *'Uncertainty and trust has gone'.*
> - *'Unsafe feeling about who and where my details are, like e-mail and ip addresses'.*
> - *'Website and mail server were temporarily unavailable'.*
> - *'Was bombarded with porn sites'.*
> - *'Could not use operating assets temporarily, asset denied access'.*

So the damage suffered varied. At the same time, it is apparent that the damage as a consequence of the most recent incident experienced was offence specific. Table 5.10 demonstrates that victims of malware, skimming and phishing are more likely than victims of other offences not to report any damage. As far as malware is concerned, a good virus scanner can prevent and remedy damage. It probably is for this reason that malware victims generally did not suffer any damage because virtually all the respondents had a virus scanner. A possible explanation for the fact that financial damages were not incurred by victimisation from skimming and phishing may be because, under certain conditions, victims of these offences were compensated by their financial service providers. Another factor which may affect phishing is that attempts at phishing may have been reported as victimisation (see Section 5.3.1).

Another pattern emerged for e-fraud and hacking. Victims of these offences, on the other hand, are more likely to report damage. Damages from e-fraud are mainly financial in nature. This is not so strange given the definition of fraud – deception intended to result in financial gain (Leukfeldt et al., 2012a). Hacking victims mainly report losses relating to the manipulation of digital data. Given the nature of the offence, this can also be explained: after all, hackers gain unauthorised access to the victim's IT. This can result in restricted access to and loss of or damage to data.

Finally, it is noteworthy that victims of DoS attacks, who – given the nature of the offence – logically report restricted access to data more often than average, were also significantly more likely than victims of other kinds of cybercrime to report image/reputational damage. Perhaps the visibility of this offence to clients may offer an explanation for this because, for example, the entrepreneur's website may have been offline due to the attack.

Table 5.10   Types of damage reported by victims as a consequence of the most recent incident

	Total (n = 447)	Malware (n = 150)	Fraud (n = 60)	Bankcard skimming (n = 47)	Phishing (n = 38)	Hacking (n = 33)	DoS (n = 32)
No damage	40.5	*47.3	**16.7	**61.7	**76.3	*24.2	25.0
Loss of time	24.8	30.0	*11.7	12.8	10.5	30.3	34.4
Financial damages	21.5	**9.3	**75.0	23.4	**0.0	18.2	15.6
Restricted access to data	13.4	12.7	5.0	4.3	5.3	**30.3	**34.4
Emotional damage	11.4	*6.0	8.3	8.5	2.6	15.2	6.3
Loss of/damage to data	5.4	6.0	0.0	0.0	2.6	**24.2	6.3
Image/reputational damage	7.4	*2.7	*0.0	*0.0	0.0	6.1	**21.9
Data leaked	1.6	1.3	0.0	0.0	0.0	3.0	0.0
Loss of customers	1.1	0.0	0.0	0.0	0.0	3.0	3.1

*Difference with 'all other victims than those in this category' ** ($p < 0.01$), * ($p < 0.05$).*

Financial damages

Rounded off, 22 per cent of one-man businesses (n = 96) suffered financial damages as a consequence of the most recently encountered cyber incident (Figure 5.26). This means that 5.9 per cent of all one-man businesses incurred damage from cybercrime. Of the 96 one-man businesses that suffered financial damages, 87 also reported the extent of the damages they incurred. Damages reported as a consequence of the most recent incident vary considerably and range from 14 to 55,000 euro. There is little point in calculating an average amount of loss because of this dispersion. We did, however, calculate the overall financial damages: it amounted to € 235,568.

There is no significant difference in the percentages of one-man businesses and SMEs who were financially disadvantaged by cybercrime (see Figure 5.26). Compared to SMEs, it seems as though the financial damages suffered by one-man businesses were not as great. The 59 SMEs that reported damages jointly reported € 442,953 euro in damages: a significantly higher amount than the amount of loss among one-man businesses (€ 235,568), spread across fewer respondents. The fact that one SME reported € 240,000 in damages does, however, contribute significantly to that difference. If we do not take into consideration this one outlier, then there is no longer any reason to suspect that there is a difference between one-man businesses and SMEs, because then damages of approximately two hundred thousand euro remain (€ 202,953).

Finally, comparing the extent of the financial damages with the results from other research is no simple task: according to McGuire and Dowling (2013) various caveats can be placed on publications in which estimates of the costs incurred through cybercrime were made. Moreover, the comparability of publications in which financial damages are reported is limited.

5.3.5   *Reactions of victims*

We asked one-man businesses that had fallen victim to cybercrime which actions they had taken as a consequence of the most recent incident that they had experienced (see Figure 5.27).[12] One in five one-man business owners took no action as a consequence of the most recently experienced cyber incident (19.0%). When entrepreneurs did take action, they were mainly self-reliant: the biggest group solved the problems arising from cybercrime themselves (34.7%) and/or took measures to prevent cybercrime victimisation in the future (20.1%). Other measures, for instance, attempting to seek compensation themselves (9.4%), contacting an interest group (5.6%) or engaging a legal service provider (2.0%), were taken by fewer respondents. The SMEs' reactions were broadly similar (see Figure 5.27). The only action taken by one-man businesses which differed from those of SMEs was the likelihood of one-man businesses contacting the police. One-man businesses were significantly more likely to do so than SMEs.

Figure 5.27   Actions taken as a consequence of victimisation (n = 447 one-man businesses, 335 SMEs)

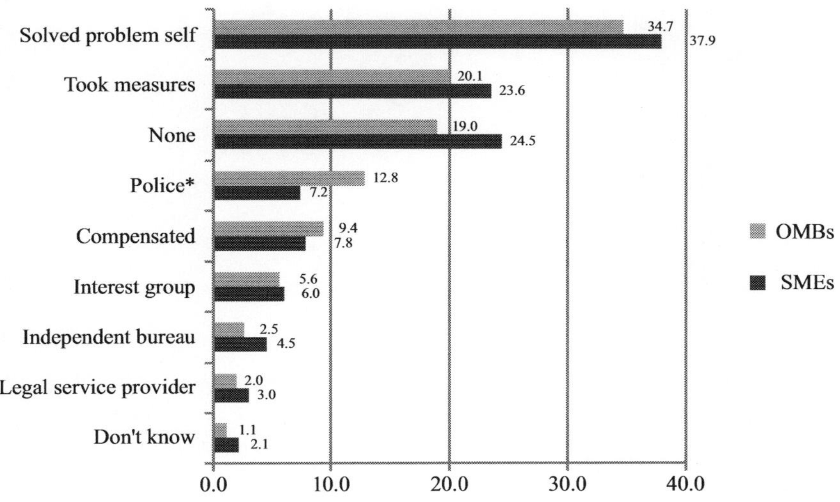

12. From 23 in-depth interviews with one-man business owners who experienced *attempts* at cybercrime, it is apparent that they mainly get in touch with the bank (n = 9). This is linked to the fact that most of the interview respondents had to deal with attempts at phishing (n = 15). In addition, some one man business owners who experienced cybercrime attempts contacted interest groups (n = 4). Despite the fact that these were merely attempts, most one-man businesses did consequently take action. The police, however, were not contacted after these attempts, because attempts were not considered to be 'worthy of contacting the police', respondents did not see the point of doing so nor were they prepared to take the time or make the effort required for this. The two respondents who did contact the police after attempts did not get any feedback about their report.

Research conducted among members of the public in the United Kingdom shows that most cybercrime victims did not take action. The reason for this that was mentioned most often is that the victims were capable of solving the problems themselves (Hernandez-Castro et al., 2013; McGuire & Downing, 2013). It emerged from the interviews with one-man business owners that no actions were taken because their protection was already adequate and the victimisation was the consequence of bad luck. A noteworthy difference with the results of the research conducted by Hernandez-Castro et al. (2013) is that if victims among members of the public take action, they tend to contact financial service providers and internet service providers, while entrepreneurs the Netherlands, if they involved a third party, were more inclined to first contact the police.
In addition to the response options given on the questionnaire, respondents were given the opportunity to give other answers. Various people one-man business owners took the opportunity to do so, mainly to clarify the measures they had taken. Text Box 5.16 contains illustrative quotes about the actions taken by one-man businesses.

> **Text Box 5.16: Explanations about the actions taken**
> - *'Informed the bank'.*
> - *'Contacted the bank'.*
> - *'Installed protective software from the bank'.*
> - *'Called in "E-Bay", the middleman, to enforce the protection E-Bay provides to buyers'.*
> - *'Informed the service provider'.*
> - *'Provider sorted it out'.*
> - *'Called the website administrator, who said: we know about the attack, it will resolve itself'.*
> - *'Better virus scan'.*
> - *'Updated the relevant software'.*
> - *'Wrote to the suspect myself'.*
> - *'Spoke to a former hacker'.*
> - *'Moved my websites to a safe host address, sites are better protected'.*
> - *'We had an old PC and we bought a new one which I think is properly protected with macfee'.*

We carried out an additional analysis to establish whether the actions taken by one-man businesses depend on the type of offence that was experienced (see Table 5.11). The results suggest that it is mainly the victims of cybercrime in the narrow sense, like hacking and malware, who are self-reliant. They were more likely than victims of other offences to be in a position to solve the problems arising from cybercrime themselves and – in cases involving hacking – to take measures to avoid falling victim to cybercrime in the future. E-fraud victims are significantly less likely to be self-reliant and are therefore more inclined to engage other parties, such as the police or legal service providers. This finding is linked to the relatively serious financial damages suffered by e-fraud victims. Just like one-man business people whose debit cards have been skimmed, e-fraud victims were therefore more inclined to try and get compensation (via other parties). Generally speaking, phishing is an offence against which no action is taken.

Table 5.11   **Actions taken by victims**

Action	Total (n = 447)	Malware (n = 150)	Fraud (n = 60)	Bankcard skimming (n = 47)	Phishing (n = 38)	Hacking (n = 33)	DoS (n = 32)
None	19.0	20.0	*8.3	21.3	**44.7	9.1	25.0
Solved problem themselves	34.7	**61.3	**3.3	**4.3	23.7	**60.6	28.1
Took measures	20.1	19.3	23.3	14.9	10.5	*36.4	18.8
Police	12.8	**4.7	**35.0	17.0	5.3	15.2	*0.0
Damages recovered	9.4	1.3	**28.3	**38.3	*0.0	0.0	0.0
Interest group	5.6	4.7	11.7	4.3	13.2	3.0	0.0
Independent firm	2.5	2.7	1.7	0.0	0.0	3.0	3.1
Legal service provider	2.0	*0.0	*6.7	2.1	2.2	0.0	0.0
Do not know	1.1	2.0	1.7	0.0	0.0	0.0	3.1

*Difference with 'all other victims than those in this category' ** ($p < 0.01$), * ($p < 0.05$).*

Contacted the police

Nearly 13 per cent (n = 57) of the one-man business owners got in touch with the police as a consequence of the most recently encountered cybercrime. Contacting the police correlates to the damage suffered as a consequence of the cybercrime (see also: Fischer et al., 2009, as cited in Schaper & Weber, 2012). Just like SMEs, one-man business owners who suffered damage were significantly more likely to contact the police than those that did not suffer damage (respectively 18.4% versus 4.4%). An additional analysis reveals moreover that the nature of the damage incurred influences the decision to contact the police. Victims who suffered financial damages, in particular, tended to contact the police. They were significantly more likely to do so than those victims who did not suffer financial damages. In comparison with victims of other offences, e-fraud victims were relatively more likely to have suffered financial damages and therefore they were significantly more likely to contact the police (see Table 5.10). Victims who suffered emotional damage were also more inclined to turn to the police (see Table 5.12).

Table 5.12   **The influence of the nature of the damage on calling in the police**

Damage	Did *not* experience this kind of damage and contacted the police	*Did* experience this kind of damage and contacted the police
Loss of time	13.3 (of n = 336)	11.7 (of n = 111)
Financial damages**	7.4 (of n = 351)	32.3 (of n = 96)
Restricted access to data	11.9 (of n = 387)	18.3 (of n = 60)
Emotional damage*	11.4 (of n = 396)	23.5 (of n = 51)
Loss of/damage to data	12.5 (of n = 423)	16.7 (of n = 24)
Image/reputational damage	12.3 (of n = 414)	18.2 (of n = 33)
Data leaked	12.7 (of n = 440)	14.3 (of n = 7)
Loss of customers	12.9 (of n = 442)	0.0 (of n = 5)

*** ($p < 0.01$), * ($p < 0.05$).*

In order to gain more insight into the reasons for contacting the police, we also asked respondents why they contacted the police as a consequence of the most recently encountered incident. SMEs were asked a similar question (see Figure 5.28).

Figure 5.28   Reason for contacting the police (n = 57 one-man businesses, 24 SMEs)

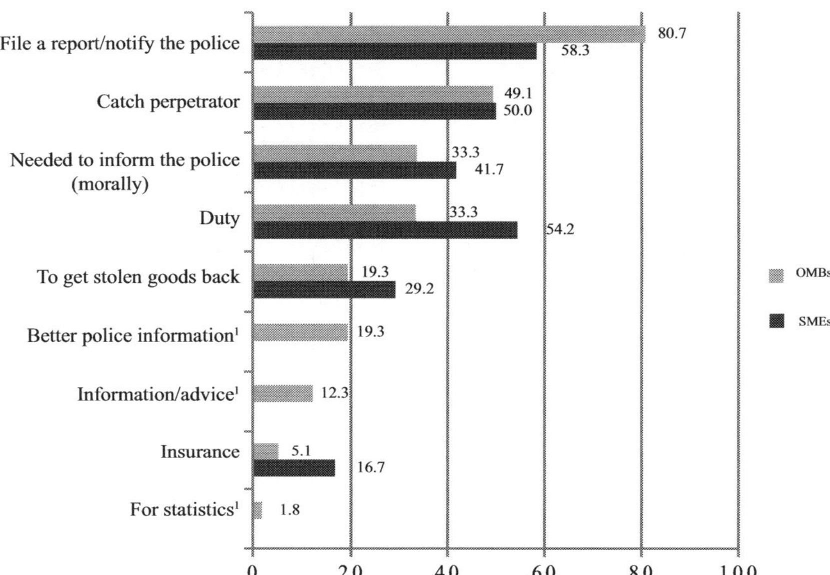

¹SMEs were not asked this.

The reason mentioned most often by one-man businesses for contacting the police was that they intended to file a report or to notify the police (80.7%). Almost half of the one-man businesses (also) indicated that they wanted the perpetrator to be caught (49.1%). A third of them were of the opinion that the police should be informed about the cybercrime incident and a similar number saw it as their duty to involve the police (33.3%). Nearly one in five one-man businesses gave as a reason for wanting to file a report that they wanted to get back what was stolen or that they wanted to contribute to improving police information (19.3%). Fewer one-man businesses mentioned that they wanted to approach the police to obtain information or advice (12.3%), for insurance purposes (5.1%) or to contribute to police statistics (1.8%).
The motives of one-man businesses for calling in the police were broadly similar to those of SMEs. More one-man businesses, however, mentioned notifying the police or filing a report as a reason than SMEs (80.7% versus 58.3%).

If reports are not filed, the police can do nothing
Mrs Alberts received an e-mail containing an invoice and paid it, but later it turned out to be a phantom invoice. She filed a report with the police online: 'We all think the police won't

> *do anything, but if things are not reported to the police, they can't do anything anyway.'*
> *Mrs Alberts did not have much confidence in the police, because in her view the police lack*
> *the knowledge required to solve these kinds of cases. The police took a statement and then*
> *she never heard from them again. The way they dealt with the case met her expectations, but*
> *she did note that the people/companies that commit these kinds of crimes are extremely dif-*
> *ficult to catch. She said that she would file a report again in future.*

One-man businesses mainly contact the police online (Figure 5.29). For this, they usually use the online reporting function on politie.nl (the Dutch police website) or the National Internet Fraud Hotline (LMIO; see also Inspectorate of Security and Justice [*Inspectie Veiligheid en Justitie*], 2015). Almost a third of the one-man businesses approached the police by going to the police station (31.6%) and 28.1 per cent contacted the police by telephone as a consequence of the most recent incident. It is quite rare for the police to visit the scene to discuss cybercrime cases (1.8%).

Figure 5.29 Ways of contacting the police (n = 57 one-man businesses, 24 SMEs)

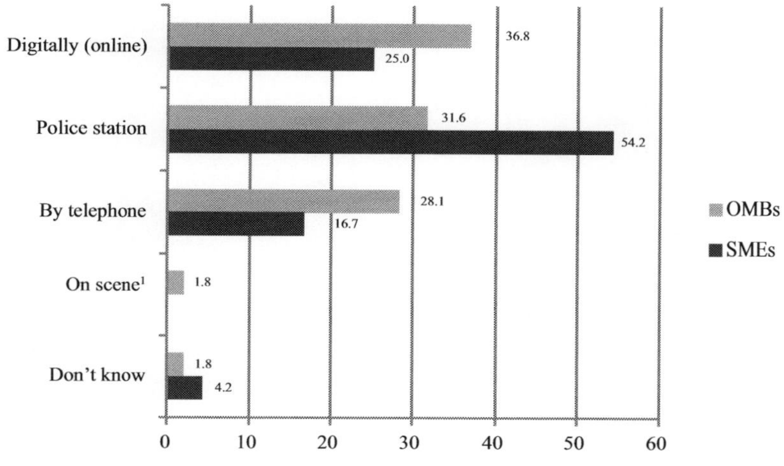

[1] SMEs were not asked this.

The reasons for choosing a specific channel to contact the police varied (see Table 5.13). One-man businesses that approached the police online did so mainly for reasons of convenience and/or to save time. Information on the internet about the options available for engaging the police online contributed to the decision to approach the police via digital means. The same applies to contacting the police by telephone. Choosing to go to the police station is principally inspired by the need for personal contact. One respondent said that the police visited the scene; the severity of the offence was the reason for this.

Table 5.13   Why was a specific channel chosen for contacting the police? (n = 56)[13]

	Total (n = 56)	Electronically (n = 21)	Police/Police station (n = 18)	By telephone (n = 16)	Came to the scene (n = 1)
Convenience/to save time	31.6	42.9	11.1	43.8	-
Because of information on internet	22.8	42.9	22.2	-	-
Because I needed personal contact	15.8	-	50.0	-	-
Because of the severity of the offence	14.0	-	22.2	18.8	100.0
Information and advice	14.0	14.3	5.6	25.0	-
I did not know there were other options	12.3	9.5	16.7	12.5	-
Because of previous positive experiences	1.8	-	-	6.3	-
On someone's recommendation	4.0	4.8	-	6.3	-

The police responded in various ways to their cybercrime workload (see Figure 5.30). When one-man businesses contact the police, the police generally registers a notification (35.1%). More than one in five of the one-man businesses that contacted the police said that an official report had actually been filed (21.1%).

Figure 5.30   What was the police response? (n = 57 one-man businesses, 24 SMEs)

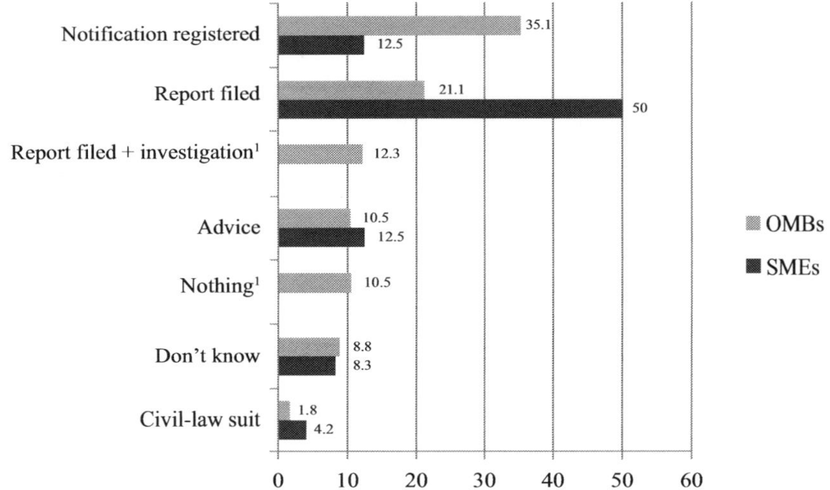

¹ SMEs were not asked this.

It is worth noting that the police registers notifications of one-man business owners more often than official reports, while the opposite is true for SMEs. The percentage of

---

13. The number of respondents per channel that indicated why they chose that channel comes to 56, while in total all 57 respondents who contacted the police were presented with this question. One of the respondents, however, did not know how the police had been contacted, so this response was not taken into consideration.

SMEs that filed a report is significantly higher than the percentage of one-man businesses that actually filed a report. Filing a report, however, does not guarantee that the police will conduct a criminal investigation. Previous research shows that the police closes the majority of cyber cases without any investigative actions (Leukfeldt, Veenstra, Domenie & Stol, 2012b). Yet 12.3 per cent of one-man businesses reported that the police filed a report and proceeded to investigate the case. In addition, 1 in 10 one-man business owners said that the police had provided advice (10.5%). The police were unable to help the same percentage of one-man businesses (10.5%) and some respondents did not know what the police response was (8.8%). Very occasionally the police told the informant that their report involved a civil case and that for this reason the police were unable to help (1.8%).

Previous research has already shown that members of the public and companies are more likely to notify the police or file a report about traditional kinds of crime than they are about cybercrime (see for instance CBS, 2015; Domenie et al., 2013; Home Office, 2013). This means, therefore, that the dark number for cybercrime is relatively high. The questions before us now are: how high is the dark number for cybercrime among companies and how much does it differ from the cybercrime dark number for members of the public? That only 12.8 per cent of one-man businesses and 7.2 per cent of SMEs involve the police in the event of cybercrime already points to the fact that the majority of cyber cases are not reported to the police. The cybercrime dark number also depends, however, on the police response. After all, if a notification or report is not filed, then the cybercrime will still remain outside the recorded crime statistics. For this reason, we also analysed the percentage of notifications or reports which were filed of all entrepreneurs who fell victim to cybercrime. Our analysis shows that 35.1 per cent of one-man businesses (n = 20) and 12.5 per cent of SMEs (n = 3) who contacted the police said that a notification was registered. That means that a notification was filed for 4.5 per cent of one-man businesses and 1 per cent of SMEs who fell victim to cybercrime.[14], [15] Fifty per cent of SMEs (n = 12) and 33.4 per cent of one-man businesses (n = 19) said that the police actually filed a report (whether or not the police proceeded to investigate the case). So reports were filed for 3.6 per cent of SMEs and 4.3 per cent of one-man businesses that fell victim to cybercrime and who contacted the police.[16, 17] Rates for notifying the police and filing reports were higher among members of the public. According to Statistics Netherlands (CBS, 2015), 13 per cent of cybercrime victims among members of the public notified the police and reports were actually filed for 7 per cent of these victims (either online or through filing a signed official report). So cybercrime among businesses remains invisible to the police to an even greater extent than cybercrime among members of the public.

---

14. Twenty out of a total of 447 one-man businesses that fell victim to cybercrime notified the police about it. That equates to $20/447 \times 100 = 4.5$ per cent of all one-man businesses that were victims of cybercrime.
15. Three out of a total of 335 SMEs that fell victim to cybercrime notified the police about it. That equates to $3/335 \times 100 = 0.9$ per cent of all SMEs that were victims of cybercrime.
16. Twelve out of a total of 335 SMEs that fell victim to cybercrime filed a report about it. That equates to $12/335 \times 100 = 3.6$ per cent of all SMEs that were victims of cybercrime.
17. Nineteen out of a total of 447 one-man businesses that fell victim to cybercrime filed a report about it. That equates to $19/447 \times 100 = 4.3$ per cent of all one-man businesses that were victims of cybercrime.

Satisfaction with the police
Of one-man businesses, 45.6 per cent were satisfied or very satisfied with the police response. A smaller group (29.8%) were dissatisfied or very dissatisfied about it. The percentage of one-man businesses that were satisfied or very satisfied about their contact with the police does not differ significantly from the percentage of satisfied or very satisfied SMEs. However, fewer one-man businesses were satisfied with their most recent contact with the police than members of the public were: Statistics Netherlands (CBS, 2015) claims that 59 per cent of the Dutch members of the public were satisfied with their most recent contact with the police. The percentage of satisfied or very satisfied members of the public is not, however, specifically related to cybercrime and so the percentage is limited in terms of comparability.

Figure 5.31   Satisfaction with contact with the police (n = 57 one-man businesses, 24 SMEs)[18]

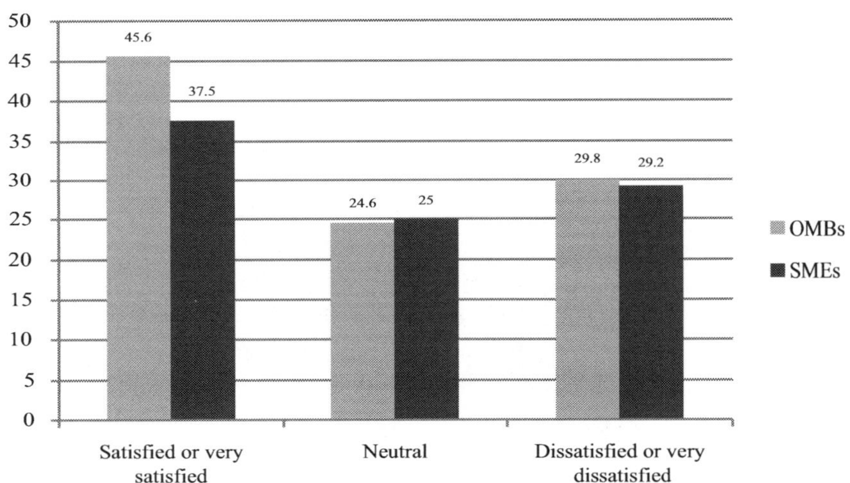

> **Satisfied with the police**
> *Mr Kuipers received an e-mail containing the so-called 'KLPD virus'. In a bogus e-mail, he was warned that illegally downloaded music or child pornography had been detected on his computer. He was ordered to make a payment within 24 hours. Mr Kuipers then called the police. The police told him that they were aware of the virus, which gave him confidence. Despite the fact that Mr Kuipers did not have to give them any details and he did not have to file a report about the incident, he was satisfied with the way the police handled the situation: they told him to go to a computer shop and have the virus removed, which he considered to be useful advice. In the event of any future victimisation, he would contact the police again.*

---

18. The percentage of SMEs that expressed an opinion about satisfaction with the police does not add up to 100 per cent because SMEs also had the option of entering 'Don't know' as a response. The two respondents who chose this option were not included in Figure 5.31.

There is a significant relationship between the police response and satisfaction with the police among one-man businesses (Table 5.14).[19] One-man businesses whose notifications or reports were not filed were mainly the ones inclined to be dissatisfied. Levels of satisfaction rose if a notification was filed and one-man businesses were most satisfied if a report was filed (whether or not the police proceeded to investigate the case). A similar finding also emerged in the first victim research into cybercrime among members of the public in the Netherlands (Domenie et al., 2013).

Table 5.14   Satisfaction among one-man businesses related to the police response (n = 57)*

	Satisfied or very satisfied	Neutral	Dissatisfied or very dissatisfied
No action taken	27.8	27.8	44.4
Notification	50.0	20.0	30.0
Report filed	57.9	26.3	15.8

Areas for improvement put forward most often by one-man businesses in terms of police response concerned giving feedback on the notification/report, being sure that a case was being handled and the speed at which the police worked (see Figure 5.32).

Figure 5.32   To what extent can the police improve their approach/handling of cybercrime according to one-man business people? (n = 57)[20]

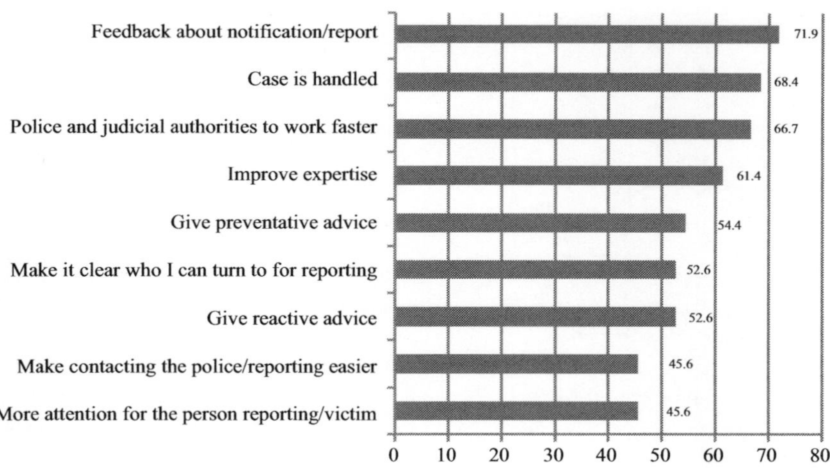

Not only one-man business people, but also SMEs, were asked how the police could improve the way they handle cybercrime. The results are, however, limited in terms of comparability because only the dissatisfied or very dissatisfied SME respondents were asked this question while the question was put to all one-man businesses (including those who were satisfied). Despite this, the results are primarily the same: dissatisfied SMEs,

---

19. Tested using Spearman's Rho, p < 0.05, $r = -0.28$, n = 57.
20. The percentages are the sum of the 'to a very large extent' and 'to a large extent' responses.

also found it important that they are given feedback about what happened to their notification/report, that the case they put forward is handled and that the speed at which the police and judicial authorities work is accelerated (see Figure 4.16 on page 99).

Views of one-man business people who did not contact the police
Rounded off, 13 per cent (n = 57) of one-man businesses who fell victim to cybercrime contacted the police. This means that 87 per cent (n = 390) of the one-man businesses did not contact the police as a consequence of the most recently encountered cybercrime. Consequently, cybercrime remains outside the field of view of the police and the criminal justice system to a large extent. Those respondents who did not involve the police were asked about their reasons for not contacting the police (Figure 5.33).

Figure 5.33   Reasons for not contacting the police (n = 390 one-man businesses, 311 SMEs)

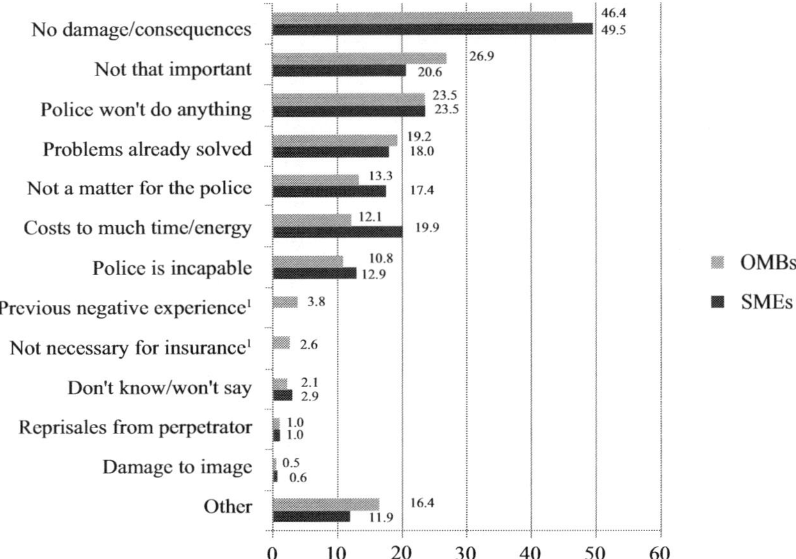

¹ SMEs were not asked this.

Lack of damage was the reason mentioned most often for not contacting the police (46.4%). We noted previously that victims who suffered damage, particularly financial damages, from cybercrime were more likely to contact the police than those who did not. This finding is in line with this. Also, some victims did not consider cybercrime victimisation to be important enough to involve the police (26.9%) and it is apparent (once again) that victims are self-reliant: some solved the problems which arose themselves (19.2%). Similar findings emerged in research into cybercrime among members of the public and businesses in England (Hernandez-Castro et al., 2013; McGuire & Dowling, 2013). McGuire and Dowling (2013, p. 7) summarised this as follows: 'Under-reporting occurred because incidents were perceived as too trivial and/or were dealt with internally'. Moreover, entrepreneurs take cost-benefit considerations into account (see also Demmer, 2014): contacting the police takes more effort than it is worth, so it is not done (12.1%).

In addition to these kinds of considerations, which show that victims consider it unnecessary to involve the police, another factor is the lack of confidence that entrepreneurs have in the knowledge and expertise of the police. Almost one in four entrepreneurs think that the police 'will not do anything anyway' about a notification or a report (23.5%) and around one in ten do not consider the police to be capable of counteracting cybercrime effectively (10.8%).

To all intents and purposes, there is little difference between the reasons given by SMEs and those put forward by one-man businesses for not involving the police. That said, a consideration that SMEs were more likely to mention than one-man businesses was that contacting the police requires too much effort.

More than 16 per cent also gave other reasons for not calling in the police. An analysis of the reasons for not contacting the police described in the open answer field shows that one-man businesses described why they did not contact the police (supplementary to or as an explanation for the selected response option(s) in the questionnaire). For instance, many respondents explained that the bank solved the problems or described why they thought that the police would not be capable of catching the perpetrator, for instance, because the perpetrator was in a foreign country. Fundamentally different reasons for not involving the police were that one-man businesses would not have thought of it and/or were not aware that they could report cybercrime to the police. For illustration purposes, a selection from the open answers is given in Text Box 5.17.

Text Box 5.17: Other reasons and explanations for not involving the police
- *'My bank had already sorted everything out'.*
- *'It is virtually impossible to tackle this kind of cybercrime'.*
- *'I thought that the police couldn't do anything about this sort of thing'.*
- *'Try and prove it'.*
- *'Mainly, the police CANNOT do anything about it. Maybe just for the stats, but that's too bad then. For this information they should create a SIMPLE website'.*
- *'International fraudster, seems to me that it is not a case for the local police, and impossible for the local police officer to just pop over to China to find out what's going on. The international sales site was held accountable for the actions of the perpetrator and they took action as an international company. What action may have been taken locally in China is not known'.*
- *'Had no idea where to file a report'.*
- *'I did not know that you should/can report it to the police'.*
- *'I didn't know it was possible'.*
- *'Didn't think of reporting the hacking of a website'.*
- *'Didn't occur to me'.*

An additional analysis showed that not contacting the police also depends (in part) on the type of cybercrime that the one-man business fell victim to most recently (see Table 5.15). We noted previously that engaging the police is linked to the damage suffered as a consequence of the cybercrime. This correlation emerged here once again: the reason mentioned most often for not contacting the police was an absence of damage or other negative consequences. That applies in particular to victims of malware and phishing. The opposite applies to victims of e-fraud and DoS attacks. They were significantly less likely than victims of other cybercrime offences to mention not having suffered damage as the most important reason for keeping the police out of it. The reason given by DoS victims not to involve the police was mainly because the offence they experienced was considered too trivial for this. Another factor that played was that this group of victims had already solved the problems thus contacting the police was rendered unnecessary. The fact that involving the police was unnecessary for insurance purposes was a reason mentioned by significantly more victims of skimming than by victims of other offences.

Table 5.15   Reasons for not contacting the police

Action	Total (n = 447)	Malware (n = 143)	Fraud (n = 39)	Bankcard Skimming (n = 39)	Phishing (n = 36)	Hacking (n = 28)	DoS (n = 32)
No damage	46.4	**60.1	**15.4	41.0	**72.2	32.1	*28.1
Not so important	26.9	30.5	20.5	5.1	25.0	39.3	*43.8
Not a matter for the police	13.3	11.9	15.4	10.3	8.3	14.3	25.0
The police will not do anything about it	21.0	18.2	30.8	12.8	16.7	25.0	25.0
The police are not capable	10.8	11.9	15.4	5.1	5.6	7.1	21.9
Previous negative experience	3.8	4.2	10.3	2.6	0.0	0.0	0.0
Not necessary for insurance purposes	2.6	0.7	5.1	*10.3[a]	0.0	0.0	3.1
Already solved	19.2	18.2	*5.1	*33.3	*2.8	32.1	*34.3
Reprisals from perpetrator	1.0	0.0	0.0	0.0	0.0	3.6	0.0
Damage to image	0.5	0.0	0.0	0.0	0.0	3.6	0.0
Takes too much time/effort	12.1	14.0	7.7	10.3	5.6	10.7	9.4
Do not know	2.1	2.1	5.1	0.0	0.0	0.0	0.0
Other	14.3	**8.4	28.2	**35.9	13.9	10.7	15.6

[a] Fisher's exact test.

*Difference with 'all other victims than those in this category' ** (p < 0.01), * (p < 0.05).*

The factors mentioned most often that may lead to companies contacting the police in the future (see Figure 5.34) are consistent with previous findings.

Once again, the reason mentioned most often for contacting the police would be if the victims suffered more financial and other damage (46.2%). Being certain that contacting the police would lead to the case being handled (30.3%) and improving feedback after a notification or report (21.5%) were also mentioned relatively frequently. In addition, self-reliance once again played a role: if one-man businesses were not able to solve the problems themselves, this increased the likelihood that the police would be contacted (25.6%). The lack of confidence in the expertise of the police noted earlier is reflected here in the desire to see police expertise improved (18.2%). In addition to this, more than one in ten victims would like information and/or tips about

Figure 5.34 Factors that would lead to victims contacting the police (n = 390 one-man businesses, 311 SMEs)

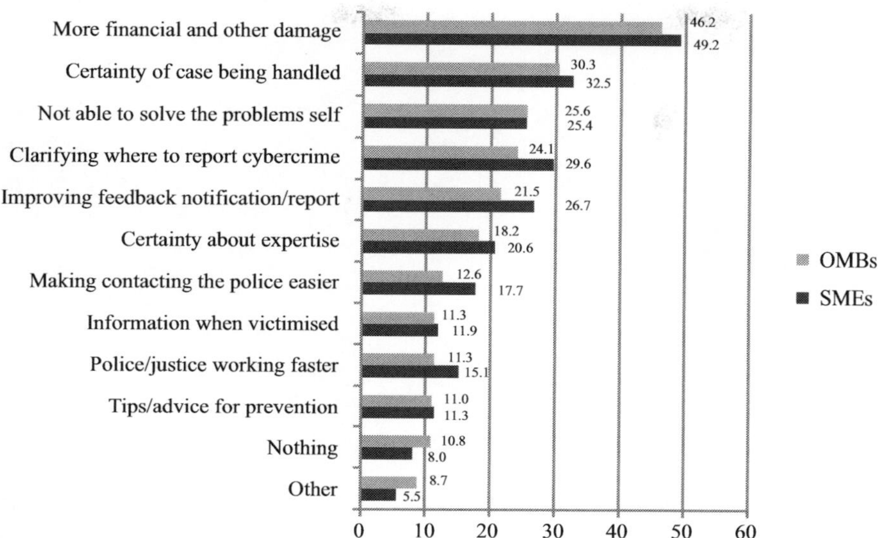

counteracting cybercrime, both in a preventative (11.0%) and reactive (11.3%) sense. Finally, more than one in ten respondents claimed that nothing would increase their willingness to turn to the police (10.8%).

Respondents were given the option of describing other factors that would lead them to contact the police in the future. The quotes from one-man business people make it clear that increasing willingness to involve the police depends on a variety of factors. A few additional clarifications are mentioned repeatedly. Several respondents tried to estimate whether the police would be capable of taking action against the suspected perpetrators. If one-man business people surmised that the police were capable of dealing with the problem, then they would be more inclined to contact them. Also, various one-man business owners said that they were not aware for which offences they could contact the police. Knowing which forms of deviant online behaviour can be reported to the police would improve reporting practices. The decision on whether or not to involve the police is also related to the nature of the offence: cybercrimes which target individuals directly do lead to contacting the police, while untargeted attacks (viruses, malware) are less likely to give cause to do so. Text Box 5.18 contains quotes about these recurring factors and a number of other considerations that play a role when deciding whether or not to contact the police.

Text Box 5.18: Quotes about factors which may lead to contacting the police
- *'If there was an indication of who the perpetrator was, or if I suspected that the offence had been committed in the Netherlands'.*
- *'If it was clear where the case came from'.*

- *'Perpetrator information'.*
- *'This is an international case which the police probably can't do much about. The only reason to file an official report would be if the insurance company required it or if it was required by the company, E-Bay in this case'.*
- *'If I knew what was an offence and what was not, and I'm not sure exactly'.*
- *'Knew that something like this could be reported'.*
- *'Didn't know that we could file a report'.*
- *'By reading somewhere that phishing could also be reported to the police?'*
- *'If there was a targeted attack, or a suspicion of intent. There is no targeted intent with infections from viruses and so on'.*
- *'If it becomes threatening'.*
- *'When it involves willful or political destruction, or theft or personal intimidation'.*
- *'If the police had enough manpower for this, which is not the case now'.*
- *'If I knew for sure that something would be done about it and that it would not cost me too much time. For a one-man business, every hour that you spend on other activities is an hour in which you don't earn any money. Then a cost-benefit analysis is quickly done and it normally tips the balance in favour of not taking action'.*
- *'If I could put into words exactly what went wrong then I would definitely communicate with the police. But often I don't understand what exactly happened but only know about the consequences'.*

Involving interest groups

In addition to questions about contacting the police, we also asked questions about contacting interest groups. The responses to these questions show that 5.6 per cent of one-man businesses that fell victim to cybercrime contacted an interest group as

Figure 5.35 One-man businesses' contact with interest groups (n = 447)

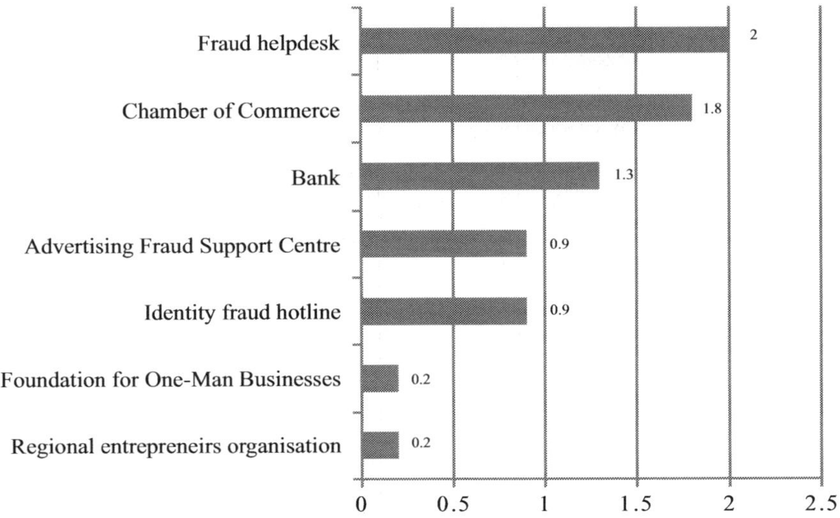

a consequence of the most recent incident (see Table 5.11). We asked one-man business owners which interest groups they had contacted (see Figure 5.35).

Interest groups were hardly, if at all, informed about cybercrime. Those one-man businesses that did contact them, were most likely to contact the fraud helpdesk (2%, n = 9) and the Chamber of Commerce (1.8%, n = 8). Six one-man businesses that called in an interest group contacted the bank (1.3%). Four contacted the Identity Fraud Hotline and/or the Advertising Fraud Support Centre (0.9%). The Foundation for One-Man Businesses in the Netherlands [*Stichting ZZP Nederland*] and/or other regional interest groups were approached by one respondent as a consequence of cybercrime (0.2%). Respondents were also given the opportunity to mention other interest groups in an open answer field. These answers revealed that ANBOS (a sector organisation for the beauty care industry) and a webshop were contacted.

The reasons mentioned most often for contacting an interest group were to obtain information and advice because, by doing so, victims wanted to increase the chance that the perpetrator would be caught and/or because victims consider it a duty to inform the interest group.

> **Fraude.nl**
> *In addition to filing an official report with the police, Mrs Alberts reported the advertising fraud to fraud.nl, to add a bit of 'force': 'The staff at fraude.nl said that they would get to work on it and, as a result, you hand it over to someone else.' Fraude.nl had received various reports about the company that had sent these invoices and they let her know that they were still busy with the case. The way fraude.nl handled the case met Mrs Alberts' expectations. She would report such incidents again in future.*

Summary

By their own account, victims of cybercrime are self-reliant: one-man businesses as well as SMEs mainly tried to solve the problems arising from cybercrime themselves and/or took steps to prevent victimisation in the future. There is a difference between the responses from victims of cybercrime in the narrow sense, like hacking and malware, and victims of e-fraud (cybercrime in the broad sense). Victims of cybercrime in the narrow sense were more likely to be self-reliant, while e-fraud victims were more inclined to contact other parties to fight cybercrime.

One-man businesses were significantly more likely to contact the police than SMEs: 12.8 per cent of one-man businesses (as opposed to 7% of SMEs) involved the police as a consequence of the most recently encountered cyber incident. Victims who suffered damage as a consequence of cybercrime were more likely to do so than victims who did not suffer damage. Financial damages, in particular, which are the kind that especially e-fraud victims face, increases the likelihood of one-man businesses calling in the police.

The reason mentioned most often for contacting the police was that entrepreneurs intended to notificate the police or to file a report. In this regard, one-man businesses indicated that they preferred to contact the police electronically, mainly because of the convenience and because it saves time. In more than a third of the instances that one-man businesses turned to the police because of cybercrime, the police recorded the notification and in one in five times that the police were contacted they filed a report. Notifying the police or filing an official report does not always mean that the police will start an investigation. According to 12 per cent of one-man businesses, the police proceeded to investigate the case after the report was filed. When converted to the total number of victims, rates for notifying the police and filing reports were higher among members of the public. Compared to the dark number for offline offences, the dark number for cybercrime is relatively high anyway, but this research shows that cybercrime among entrepreneurs remains outside recorded crime to an even greater extent.

The group of one-man businesses that were satisfied with the police response was larger than those who were not. Moreover, one-man businesses were more likely to be satisfied with their contact with the police than SMEs were. This satisfaction was linked to the police response: levels of satisfaction among one-man businesses rose if their notification was registered and one-man businesses were most likely to be satisfied if an official report was filed (whether or not the police proceeded to investigate the case). One-man businesses and SMEs identified similar areas for improvement to the police response. These areas included giving feedback on the notification/report, increasing the certainty that a case was being handled and the speed at which the police worked.

Given that only 13 per cent of one-man businesses involved the police, the issue of cybercrime remains largely invisible to the investigative authorities. Reasons for not involving the police are lack of damage, the fact that the offence is considered too trivial and because victims are able to solve the problems which arose due to cybercrime themselves. This finding is not new: earlier research led to similar results (Hernandez-Castro et al., 2013; McGuire & Downing, 2013). According to one-man businesses, the likelihood of contacting the police increases: if financial and other kinds of damage increase (46.2%); they are guaranteed that their case will be handled (30.3%); if they are not able to solve the resulting problems themselves (25.6%); if filing a report is made easier (24.1%) and/or if the feedback after notifying the police or filing an official report is improved (21.5%).

A total of 5.6 per cent of the one-man businesses got in touch with an interest group. Specifically, the fraud helpdesk and the Chamber of Commerce were the ones who were called in. Reasons mentioned for involving an interest group were to obtain information and advice, to increase the chance that the perpetrator would be caught and/or because victims considered it their duty to inform the interest group.

5.3.6   *Intended reporting behaviour*

A large part of the issue of cybercrime among entrepreneurs remains invisible to the police and the criminal justice system. This is because entrepreneurs generally do not contact the police when they fall victim to cybercrime (see Section 5.3.5). This can mainly be attributed to self-reliance – entrepreneurs solve their problems themselves – and a lack of damage/consequences. Entrepreneurs also pointed to problems relating specifically to the police, such as a lack of confidence in the cybercrime expertise of the investigative authorities, that stops them from contacting the police in the prevailing situation. Despite this, the majority of the entrepreneurs surveyed, one-man businesses as well as SMEs, claimed that they would file a report in the event of future cybercrime victimisation (see Figure 5.36). There is a difference between intentions to report incidents to the police and actual reporting behaviour: the majority of the entrepreneurs said that they would report this kind of crime to the police, but when they are actually confronted with cybercrime, they tend not to contact the police. This considerable discrepancy between stated and actual reporting behaviour makes it clear that the police must not base their policy on what members of the public say they will do should they fall victim.

Figure 5.36   Intended reporting behaviour (n = 1,622 one-man businesses, 1,203 SMEs)*

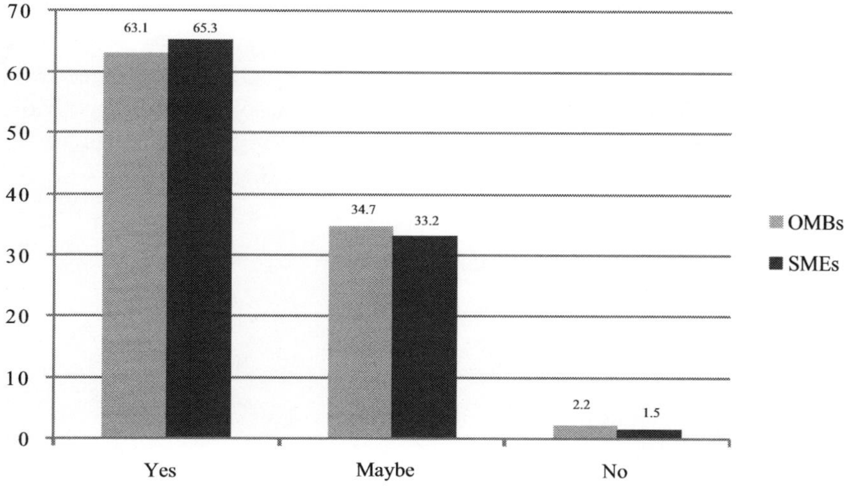

An additional analysis shows that there is a difference between the intended reporting behaviour of one-man businesses that became cybercrime victims and those that did not. Of those one-man businesses that were not victims, 76.2 per cent said that they would file a report in the event of future cybercrime victimisation. One-man businesses that fell victim to cybercrime were significantly less inclined to file a report in the future: 29.4 per cent said that they would. There was, however, no difference in intended future reporting behaviour between those who were victims in the past and did contact the police, and those who were victims and did not contact the police. Also, it cannot be demonstrated statistically that levels of satisfaction with the police regarding a previous incident would influence future willingness to report among one-man businesses. This is because only 57 victims indicated how satisfied they were about their experience of police response in the past. Were we to make a comparison within this group between victims who intended and those who did not intend to file a report in the future, it would lead to statistically unreliable results. Although previous victimisation thus determines the likelihood of one-man businesses calling in the police in the future, it does not demonstrably apply to previous experience with the police. It may be that one-man businesses that fell victim to cybercrime found that they could solve the problems themselves, as a result of which they are less likely to say that they would go to the police in the future. However, an additional analysis revealed that demonstrated self-reliance also did not significantly influence the intention to contact the police in the event of future victimisation. Follow-up research would therefore have to offer more insight into the reasons behind the victims' reluctance to involve the police in the event of future victimisation.

In addition to the question of whether entrepreneurs would file a report on cybercrime in future, we also asked respondents about their preferred channel for filing a report should they do so in future (see Figure 5.37). Half of the one-man businesses indicated that they prefer electronic options for filing reports (online) (49.1%). A quarter said that they would prefer to file a report personally at the police station (25.6%). Less than a quarter (18.1%) would prefer to file a report by telephone and 7.1 per cent attached most importance to contact with the police taking place at the scene. One-man businesses that fell victim to cybercrime and called in the police did so according to the preferred methods: they were most likely to contact the police electronically, followed by contact at the police station, telephone communication and a visit by the police at the scene (see Figure 5.29).

Figure 5.37   Preference for type of reporting in the event of future victimisation (n = 1,622 one-man businesses, 1,203 SMEs)**

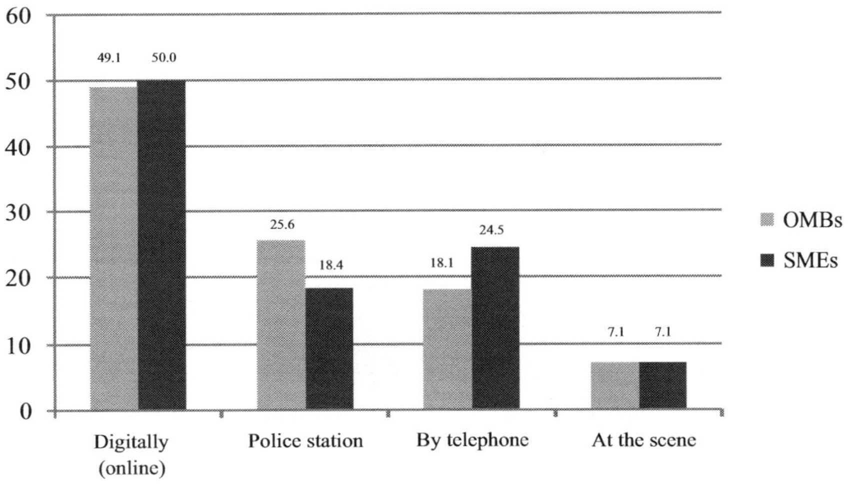

For future reporting, the order of preference among one-man businesses differed from that of SMEs: while the preferred method among both groups of entrepreneurs was electronic contact with the police, among one-man businesses this method was followed by going to the police station, while SMEs indicated that, after online reporting, they would prefer to contact the police by telephone. Perhaps the convenience and/or time saved by contacting the police by telephone play a stronger role among SMEs than among one-man businesses. We were not, however, able to determine this statistically because we did not ask one-man businesses *why* their preference in the future would be for a specific reporting channel. Moreover, the earlier finding (that a discrepancy is to be expected between intended and actual behaviour) should be taken into account.

Summary

As was the case among SMEs, there was also a difference between demonstrated and intended reporting behaviour among one-man businesses: more than 60 per cent of one-man businesses said that they would file a report on cybercrime in the future, while not more than 13 per cent of victims are actually doing so currently. One-man businesses as well as SMEs said that they would prefer a digital platform for involving the police in the future. Unlike SMEs who mainly contacted the police by visiting the police station, one-man businesses indicated that they contacted the police online, which is in line with their preference.

5.4　　　THE ROLE OF PUBLIC AND PRIVATE PARTIES WHEN TACKLING CYBERCRIME

In this section, we provide insight into the role that one-man businesses assign to public and private parties when it comes to tackling cybercrime. We start by discussing who is responsible for security on the internet according to one-man businesses. We then go on to discuss the extent to which one-man business people have confidence in the police with regard to fighting cybercrime. In the third sub-section, we give insight into awareness among one-man businesses about government measures to counter cybercrime and whether they utilise these measures. This is followed by a description of the reasons that one-man businesses have for either using or not using these government measures. Finally, we discuss the willingness on the part of one-man business people to help the police in their efforts to fight cybercrime.

5.4.1　　Responsibility for online security

We asked one-man business people who they consider to be responsible for security on the internet. The results are given in Figure 5.38. Just like SMEs, one-man business owners generally laid the responsibility on themselves: no fewer than 89.7 per cent were of the opinion that they themselves were responsible for their security on the internet. Research into cybercrime among members of the public also shows that 85.1 per cent are prepared to safeguard their own security on the internet (Domenie et al., 2013). The same impression emerged from the in-depth interviews.

Personal responsibility

Mr Van Houten thinks that it is the duty of entrepreneurs themselves to ensure that they are safe when online. For one-man businesses, as is the case for consumers, there is a lot of information about safe internet practices to be found on the web. Entrepreneurs should familiarise themselves well about the dangers of being online and use quality marks. Banks have a phased plan for safe banking, which entrepreneurs should take to heart. The government also pays attention to cybercrime. In short: there is plenty of information available, but personal responsibility and alertness are deciding factors. according to Mr Van Houten.

Figure 5.38   Responsibility for security on the internet (n = 1,622 one-man businesses, 1,203 SMEs)[21]

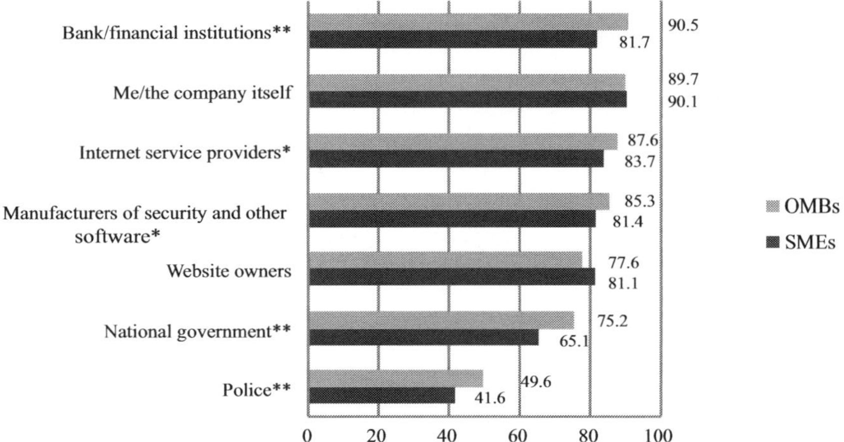

Of the one-man businesses surveyed, 90.5 per cent were of the opinion that banks and financial institutions are (also) responsible for security on the internet. Once again, this finding is consistent with the view of members of the public (Domenie et al., 2013). Fewer SMEs, however, agreed with this opinion (81.7%). In addition, internet service providers (87.6%) and manufacturers of security and other software (85.3%) were considered to be parties responsible to a large or very large degree. Once again, SMEs were less likely to lay the responsibility at the door of these parties.

More than three quarters of one-man business people laid the responsibility for the security on the internet at the door of the national government (75.2%). Almost two thirds of the SME sector agreed with this (65.1%); however, fewer SMEs than one-man business people were inclined to agree. The conclusion must be that one-man business people are more inclined than SMEs to lay the responsibility, or part of it, on other parties.

As was the case among SMEs, one-man business people considered the police to be last in the line of those responsible for security on the internet. Once again, there is a

---

21. Percentage of respondents who agreed or agreed completely with the questions posed.

parallel here with the opinion of members of the public: at only 29.0 per cent, members of the public were least likely to place responsibility for security on the internet at the door of the police (Domenie et al., 2013).

> **Responsibility of the police**
> *Mr Van der Kooi does not think that the police are responsible for security on the internet. He feels that you yourself are responsible for this. That you need to be aware of the risks and must think about what you're doing. He does, however, think that the police are on the case and he does consider it a duty of the police to prevent and fight cybercrime.*

In conclusion, members of the public, one-man businesses and SMEs were of the opinion that fighting cybercrime is not something that should be taken on by the police alone. The overall impression is that it is seen as the shared responsibility of various parties, and primarily of those involved themselves. This finding is consistent with Dutch government policy and the results of previous research which states that security in cyberspace is a shared responsibility (Intomart GfK, 2013; Coalition Agreement [*Regeerakkoord*], 2012). This same view of shared responsibility emerged in the in-depth interviews with one-man business people. For instance, a respondent said that, while most of the responsibility lies with users themselves, government institutions and banks are responsible for raising awareness: 'If you go swimming in dangerous waters, despite the warning signs, you can hardly expect the government to close the whole beach'.

5.4.2   *Confidence in the police regarding fighting cybercrime*

All one-man business people were asked about the level of confidence they have in the police. They were first asked about how much confidence they have in the police as far as the fighting of crime in general is concerned (Figure 5.39).

Figure 5.39   Confidence in the police in general (n = 1,622 one-man businesses, 1,203 SMEs)

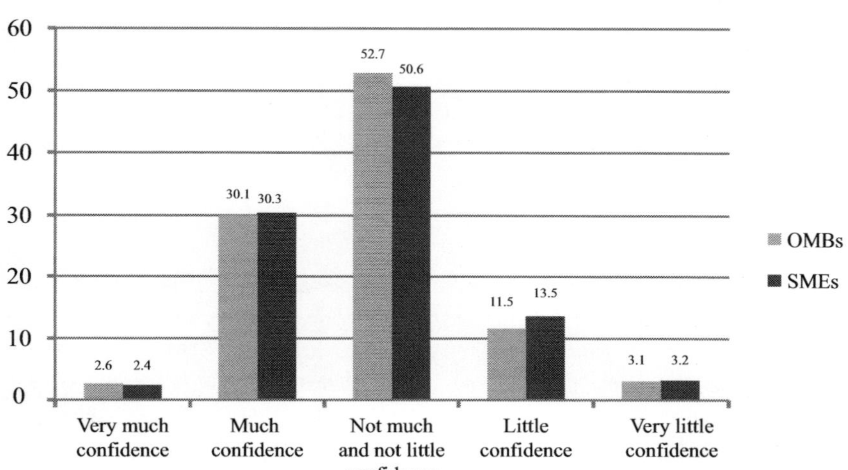

Almost a third of one-man business people said they had confidence or a great deal of confidence in the police when it comes to fighting crime in general (32.7%). The biggest group said that they did not have much confidence, but also not too little confidence in the police. The percentages did not differ from the SME sector: most SMEs also did not have a great deal of confidence nor too little confidence in the police (50.6%).

We subsequently asked one-man business people about the confidence they had in the police where it concerned fighting cybercrime (see Figure 5.40). The results revealed that one-man business people have less confidence in the capacity of the police to fight cybercrime compared to fighting crime in general: 20.7 per cent (versus 32.7%) said they have confidence or a great deal of confidence in the capacity of the police to fight cybercrime. More than half did not have much nor did they have too little confidence in the police (54.0%) and a quarter had little, very little or no confidence in the competence of the police when it comes to tackling cybercrime (25.3%). Once again, the percentages of SMEs did not differ from those of the answers given by one-man businesses.

Figure 5.40   Confidence in the police regarding cybercrime (n = 1,622 one-man businesses, 1,203 SMEs)

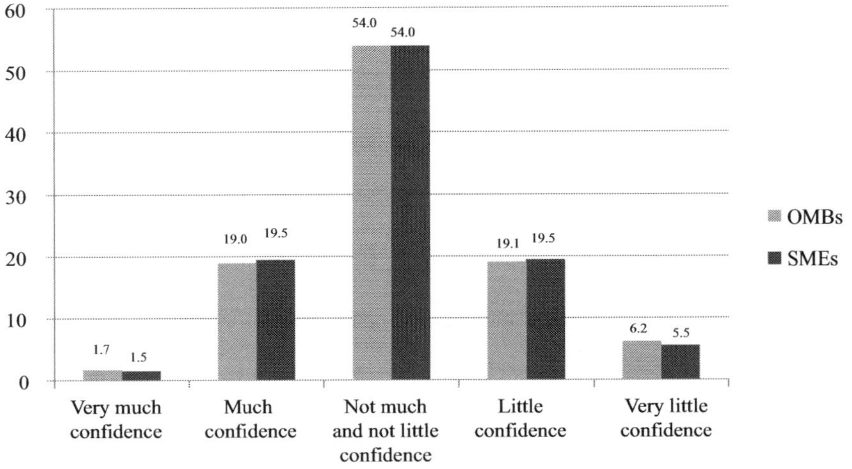

Confidence in the police
Mrs Thiemen said she had no confidence in the police when it comes to cybercrime. Despite the fact that they have a special team for this, they are looking at the big picture and so she thinks that they won't go to any trouble for small amounts. But for her 2,300 euro was a lot of money and she would have liked to have seen the perpetrator caught. Despite this, she would still notify the police in the future to provide them with information with the hope that they would do something about it if they get plenty of reports.

To gain better insight into the level of confidence that one-man business people have in the police, we then presented them with two statements: 'When it really comes down to it, the police will do their utmost to help you' (Statement 1, Figure 5.41) and 'When it really comes down to it, the police will be there for you' (Statement 2, Figure 5.42) (Van Dijk, 2007). Of one-man business people surveyed, 55.4 and 56.6 per cent respectively agreed or completely agreed with these two statements. The answers given by SMEs did not differ from those of the one-man businesses: more than half of SMEs also agreed or completely agreed with the statements.

Figure 5.41   Confidence in the police: Statement 1 (Van Dijk, 2007) (n = 1,622 one-man businesses, 1,203 SMEs)

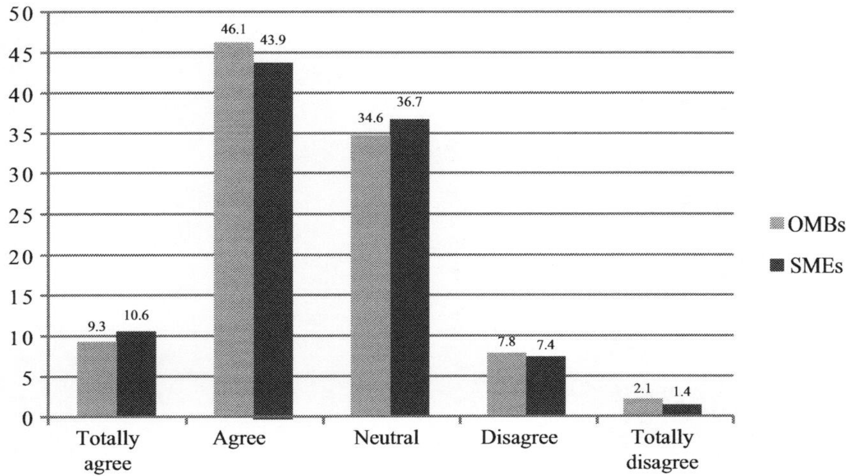

Figure 5.42   Confidence in the police: Statement 2 (Van Dijk, 2007) (n = 1,622 one-man businesses, 1,203 SMEs)

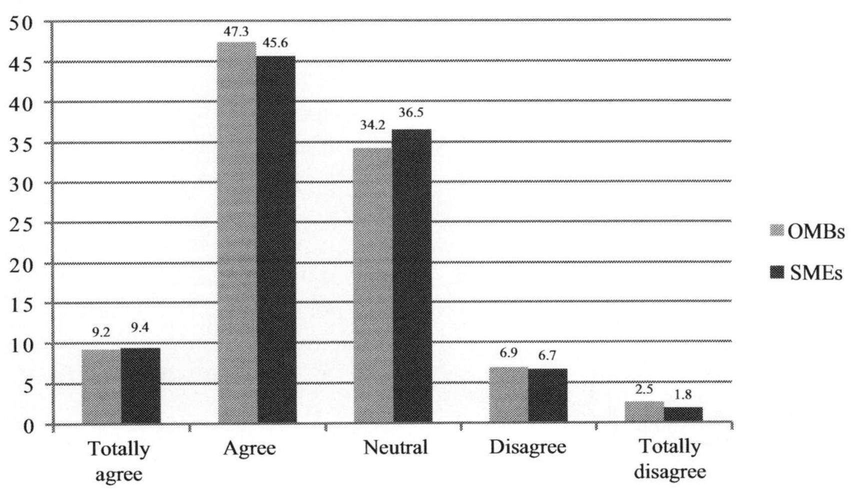

5.4.3   *Government measures to counter cybercrime*

The authorities have deployed various initiatives in the battle against cybercrime. One-man business people were asked which of these initiatives they knew about and, if so, whether they used them. The results are given in a stacked graph in Figure 5.43. The total percentage given with each bar indicates the percentage of one-man business people that is familiar with and has used the initiative in question. For instance, 27.4 per cent of one-man business people knew about the National Internet Fraud Hotline (LMIO), but only 1.8 per cent of them had actually used it (n = 30). So the remaining 71.6 per cent did not know about the LMIO.

Figure 5.43   One-man business people who knew about and used government initiatives (n = 1,622)

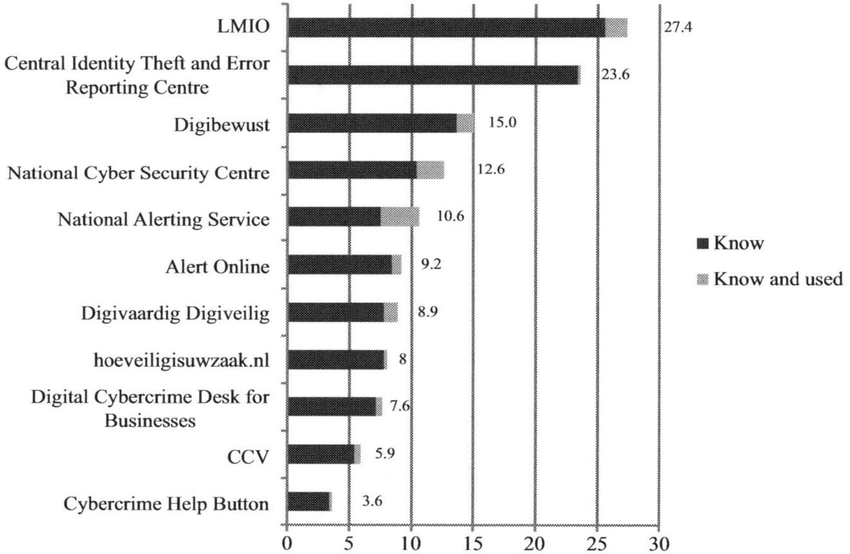

One-man business people surveyed in this research project were not familiar with many government measures designed to counter cybercrime. Only 42.4 per cent knew one or more of the initiatives mentioned on the questionnaire. Even fewer one-man business people who knew about a government initiative also made use of it: not more than 7.3 per cent knew of and used one or more of these measures. This can be explained by the fact that it was not necessary for them to use the government initiative: of one-man businesses which did not use an initiative, 72.7 per cent had not fallen victim to cybercrime in the previous year. Further on we provide insight into the reasons why respondents may or may not have made use of a government initiative.

After the LMIO at 27.4 per cent, almost a quarter of one-man business people (23.6%) knew of the Central Identity Theft and Error Reporting Centre [*Centraal Meld- en informatiepunt Identiteitsfraude en -fouten* (CMI)]. A fraction of them used the services of the CMI (n = 4). Digibewust (Dutch for 'digital awareness') and the National Alerting Service [*Waarschuwingsdienst*] of the Computer Emergency Response Team have since joined forces and have continued their services on www.veiliginternetten.nl (Dutch for 'safe internet practices'). The websites were known to 15.0 and 10.6 per cent respectively. The National Alerting Service was used by 3.1 per cent, the biggest group to use government initiatives. Relatively speaking, respondents were less likely to know hoeveiligisuwzaak.nl (Dutch for 'how safe is your businesses') (8.0%); the Digital Cybercrime Desk for Businesses (7.6%) and the safe business practices website for cybercrime of the Centre for Crime Prevention and Security (CCV) (5.9%). These are government initiatives specifically targeting companies and their online security. One-man business people were least likely to know the Cybercrime Help Button [*Hulpknop Cybercrime*] (3.6%).

Reasons for deciding whether or not to use government measures (in-depth interviews)
The one-man business people who were interviewed were also hardly aware of government initiatives to counter cybercrime and did not know where they should turn for more knowledge about counteracting cybercrime. Some did, however, know about advertising campaigns like 'Hang up, click it away and call your bank' and campaigns that do not specifically target entrepreneurs: 'Nice for older people maybe, but for the rest these kinds of campaigns aren't really useful for one-man businesses', said one of the respondents.
Some of one-man business people who knew about the government initiatives but had not used them said that they had not done so because they knew enough about the subject to tackle cybercrime themselves, for instance, because they were IT specialists by trade. Other people mentioned that protection against cybercrime was something they would have to take care of themselves, not the government: 'What you should use is your common sense'.
Respondents felt that they should get more support in the prevention and fighting of cybercrime. Support from the sector, in particular, was thought to be minimal: 'When I started my own company, I went to several meetings, but cybercrime was never mentioned'. Another respondent agreed with this: 'Information in the sector and from the trade union is very poor. It begins when you start a business and there is hardly any information, if at all. You get a chamber of commerce number and it's up to you whether you sink or swim. When I started my own company, I drew up a plan myself and the chamber of commerce gave some coaching, but as far as cybercrime was concerned, I didn't get any information'.
Respondents urged the government to inform entrepreneurs and/or offer companies a central point of contact where they could get information about what to do to counter cybercrime. This should preferably have customised information for each sector. Perhaps the government could even offer a service which would involve them coming to the company to see what could be changed. If this is not possible, then an online workshop would be good: 'Not too long and complicated, but brief and to the point'. Finally, they recommended making more commercials aimed at prevention.

5.4.4 *Willingness among one-man businesses to cooperate with fighting cybercrime*

In conclusion, respondents were asked the following questions concerning the role of public and private parties in tackling cybercrime: 'Are you prepared to help the police as a police volunteer in fighting cybercrime?' Figure 5.44 presents the responses given by one-man business people to these questions.

Figure 5.44   Willingness to help as a police volunteer (n = 1,622)

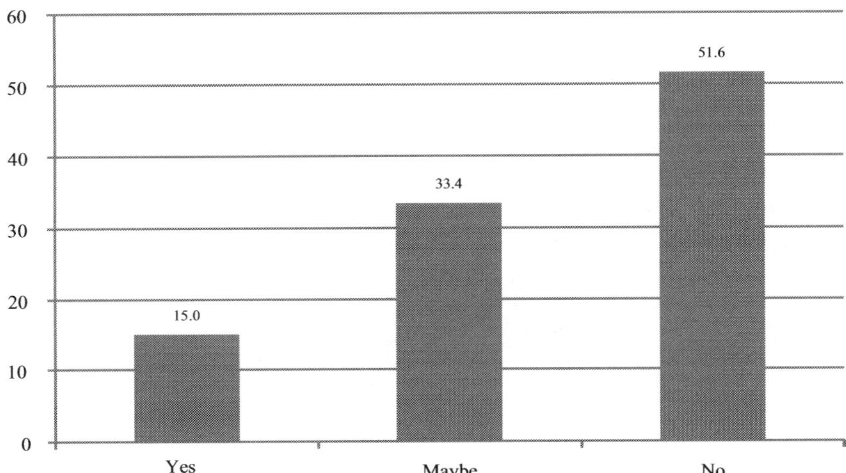

More than half of one-man businesses surveyed said that they would not be prepared to help the police in their mission against cybercrime (51.6%). A third were not sure and 15.0 per cent said they would be prepared to offer assistance. That may seem like a small minority, but if even one tenth of the 15.0 per cent were to put their words into actions (compare Section 5.3.6), then the sample of 1,622 one-man business people presented here would still yield around 24 volunteers. It was possible for respondents to clarify their answers to this question. A total of 409 clarifications were given. We grouped these clarifications as much as possible: 343 clarifications have been incorporated in Figure 5.45.

Of the one-man businesses surveyed, 8.6 per cent said that they would be prepared to help the police to detect cybercrime by filing a report or notifying the police when they are confronted with cybercrime. For instance, two respondents said: 'A simple hotline that you can send bogus e-mails to and report other things, that would be a very good thing' and 'I would love to be able to send my phishing e-mails through to a national investigation team so that they can combine these e-mails and unmask the perpetrators'.

Some of the respondents would like to help but have no idea how (4.5%) or would let it depend on how much time or energy it would take (2.2%). Thirty-six one-man businesses said that they would be prepared to help by taking part in research (1.5%). For the rest, there were one-man businesses that said they would like to use their expertise

Figure 5.45 Clarification on helping as a police volunteer (n = 343)

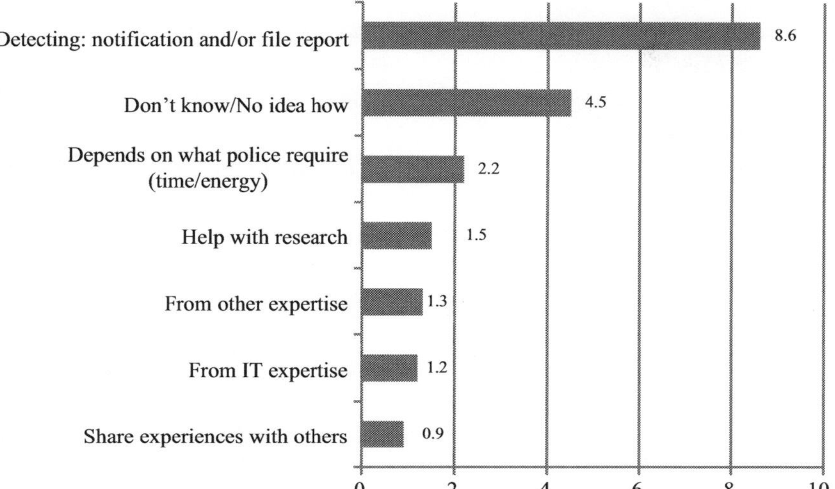

to assist the police: as an IT specialist (1.2%) or as some other kind of expert (1.3%). A respondent explained: 'As an IT expert I would very much like to use my expertise and time if this would contribute to reducing cybercrime. I think that the police should make much more use of as many volunteers and experts as possible who work in the IT sector. I would help straight away if they asked me to'.

Finally, there were 15 one-man business owners (0.9%) that would be prepared to help by sharing their experiences and, by doing so, prevent others from becoming victims: 'For instance, by taking part in a focus group or panel like various newspapers also do'. One of the respondents said the following on the subject: 'I think that fighting cybercrime is something that we should do together with all the parties involved, so that's why I would very much like to help'. Text Box 5.19 contains a few other quotes.

Text Box 5.19: Quotes from one-man businesses about willingness to help as a police volunteer

- *'Occasionally completing a questionnaire, answering questions and letting other people see what I do for protection. In exchange for good tips, obviously'.*
- *'By reporting unreliable websites and LinkedIn, Facebook or Twitter accounts which have been taken over. But I'm not sure what kind of information the Police need exactly'.*
- *'By serving as bait, for instance, to find out who a "phishing" attacker is'.*
- *'Makes no difference to me how I can assist them. I think it's a good initiative that they are focusing on it'.*
- *'I am by no means computer illiterate and I'm on the internet a lot and if I were to come across something that I thought was dodgy, I'd be able to report it very quickly. Only, really, where and with whom, would I find the real cyber police?'*

Summary

One-man business people laid the responsibility for online security with several parties. It is considered to be the shared responsibility of parties such as the banks, internet service providers and manufacturers of security and other software. One-man business people mainly laid the responsibility at their own door. They considered the police to be responsible to a lesser degree.

Even though the authorities are investing in several government measures which are intended to help one-man business people to counter cybercrime, not even half of them were aware of one or more of the most well-known initiatives. Even fewer had used the initiatives. Government initiatives which specifically target companies are hardly known to one-man business people.

Not all one-man business people had the same amount of confidence in the police when it comes to fighting cybercrime. The majority have their doubts. Some of them even had little, very little or no confidence in the competence of the police when it involves tackling cybercrime. Despite this, a considerably larger group were of the opinion that, when it really comes down to it, the police would do their utmost to help them.

More than half of one-man businesses surveyed said that they would not be prepared to help the police in their mission against cybercrime. This may not only be due to unwillingness; some of them said that they would like to help, but are not sure how. They are also unsure of the areas in which the police would like help. That said, 15.0 per cent said that they would be prepared to help the police. If even one tenth of them were to put their words into actions (compare Section 5.3.6) then the sample presented here encompasses around 24 volunteers.

6 | CONCLUSIONS AND FINAL CONSIDERATIONS

This report offers insight into cybercrime among SMEs and one-man businesses in the Netherlands. In this concluding chapter, we give answers to the five main questions that are the focus of the report:

1. What activities do businesses undertake in cyberspace?
2. What protective measures do businesses take against cybercrime?
3. What is the nature and extent of cybercrime victimisation among businesses and what actions are taken by businesses in the Netherlands who have fallen victim to cybercrime?
4. What factors are associated with victimisation among businesses?
5. Which role do companies assign to public and private parties with regard to tackling cybercrime?

This chapter concludes with a number of considerations derived from the research findings that may contribute to police and other policy on the fighting of cybercrime.

6.1 ONLINE ACTIVITIES

Entrepreneurs prove themselves to be active internet users. The online activities undertaken the most are e-mailing, internet banking and looking for specific information online (targeted searching). Internet activities for business purposes, like placing and processing orders online, are more likely to be carried out by SMEs than by one-man businesses. Online chatting, for example on WhatsApp, is more popular among one-man business owners. The interconnectedness of private and business internet use among one-man business owners may offer an explanation for this.

Social media is also popular. More than 60 per cent of the SME sector use social media. Almost 90 per cent of the one-man business owners have at least one profile for social media. Although one-man business owners may use private accounts for business purposes – their private and business internet use is strongly interwoven – almost 46 per cent said that they also have a company profile. YouTube, Facebook, Twitter and LinkedIn are the most popular social networks.

In short, SMEs as well as those who have one-man businesses are all active internet users. The internet is principally used for traditional business processes, for instance, getting information, communicating and managing banking affairs. Targeted use of company profiles on social media is less widespread.

6.2   PROTECTIVE MEASURES

The functioning of IT is vital for entrepreneurs: by their own admission, entrepreneurs said that they are dependent on IT to a large or very large degree. Moreover, this applies to more SMEs (73.9%) than one-man businesses (63.2%). SMEs are also more likely to keep confidential information on their private and company computers than one-man business owners (65.1% versus 45.1%). ICT dependency and the fact that confidential information is stored are reflected in the finding that the majority of business people – more so among SMEs (83.7%) than one-man business owners (67.7%) – considered it to be important or very important to protect digital information. SMEs are more inclined than one-man business people to opt to engage an external company for this (47.4% versus 20.0%). Conversely, more one-man business owners take care of their information security themselves than SMEs do (80% versus 52.6%). In this light, SMEs are dependent when it comes to protecting their IT: they have to be able to rely on the expertise of external companies. The question for one-man business owners is whether they are capable of arranging adequate IT protection themselves.
Almost all entrepreneurs have undertaken one or more technical measures to protect themselves against cybercrime. These mainly involved installing the obvious security software, such as virus scanners or firewalls. Protecting networks, keeping software up-to-date and backing up are also protective measures that are undertaken often. Advanced security techniques, for instance the use of encryption, are used by far fewer respondents. In addition to technical measures, the majority of one-man business owners apply at least one of their own rules for safe internet practices (96.5%). An example would be rules applied for opening potentially unsafe files and for disclosing information. More than three quarters of SMEs use at least one policy measure for safe internet practices. They mainly focus on raising awareness among employees (60.3%) and drawing up rules about handling (38.0%) and disclosing (35.0%) confidential private and company-related information online. Various physical measures are also undertaken. Seventy-eight per cent of SMEs and almost 60 per cent of one-man businesses apply physical measures, for instance, securing rooms where vital IT equipment is kept or securing computers using cable locks. More than half of the entrepreneurs interviewed are confident that the measures that they have taken would protect them against cybercrime. The question is whether this confidence is justified.

6.3   VICTIMISATION

The percentages of those who fell victim to one or more kinds of cybercrime are 28.5 per cent for SMEs and 27.9 per cent for one-man businesses. According to the most recent Corporate Sector Crime Monitor in Holland, 31 per cent of businesses fell victim to mainly traditional kinds of crime (WODC, 2011). Therefore cybercrime occurs to a similar extent. Businesses are most often confronted with malware, e-fraud, phishing and hacking. Even though it seems as though some kinds of cybercrime – like advertising fraud – specifically target entrepreneurs, the most common types of cybercrime are not typically a problem with which SMEs or one-man businesses have to contend. Previous research among members of the public and larger companies also showed that these kinds of cybercrimes occur most frequently. It can therefore be concluded that, as a consequence of the digitisation of society, cybercrime is a phenomenon that affects society as a whole. This research did not produce evidence that attacks are becoming more targeted (for instance, spear phishing). Instead, our findings point to cybercrime, seen as a whole, being based on a dragnet method: start with a broad and rather untargeted approach and see what ends up in your net.

6.3.1 Risk factors for one-man businesses

We identified and listed the attributes of one-man businesses that influence the probability of victimisation. The findings are in line with the results of previous research among members of the public: victims are younger than non-victims (up to and including 45 years), they distinguish themselves by their more active internet behaviour and they have less self-control. Moreover, protective measures (physical or technical) do not demonstrably contribute to preventing victimisation. Company attributes, insofar as they were investigated, also do not affect the likelihood of becoming a victim of cybercrime. Because age and self-control are factors that are difficult to influence, the analysis shows that, in order to prevent cybercrime victimisation, it is important to be cautious when using the internet. Self-imposed rules, like having rules for disclosing information online or making online payments, can contribute to the prevention of victimisation.

6.3.2 The way in which cybercrime is committed

Victims of cybercrime do not know much about the way in which cybercrime is committed. Entrepreneurs who fell victim to cybercrime did not generally know who the perpetrator was, from which country the cybercrime was committed and how the perpetrator set to work. In particular, knowledge about the modi operandi for cybercrimes in the narrow sense, for instance malware and hacking, was lacking. Fewer respondents knew about the modi operandi for these crimes than about e-fraud modi operandi. This can be explained by the fact that in e-fraud – as opposed to, for instance, malware or hacking – there is generally interaction between the perpetrator and the victim.

To the extent that respondents were able to indicate from which country the cybercrime to which they had fallen victim was committed, 8.4 per cent of SMEs and almost 15 per cent of one-man business people noted that the cybercriminal operated from abroad. So if entrepreneurs were to file reports for these kinds of offences, the police will be confronted with suspects operating from outside the country. Although cybercrime thus regularly crosses national borders, most cybercrimes are committed from within the country (as far as was known).

6.3.3 *Impact and damage*

More than two fifths of the entrepreneurs who fell victim to cybercrime did not suffer any damage. Damage and the extent to which entrepreneurs felt it was serious to be confronted with cybercrime are related: the greater the financial damage, the worse entrepreneurs felt about becoming a victim of cybercrime. By no means all business people consider falling victim to cybercrime to be serious: 26.3 per cent of SMEs and 34.2 per cent of one-man businesses labelled the most recent cybercrime incident as serious. So although it is not rare for entrepreneurs to become cybercrime victims, the consequences of this must not be overestimated.

Loss of time, financial damages and restricted access to information are the most commonly reported kinds of damage. Damages depended on the type of offence that the entrepreneur fell victim to: hacking leads to restricted access and/or manipulation of computer data while e-fraud leads to financial damages.

SMEs and one-man businesses reported suffering financial damages to a similar extent. However, there is not much point in calculating and/or comparing the average damages for SMEs and one-man businesses. Reported losses varied too widely and the sample sizes were too small to be able to do so. Nevertheless, the overall amount of loss that SMEs and one-man businesses reported in the research was calculated. Combined, the damages reported by the 1,203 SMEs in our research amounted to 442,953 euro (n = 59). That amount of loss was strongly influenced by an outlier from one SME who suffered 240,000 euro in damages. The 1,622 one-man businesses in our research together suffered 235,568 euro in damages as a consequence of the most recent cybercrime incident (n = 87).

6.3.4 *Reactions of victims*

Almost a quarter of the SMEs and a fifth of the one-man businesses did not take any action after falling victim to cybercrime. Entrepreneurs who did take action generally proved to be self-reliant: they took action in attempts to solve the problems which had arisen as a consequence of cybercrime themselves and/or took measures to prevent cybercrime in the future. The extent of self-reliance among entrepreneurs depended on the type of cybercrime they experienced. Victims of cybercrimes in the narrow sense, like malware and hacking, are more likely to be self-reliant than e-fraud victims. E-fraud victims are more likely to contact other parties.

The majority of the entrepreneurs did not contact the police when falling victim to cybercrime. The percentages of those who did not contact the police as a consequence of cybercrime victimisation are 92.8 per cent for SMEs and 87.0 per cent for one-man businesses. So cybercrime remains largely outside the police's field of vision.

The reason mentioned most often for not calling in the police is generally an absence of damage. Analyses demonstrate that the greater the financial and other kinds of damage, the more frequently business people opt to contact the police. As noted previously, damages and the perceived severity of victimisation are linked. We can see this correlation reflected here. In addition to an absence of damages, the reason that the incident was too trivial is one of the other main arguments given for not involving the police. Self-reliance also plays a role: because entrepreneurs have the capacity to solve cybercrime problems themselves, they do not contact the police. Finally, confidence in the police affects the decision of whether or not to engage the police: 23.5 per cent of SMEs and one-man businesses alike suspect that the police 'won't do anything anyway' to counter cybercrime. Following on from this, it emerged that confidence in the police force when it comes to fighting cybercrime is not as strong as the level of confidence in the police when it involves tackling traditional crime, which in itself is not high but also not low.

Despite the fact that the majority of victims do not contact the police, 7.2 per cent of SMEs and 12.8 per cent – a significantly larger group – of one-man businesses did do so. When entrepreneurs do turn to the police, they do so mainly because they want to notify the police or file a report on the crime. However, notifications or reports are not registered in all cases. The police registered only 1 per cent of all notifications and 3.6 per cent of all reports of SME victims. Of the one-man businesses who fell victim to cybercrime, 4.5 per cent said the police actually registered a notification and according to 4.3 per cent the police filed an official report. From this it can be concluded that the extent to which cybercrime among businesses is part of the recorded police statistics is small. The most recent Security Monitor conducted by Statistics Netherlands (CBS, 2015) showed that 13 per cent of members of the public reported cybercrime and that 7 per cent of these actually filed a report. So the police lack insight into the nature and extent of cybercrime, particularly where it affects businesses.

Entrepreneurs who contact the police are more likely to be satisfied or very satisfied with the police action than they are to be dissatisfied or very dissatisfied. Satisfaction among entrepreneurs is related to the police response. If the police file a report, entrepreneurs are more satisfied with the police action than if the police opt for another method of handling the report. However, this finding was only demonstrated statistically for one-man businesses because the number of SMEs which contacted the police was too small to be able to carry out a similar analysis on this target population. More than three fifths of the SMEs and one-man businesses said that they intended to report cybercrime to the police were they to fall victim to cybercrime in the future. This is not consistent with the finding that the majority of the entrepreneurs did not involve the police when they actually did fall victim. So there is a difference between intended and actual reporting behaviour. This considerable discrepancy between stated and actual reporting behaviour makes it clear that the police must not base their policy on what members of the public say they will do should they fall victim.

Even though the results may give cause for optimism about satisfaction with the police among entrepreneurs, various areas for improvement with regard to the police response were identified. Improvements could be made to feedback to victims about notifications and reports, the certainty that a case was being handled and the speed at which the police worked. The police could also benefit from the willingness of entrepreneurs to contribute to tackling cybercrime as police volunteers. SMEs were not asked about this, but 15.0 per cent of one-man business owners are prepared to help the police. With regard to filing reports, the research showed that respondents do not always do what they say they will, but if even one tenth of the 15.0 per cent were to put their words into actions, then the sample of 1,622 one-man business people presented here would still yield around 24 volunteers. These are people who the police could recruit as police volunteers.

6.4   THE ROLE OF PUBLIC AND PRIVATE PARTIES WHEN TACKLING
             CYBERCRIME

It has already been noted that the police are only called in to a limited extent when it comes to cybercrime victimisation. The role of interest groups in the tackling of cybercrime is even smaller. Rounded off, 6 per cent of entrepreneurs contacted an interest group after falling victim to cybercrime. Yet entrepreneurs feel that roles for tackling cybercrime should be reserved for various other parties, alongside themselves. Four fifths of entrepreneurs consider financial institutions, internet service providers and software manufacturers to be responsible for internet security. Entrepreneurs feel that the police are the last on the list of parties responsible for security on the internet (see also Intomart GfK, 2013). In conclusion, it can be stated that entrepreneurs, just like the Dutch government (Regeerakkoord, 2012), see security on the internet to be a responsibility shared by several parties, from the private as well as the public sector. Various government initiatives have been developed which aim at contributing to the tackling of cybercrime against businesses. Examples of these are the National Internet Fraud Reporting Centre (LMIO) and websites like waarschuwingsdienst.nl. We asked one-man business owners whether they were aware of such measures and whether they had used them. Fewer than half of the one-man business owners know one or more of these initiatives against cybercrime and not even 10 per cent have ever used them. By their own account, entrepreneurs are self-reliant and are capable of protecting themselves against cybercrime. They say that it is for this reason that they do not use these kinds of initiatives. At the same time, one-man businesses mentioned during the in-depth interviews that they require more support when it comes to preventing and fighting cybercrime, particularly from actors within their own sector. So there is probably a larger role for interest groups than is currently being assigned to these organisations. It is therefore advisable to, by evaluating the ways in which support for companies is currently being organised, offer insight into more effective options to help entrepreneurs in their battle against cybercrime.

6.5   FINAL CONSIDERATIONS FOR POLICE AND OTHER APPROACHES FOR
           TACKLING CYBERCRIME AGAINST COMPANIES

Prevention is the principal strategy against crime, also against cybercrime. It is therefore reassuring to know that virtually all entrepreneurs take technical measures to prevent cybercrime. However, since virtually all entrepreneurs take technical measures, like using virus scanners, our research could not demonstrate whether such measures contribute to the prevention of victimisation. After all, if everyone took technical measures, then no comparison can be made between a group that did and a group that did not use such measures. That this research could not demonstrate that taking technical measures reduces the likelihood of victimisation thus does not mean that such measures are not important in the prevention of cybercrime.

This study has shown that 'exercising caution when on the internet' is important for the prevention of victimisation. Rules, including those that people apply to themselves, can help in this. Who is, in this respect, going to create awareness? According to entrepreneurs, safeguarding the internet is not a task that can be assigned directly to the police. The question is thus whether police should claim responsibility for stimulating prevention awareness. There are already various governmental and other websites for that purpose, but they are little known and infrequently visited. It does not seem logical that the police should take it upon themselves to improve this situation. Stimulating safe behaviour on the internet more likely is a job for national government and sector or interest groups.

Cybercrime victims do not generally file reports when victimised. Consequently, cybercrime remains largely invisible to the police and the criminal justice system. This applies to cybercrime among members of the public, but to an even greater extent to cybercrime among businesses. Fighting crime requires an understanding of the nature and extent of the problem. This observation is thus a problem for the fight against cybercrime. Encouraging people to contact the police in cases involving cybercrime victimisation may ostensibly contribute to the fighting of cybercrime. However, in reality, an absence of expertise and capacity within the police force, and reluctance to prioritise this kind of crime, means that the police are limited in their ability to effectively fight cybercrime (Leukfeldt et al., 2012b). From this perspective, it is questionable whether it would be prudent to put efforts into increasing the rate of reporting. The fact is that it would mean an increase in the police's cybercrime workload while it is doubtful whether criminal investigations could be carried out into the cybercrime cases put forward. A downside of this strategy may be that levels of satisfaction with the police response – and with this willingness to file a report – may ultimately fall. In addition, it is at any rate questionable whether the traditional case-oriented police approach would suffice against cybercrime. After all, cybercrimes can be committed quickly and simultaneously in large quantities and the extent of cybercrime – in our increasingly digitising society – is only expected to expand. In this light, fighting cybercrime by using the traditional case-oriented police approach is extremely demanding for the police. It thus seems recommendable to invest in other strategies to tackle cybercrime as well.

First, despite the aforementioned objections, reporting cybercrime to the police should be made easier (via digital means). By using the information the police gathers from these reports, insight in the nature and extent of cybercrime is gained. This information should primarily be used to achieve successes that transcend individual cases. Stimulating reporting practices includes an appeal to the moral principles of entrepreneurs to report incidents. For this reason, managing the expectations of victims is important. It should be made clear that one individual report is unlikely to lead to an investigation. As entrepreneurs may well wonder what they ultimately stand to gain from reporting cybercrime if this is the approach, investigative successes should be communicated. By doing so, it will be made clear to entrepreneurs that the police are working on the online security of businesses.

Another alternative strategy is in line with the observation that entrepreneurs tend to be self-reliant and that, according to entrepreneurs, tackling cybercrime is the shared responsibility of public as well as private parties. Entrepreneurs see the police as their last resort. This means that, depending on the incident, some consideration should be given to whether criminal prosecution is an appropriate approach for the problem. If not, then the police – together with other parties – could help victims to solve the problems arising from cybercrime themselves (thus promoting the self-reliance that they already have). In this regard, the finding that few entrepreneurs have a plan to address problems in case they fall victim is an important one. Encouraging entrepreneurs to draw up such a plan is in line with this strategy, and the Chamber of Commerce and/or sector organisations could play a role in this.

Various strategies could be applied in combination with one another. Encouraging police contact does not necessarily have to lead to an (unwanted) heavier workload. After all, through good communications with victims, it can be made clear that just notifying the police about cybercrime ultimately contributes to the case transcending fighting of cybercrime. In the process, by working together with other parties, the police can contribute to the self-reliance and problem-solving capacities of entrepreneurs who are confronted by cybercrime. Combining these strategies will contribute to a 'selection at the gate' principle: criminal prosecution will then be applied to a selection of cases, which actually require such an approach because other strategies are not effective enough. The investigative authorities can then place their focus fully on these cases.

In the process, the police will be – even in minor cases – confronted with crime that crosses borders. Even though the majority of cybercrimes are committed within the country as opposed to from abroad, and so the police must first draw up a domestic cybercrime policy, they must also have an investigative policy aimed at addressing minor international cybercrimes. Another reason for doing so is that it may become clear from tackling minor international cases that they belong to the repertoire of a criminal group of repeat offenders.

This report focuses on various kinds of cybercrime. Unless otherwise indicated, the clarifications presented below about the cybercrimes surveyed in this study are based on the 'Guide to offences with a digital component' [*Handreiking voor delicten met een digitale component*] (Leukfeldt et al., 2012a). Besides a description of the cybercrimes studies, it is described how the offences have been made punishable in Dutch criminal law.

Cyber extortion
Extortion is the obtaining of money or property from a person or organisation through threats and/or violence. Cyber extortion uses digital means to achieve this. Extortion is punishable under Section 317 of the Dutch Criminal Code.

Cyberstalking
Cyberstalking is the generic name for the systematic and relentless online harassment and/or threatening of a person. In the Dutch Criminal Code, stalking is called 'belaging' and is made punishable in Section 285b of the Dutch Criminal Code.

Online blackmail
The focus in blackmail, be it in cyberspace or otherwise, is threatening a person with libellous defamation or disclosing a secret (online or otherwise) with the objective of obtaining money or goods. Blackmail is punishable pursuant to Section 318 of the Dutch Criminal Code.

Theft of data
Theft is the unlawful appropriation of any property that belongs (entirely or in part) to another (Section 310 of the Dutch Criminal Code). In this case it concerns the theft of digital data, such as text files, photographs or e-mails. For this it is necessary to hack (138ab) and it may involve intercepting and recording data (Section 139c of the Dutch Criminal Code).

Destruction of data
The destruction of data involves the wilful and unlawful modification and deletion of data, making it unusable or inaccessible, or adding other data to it. Destruction of data is punishable under Section 350a of the Dutch Criminal Code.

Online fraud or scamming
Fraud is wrongful deception intended to result in the financial or personal gain (Section 326 of the Dutch Criminal Code). Scamming can take place online too, for instance, on auction sites.

Online identity abuse
Identity abuse is the illegal use of a created/assumed identity, in this case on the internet. Identity fraud was made punishable separately under Section 231b of the Dutch Criminal Code on 1 May 2014.

Phishing
Phishing is extracting information using digital means (for instance, e-mails or text messages), the ultimate objective being identity abuse and/or fraud. Phishing falls under the heading 'fraud' and is therefore punishable pursuant to Section 326 of the Dutch Criminal Code. It may also involve forgery of documents (Section 325 of the Dutch Criminal Code).

Online libel/slander
Cyber defamation is the wilful tarnishing of a person's honour or reputation using IT or accusing a person of a specific fact (regardless of whether it is true or not), with the objective of making this fact known (Section 261 of the Dutch Criminal Code). Online slander constitutes defamation if the perpetrator is aware that the fact that he or she is accusing the victim of is not true (Section 262 of the Dutch Criminal Code).

Cyber espionage
Cyber espionage focuses on obtaining confidential information of financial or political value, or on direct financial gain (GOVCERT, 2011). Espionage has not been made punishable in the Dutch Criminal Code as an offence in and of itself. Other offences have been made punishable, however, for instance, the intercepting and/or recording of data or the placement of equipment for this purpose. These are punishable under Sections 139c and 139d of the Dutch Criminal Code.

Hacking
Hacking is gaining access to a computerised work without permission and is punishable as computer intrusion under Section 138a of the Dutch Criminal Code.

Unauthorised use of a company network
The unauthorised of a company network is a form of hacking and can be done with the aim of using the processing capacity of a computerised system (Section 138ab(3), preamble and under a of the Dutch Criminal Code).

Defacing
Defacing is the modifying, replacing or destruction of a website without permission. This constitutes hacking because a computerised system (the server) has to be broken

into to be able to modify a website (138ab of the Dutch Criminal Code). In addition to this, Sections 350a and 350b of the Dutch Criminal Code apply because digital information is unlawfully and wilfully altered, deleted or rendered unreliable/ inaccessible.

Malware

Malware is the generic name for malicious software. Examples include viruses, worms and Trojan horses. It may involve various offences punishable by law, for instance, computer intrusion and destruction or damage to data (Sections 138ab, 350a and 350b of the Dutch Criminal Code).

DoS attacks

The National Cyber Security Centre (NCSC) defines denial-of-service (DoS) attack as follows: 'In a DoS attack, a computer or network system is so heavily loaded or manipulated that the system is disabled, or that a service offered, be it online or not, is no longer available for legitimate users' (*Nationaal Cyber Security Centrum*, 2012, p. 77). Various sections of the law apply to DoS attacks, but according to the NCSC Section 138b of the Dutch Criminal Code specifically focuses on making such attacks punishable.

Skimming

Skimming is unlawfully obtaining and copying information (using technical means) from the magnetic strip on debit, credit or value cards. An important provision with regard to skimming is Section 232 (1) of the Dutch Criminal Code. This section makes punishable the deliberate forgery or counterfeiting of a debit, credit, value card etc. with aim of obtaining financial or other gain.

REFERENCES

Bighelaar, S. van den & Akkermans, M. (2013). *Bevolkingstrends 2013: Gebruik en gebruikers van sociale media* [Demographic trends 2013: Use and users of social media]. Den Haag/Heerlen: CBS.

Bosler, A.M. & Holt, T.J. (2009). Online activities, guardianship, and malware infection. *International Journal of Cyber Criminology*, 3(1), 400-420.

Brewer, R. (2014). Advanced persistent threats: minimising the damage. *Network Security*, April 2014, p. 5-9.

CBS (2012a). *Integrale Veiligheidsmonitor 2011. Landelijke rapportage* [Security Monitor 2011. National report]. Den Haag/Heerlen: CBS.

CBS (2012b). *Integrale Veiligheidsmonitor 2011. Tabellenrapport* [Security Monitor 2011. Tables]. Den Haag/Heerlen: CBS.

CBS (2014). *ICT, kennis en economie 2014* [ICT, knowledge and economy 2014]. Den Haag/Heerlen: CBS.

CBS (2015). *Veiligheidsmonitor 2014* [Security Monitor 2014]. Den Haag/Heerlen: CBS.

Chamber of Commerce (28 September 2009). *Cybercrime*. Amsterdam: Chamber of Commerce.

Counsil of Europe (COE) (1990). *Computer-related crime: Final report of the European Committee on Crime Problems*. Straatsburg: Counsil of Europe.

Cresanti, R. (2014). 21st Century Technology Attracts 21st Century Criminals. *Franchising World*, November 2014, p. 24-26.

Demmer, H.C. (2014). *Het E-loket: onderzoek naar de wensen van het MKB en de Juridische gevolgen voor het E-loket indien deze wensen zouden worden uitgevoerd* [The E-desk: research into the wishes of SME's and their juridical implications]. Leeuwarden: Lectoraat Cybersafety (bachelor thesis).

Dimopoulos, V., Furnell, S., Jennex, M. & Kritharas, I. (2004). *Approaches to IT Security in Small and Medium Enterprises*. Paper presented on the 2nd Australian Information Security Management Conference, Perth (Western Autralia), 26 November 2004.

Doldersum, W. (2015). *Non-respons onderzoek: slachtofferschap van cybercrime Onder ZZP'ers* [Non-response research: cybercrime victimisation among one man businesses]. Leeuwarden: Lectoraat Cybersafety (student report).

Domenie, M.M.L., Leukfeldt, E.R. & Stol, W.Ph. (2011). *Verantwoording pilotslachtofferonderzoek cybercrime* [Research methodology of the pilot study on cybercrime victimisation]. Leeuwarden: Lectoraat Cybersafety.

Domenie, M.M.L., Leukfeldt, E.R., Wilsem, J.A. van, Jansen, J. & Stol, W.Ph. (2013). *Slachtofferschap in een gedigitaliseerde samenleving: Een onderzoek onder burgers naar e-fraude, hacken en andere veelvoorkomende criminaliteit* [Victimisation in a Digitised Society. A Survey Among Members of the Public Concerning E-Fraud, Hacking and other High-Volume Crimes]. Den Haag: Boom Lemma uitgevers.

Ernst & Young (2011). *ICT Barometer over cybercrime* [ICT Barometer about cybercrime]. Amsterdam: Ernst & Young LLP.

Featherman, M.S. & Pavlou P.A. (2003). Predicting e-services adoption: a perceived risk facets perspective. *International Journal of Human-Computer Studies, 59*(4), 451-474.

Federation of Small Businesses (FSB) (2013). *Cyber security and fraud: The impact on small businesses.* Retrieved from: <www.fsb.org.uk/policy/assets/fsb_cyber_security_and_fraud_paper_final.pdf>.

Foubert, J. (2012). *De psychosociale gezondheid van buurtbewoners die getroffen zijn door grondwaterverontreiniging: de rol van site-specifieke stressoren en communicatie tussen bewoners* [The psychosocial wellbeing of neigbourhood residents who were affected by the pollution of groundwater: the role of site-specific stress factors and communication between residents]. Gent: Universiteit Gent.

Gottfredson, M. & Hirschi, T. (1990). *A General Theory of Crime.* Stanford: Stanford University Press.

GOVCERT.NL (2011). *Cybersecuritybeeld Nederland: December 2011* [Cyber Security in the Netherlands: December 2011]. Den Haag: GOVCERT.NL.

Grasmick, H.G., Tittle, C.R., Bursik, R.J. & Arneklev, J.A. (1993). Testing the core empirical implications of Gottfredson and Hirschi's general theory of crime, *Journal of Research in Crime and Delinquency, 30*(1), 5-29.

Gunderson Hunt, K. (2013). Firewall Under Fire: Could a Cybercrime Send You Up in Flames? *Journal of Property Management,* Jan-Feb 2013, p.48-53.

Gupta, A. & Hammond, R. (2005). Information systems security issues and decisions for small businesses. *Information Management & Computer Security, 13*(4), 279-310.

Hagen, J.M., Sivertsen, T.K. & Rong, C. (2008). Protection against unauthorized access and computer crime in Norwegian enterprises. *Journal of Computer Security, 16*(3), 341-366.

Hernandez-Castro, J. & Boiten, E. (2014). Cybercrime prevalence and impact in the UK. *Computer Fraud & Security,* February 2014, p. 5-8.

Hernandez-Castro, J., Boiten, E. & Barnoux, M. (2013). *Second survey on the prevalence and impact of cybercrime victimisation.* Canterbury: University of Kent, Interdisciplinary Research Centre in Cyber Security.

Higgins, G.E. (2007). Examining the Original Grasmick Scale: A Rasch Model Approach. *Criminal Justice and Behavior, 34*(2), 157-178.

Hoevenagel, R. (2013). *Cybercrime in het bedrijfsleven.* Zoetermeer: Panteia.

Home Office (2013). *Crime against businesses: Headline findings from the 2012 Commercial Victimisation Survey.* Retrieved from: <www.gov.uk/government/uploads/system/uloads/attachment_data/file/147935/crime-business-prem-2012-pdf.pdf>.

Hong, I.B. & Cha, H.S. (2013). The mediating role of consumer trust in an online merchant in predicting purchase intention. *International Journal of Information Management, 33*(6), 927-939.

Hutchings, A. & Hayes, H. (2009). Routine Activity Theory and Phishing Victimisation: Who Gets Caught in the 'Net'? *Current Issues in Criminal Justice, 20*(3), 433-451.

Inspectie Veiligheid en Justitie (2015). *Aanpak van internetoplichting door de politie. Inspectieonderzoek naar een vorm van cybercrime* [The fight against e-fraud by the police. Research on a form of cybercrime]. Den Haag: VenJ.

Intomart GfK (2013). *Rapportage Cyber Security* [Cyber Security Report]. Intomart GfK Bv. Retrieved from: <https://www.nctv.nl/Images/rapportage-cybersecurity-18-10-2013_tcm126-520009.pdf>.

Jansen, J., Veenstra, S. & Stol, W.Ph. (2013a). *Bedrijf en digitale veiligheid: Evaluatie van het Digitaal Bedrijven-loket Cybercrime* [Companies and digital security: evaluation of the cybercrime desk for businesses]. Leeuwarden: NHL Hogeschool, Lectoraat Cybersafety.

Jansen, J., Leukfeldt, R., Kerstens, J., Veenstra, S., van Wilsem, J. van & Stol, W.Ph. (2013b). Slachtofferschap in een gedigitaliseerde samenleving en kansen voor Preventie [Victimisation in a digitised society and chances for prevention]. In: Jansen, J. & Stol, W.Ph. (eds.) *Cybercrime en de politie* [Cybercrime and the police]. Den Haag: Boom Lemma uitgevers.

Jewkes, Y. & Yar, M. (2008). Policing cybercrime in the twenty-first century. In: Newburn, T. (red.). *Handbook of policing*. Cullompton: Willan Publishing.

Kjaerland, M. (2006). A taxonomy and comparison of computer security incidents from the commercial and government sectors. *Computers & Security, 25*(7), 522-538.

Klinkenberg, S. (2004). *Constructie en Validitatie van een Algemene Computervaardigheid Vragenlijst (ACV)* [Construction and validation of a general computer skills questionnaire]. Amsterdam: Universiteit van Amsterdam.

Koldijk, H.P. (2011). *Monitor Digitaal Bedrijvenloket Cybercrime: Politie Flevoland* [Monitor of the cybercrime desk for businesses: Flevoland regional police force]. Leeuwarden: NHL Hogeschool.

Leukfeldt, E.R. (2014). Phishing for suitable targets in the Netherlands: routine activity theory and phishing victimization. *Cyberpsychology, Behavior, and Social Networking, 17*(8), 551-555.

Leukfeldt, E.R., Domenie, M.M.L. & Stol, W.Ph. (2010). *Verkenning cybercrime in Nederland 2009* [Exploring cybercrime in the Netherlands 2009]. Den Haag: Boom Juridische uitgevers.

Leukfeldt, E.R., Kentgens, A., Frans, B., Toutenhoofd, M.H., Stol, W.Ph. & Stamhuis, E. (2012a). *Alledaags politiewerk in een gedigitaliseerde wereld: Handreiking voor delicten met een digitale component* [Everyday police work in a digitised world: guidelines for handling offences with a digital component]. Den Haag: Boom Lemma uitgevers.

Leukfeldt, E.R., Veenstra, S. Domenie, M.M.L., & Stol, W.Ph. (2012b). *De strafrechtketen in een gedigitaliseerde samenleving. Een onderzoek naar de strafrechtelijke afhandeling van cybercrime* [A study into the functioning Functioning of the Dutch Criminal Justice System in Combating Crime in a Digitized Society]. Leeuwarden: NHL Hogeschool, Lectoraat Cybersafety.

Loether, H.J. & McTavish, D.G. (1980). *Descriptive and Inferential Statistics. An Introduction (2nd Edition)*. Boston: Allyn and Bacon Inc.

Ma, Q., Ono-Kihara, M., Cong, L., Pan, X., Xu, G., Zamani, S., Ravari, S.M. & Kihara, M. (2009). Behavioral and psychosocial predictors of condom use among university students in Eastern China. *AIDS care, 21* (2), 249-259.

McAfee (2013). *SMB is the new cybercrime target*. Retrieved from: <www.mcafee.com/au/resources/misc/smb-is-the-new-cybercrime-target.pdf>.

McGuire, M. & Dowling, S. (2013). *Cyber crime: A review of the evidence*. Home Office. Retrieved from: <https://www.gov.uk/government/uploads/system/uploads/attachment_data/file/246749/horr75-summary.pdf>

Motivaction (2012). *Cyber security awareness: Een onderzoek naar kennis, bewustzijn en gedrag ten aanzien van cyber security* [Cyber security awareness: a study on knowledge, awareness and behaviour regarding cyber security]. Amsterdam: Motivaction.

Mullan, B., Wong, C. & Kothe, E. (2013). Predicting adolescent breakfast consumption in the UK and Australia using an extended theory of planned behavior. *Appetite, 62*, 127-132.

Murphy, C., Coover, D. & Owen, S. (1989). Development and validation of the Computer Self-Efficacy Scale. *Educational and Psychological Measurement, 49*, 893-899.

Nationaal Cyber Security Centrum (2012). *Cybercrime: Van herkenning tot aangifte* Cybercrime: from recognition until filling a report]. Den Haag: Nationaal Cyber Security Centrum.

Næringslivets SikkerhetsRad (NSR) (2012). *Mørketallsundersøkelsen: Informasjonssikkerhet og datakriminalitet.* Oslo: NSR.

Ng, B.Y., Kankanhalli, A. & Xu, Y.C. (2009). Studying users' computer security behavior: A health belief perspective. *Decision Support Systems, 46*(4), 815-825.

Ngo, F.T. & Paternoster, R. (2011). Cybercrime victimization: An examination of individual and situational level factors. *International Journal of Cyber Criminology, 5*(1), 773-793.

Ochsner, S., Scholz, U. & Hornung, R. (2013). Testing phase-specific self-efficacy beliefs in the context of dietary behaviour change. *Applied Psychology: Health and Well-Being, 5*(1), 99-117.

Ponemon Institute (2012). *The human factor in data protection.* Traverse City: Ponemon.

PricewaterhouseCoopers (2011). *Cybercrime: protecting against the growing threat.* Retrieved from: <www.pwc.de/de_DE/de/risiko-management/assets/ global_economic_crime_survey.pdf>.

PricewaterhouseCoopers (2013). *2013 Information security breaches survey.* Retrieved from: <www.pwc.co.uk/assets/pdf/cyber-security-2013-technical-report.pdf>.

RAND (2008). *The National Computer Security Survey (NCSS): Final Methodology.* Santa Monica, Canada: RAND Corporation.

Regeerakkoord (2012). *Bruggen slaan: regeerakkoord VVD-PVDA* [Building bridges: coalition agreement VVD-PVDA]. Retrieved from: <https://www.rijksoverheid.nl/documenten/rapporten/2012/10/29/regeerakkoord>

Rundmo, T. & Nordfjærn, T. (2013). Predictors of demand for risk mitigation in transport. *Traffic Psychology and Behaviour, 20*, 183-192.

Sam, H.K., Othman, A.E.A. & Nordin, Z.S. (2005). Computer Self-Efficacy, Computer Anxiety, and Attitudes toward the Internet: A Study among Undergraduates in Unimas. *Educational Technology & Society, 8*(4), 205-219.

Schaper, M.T. & Weber, P. (2012). Understanding Small Business Scams. *Journal of Enterprising Culture, 20* (03), 333-356.

Scholz, U., Nagy, G., Göhner, W., Luszczynska, A. & Kliegel, M. (2009). Changes in self-regulatory cognitions as predictors of changes in smoking and nutrition behavior. *Psychology & Health, 24*(5), 545-561.

SER (2010). *Zzp'ers in beeld: een integrale visie op zelfstandigen zonder personeel* [One man businesses in the picture: an integral vision on one man businesses]. Den Haag: SER.

Stol, W.Ph. (1999). ICT-criminaliteit bestaat niet [ICT crime does not exist]. *Tijdschrift voor de politie, 61*(5), 29.

Stol, W.Ph. (2008). Cybercrime. In: Stol, W.Ph. & van Wijk, A. (red.), *Inleiding criminaliteit en opsporing* [An introduction in crime and law enforcement]. Den Haag: Boom Juridische uitgevers.

Stol, W.Ph. (2012). Cyberspace and safety. In: Leukfeldt, E.R. & Stol, W.Ph. (eds.), *Cyber safety: An introduction.* Den Haag: Eleven International Publishing.

Stol, W.Ph., Treeck, R.J. van, Ven, A.E.B.M. van der (1999). *Criminaliteit in cyberspace. Een praktijkonderzoek naar aard, ernst en aanpak in Nederland* [Crime in cyberspace. A research into the nature, severity and approach in the Netherlands]. Den Haag: Elsevier.

Syntens (2006). *Eindrapportage nulmeting: In het kader van het MKB-experiment van het Nationaal Project Aanpak Cybercrime* [Final report of the baseline study regarding an SME experiment of the National Project Against Cybercrime]. Nieuwegein: Syntens.

Torkzadeh, G. & Koufteros, X. (1994). Factorial validity of a computer self-efficacy scale and the impact of computer training. *Educational and psychological measurement*, 54(3), 813-821.

Van Dijk, T. (2007). *100%: Een onderzoek naar het vertrouwen van burgers in de politie* [100%: a research into the trust of the public in the police]. Retrieved from: <www.rijksoverheid.nl/bestanden/documenten-en-publicaties/rapporten/2007/08/10/100-een-onderzoek-naar-het-vertrouwen-van-burgers-in-de-politie/1164.pdf>.

Van Wilsem, J.V. (2010). Gekocht, maar niet gekregen: Slachtofferschap van online oplichting nader onderzocht [Bought, but never received: Victimisation of online fraud]. *Tijdschrift voor Veiligheid*, 9(4), 16-29.

Veenstra, S., Zuurveen, R., Jansen, J., Kloppenburg, S. & Stol, W.Ph. (2014). *MKB en cybercrime: Slachtofferschap onder het Nederlandse Midden- en Kleinbedrijf in een gedigitaliseerde samenleving* [SME and cybercrime: victimisation among Dutch Small and Medium sized Enterprises in a digitised society]. Leeuwarden: Lectoraat Cybersafety.

Verizon (2012). *2012 Data breach investigations report*. Retrieved from: <www.verizonenterprise.com/resources/reports/rp_data-breach-investigations-report-2012-ebk_en_xg.pdf>.

WODC (2011). *Monitor Criminaliteit Bedrijfsleven 2010: Feiten en trends inzake aard en omvang van criminaliteit in het bedrijfsleven* [Monitor of Crime against Companies: facts and trends regarding the nature and extent of crime against companies]. Den Haag: WODC.

ZZP Barometer (2014). *Themarapport 'Social media & netwerken'* [Theme report 'social media and networking']. Retrieved from: <http://zzpbarometer.nl/2014/12/themarapport-social-media-netwerken/>.